THE GREATEST
POLAR EXPLORATION
STORIES EVER TOLD

THE GREATEST
POLAR EXPLORATION
STORIES EVER TOLD

EDITED AND WITH AN INTRODUCTION

BY TOM MCCARTHY

LYONS
PRESS

ESSEX, CONNECTICUT

An imprint of Globe Pequot, the trade division of
The Rowman & Littlefield Publishing Group, Inc.
4501 Forbes Blvd., Ste. 200
Lanham, MD 20706
www.rowman.com

Distributed by NATIONAL BOOK NETWORK

British Library Cataloguing in Publication Information available

Library of Congress Cataloging-in-Publication Data Available
ISBN: 978-1-4930-7100-5 (pbk.)
ISBN: 978-1-4930-7101-2 (electronic)

Contents

Introduction

The newspaper advertisement for volunteers to accompany Ernest Shackleton on his planned traverse of Antarctica was frank in its offering.

> Men wanted for hazardous journey. Low wages, bitter cold, long hours of complete darkness. Safe return doubtful. Honour and recognition in event of success.

Still, hundreds applied. There were few chances left to be the first to reach the last challenge on Earth.

As the twentieth century came of age, explorers had uncovered most of the world's mysteries, sailing to the far corners of the globe, ascending many of its most forbidding peaks, crossing its greatest deserts, and penetrating its thickest jungles.

Frozen, alien, inhospitable, dangerous, and close to impossible to reach, there were only two tiny dots on the globe that human beings had not yet set foot on—the North and South Poles.

Herein you will find visceral, exciting, and stunning stories of perseverance, of extra-human endurance in the worst of conditions. The men had committed themselves to a mission, knowing that in many cases failure meant death. Their bravery was unquestioned, though perhaps their sanity was debatable. For little money and a guaranteed frozen hell, they were willing to traverse a frozen often sunless landscape to be the first to reach the North or South Pole.

Many of these explorers would die, to put in most kindly, unpleasantly.

Roald Amundsen and Robert Falcon Scott raced to death to be the first to set foot on the South Pole. Scott died just short of the South Pole while Amundsen went on to world fame and honors. John

Franklin would as well, with all his crew, on his third expedition. Charles Hall, who had survived everything the Arctic could throw his way and flourished doing so, was killed by his own men, poisoned—though karma would have a say about the fate of the survivors.

The drama of Arctic exploration would continue for some time in the warm halls of symposia for Robert Peary and Frederick Cook, who both claimed to have reached the North Pole first.

These stories will both inspire and inform—and answer questions about the limits of human endurance.

Many men would die during their challenging, frozen journeys, and their deaths were protracted and excruciatingly painful. Yet groups of hopeful adventurers continued to try again.

There are stories, wrought by the challenging landscape and weather, that made these explorers household names and heroes: Peary, Scott, Amundsen, Shackleton, Franklin, Cherry-Garrard, Scott, Kane, Cook.

Each of these men knew success would bring glory to their countries and financial security and fame and eminent places in history for themselves. Each knew also the odds of success were slim and the chance of dying great.

Nations held their collective breaths for news of each expedition and those years later were termed the Heroic Age of Exploration—there were simply no other endeavors that captured the world's attention like the various races to the poles.

Their suffering was not always of the dramatic, perhaps even cinematic ilk, say, pulling themselves from a sled teetering over the hidden abyss of an all-too-common crevasse or crossing the torrent of an arctic river with death all but certain with one slip.

Heroics could come in more subtle ways. The crew of Ernest Shackleton's *Endurance* found themselves locked in ice, their only certainty was knowing that their sturdy ship would be crushed and they would be stranded on an ice flow nearly 1,000 miles from safety.

Their only question was when.

As the ice exerted more pressure, the *Endurance* began to leak. Men were needed below, to stem the leak and try to repair a broken pump, but first they needed to clear the area.

Here is how one of the brave souls doing the work relayed the task with the nonchalance of a man on a Sunday stroll.

"This is not a pleasant job," he wrote. "We have to dig a hole down through the coal while the beams and timbers groan and crack all around us like pistol-shots. The darkness is almost complete, and we mess about in the wet with half-frozen hands and try to keep the coal from slipping back into the bilges. The men on deck pour buckets of boiling water from the galley down the pipe as we prod and hammer from below, and at last we get the pump clear, cover up the bilges to keep the coal out, and rush on deck, very thankful to find ourselves safe again in the open air."

Or consider the actions of one member of John Franklin's Coppermine Expedition:

At this time Dr. Richardson, prompted by a desire of relieving his suffering companions, proposed to swim across the stream with a line and to haul the raft over. He launched into the stream with the line round his middle but when he had got a short distance from the bank his arms became benumbed with cold and he lost the power of moving them; still he persevered and, turning on his back, had nearly gained the opposite bank when his legs also became powerless and, to our infinite alarm, we beheld him sink. We instantly hauled upon the line and he came again on the surface and was gradually drawn ashore in an almost lifeless state.

Each of the journeys recounted in this collection offers the same underratedness, the identical "we are nearly dead but have work to do" insouciance toward our calling.

One can only read of their privations with awe and head-shaking respect.

The Greatest Polar Expedition Stories Ever Told recaptures the spirit, drama, and tragedy of a time in history that will never come again.

Part I

The Call of the North

Chapter One

The Quest for the North Pole

John Buchan

WHEN SCEPTICAL PEOPLE SAY THAT POLAR EXPLORATION HAS BEEN OF no benefit to mankind, it is permissible to think that their judgment is as unsound as their point of view is limited. Not only have polar explorers added enormously to the scientific knowledge of the world, but they have also materially aided commerce. But even if these voyages had been barren of scientific and commercial results, they would have been infinitely worth making.

For among polar explorers are many men who must be universally regarded as heroes. No training was more rigorous and dangerous, no work has ever called for more endurance, resource, and courage. A nation which is without its heroes is in a sad plight; a nation which has them and ignores their example can only be looked upon with pity. The spirit of high adventure is one that no country can afford to neglect.

The history of geographical discovery is, in its initial stages, almost solely one of conquest. Men, either for their own or their country's profit—and sometimes for both—went out in search of unknown lands because they wanted to trade with them.

Not until the fifteenth century did English seamen begin to turn their attention to the North. They were more or less forced to do so. Portugal and Spain were all-powerful in the East and West, and so England began earnestly to think of discovering a way to Cathay and the Spice Islands by a northern route. But if we were a little slow in beginning to pay attention to the Arctic regions, we have every cause to be satisfied with our work after we had once begun it. The fifteenth century saw considerable activity as regards Scandinavia, but it was not until 1505 that a charter was granted to the Company of Merchant Adventurers, and from that year we can date our real interest in Arctic discovery.

It is well, perhaps, to bear in mind, while thinking of polar exploration, that there is a marked difference between the two polar regions. The Arctic is an ocean surrounded by continental lands; the Antarctic is a continental land surrounded by oceans.

In 1553 Sir Hugh Willoughby set out to try and find a northeast passage to the Indies. On this voyage—in which Willoughby lost his life—Novaya Zemlya was discovered, and Richard Chancellor, who took part in the expedition, reached Archangel; and then, travelling overland to Moscow, was received graciously by Ivan the Terrible, the Tsar of Russia. This visit was of importance because it helped to establish trade between England and Russia.

Competition to find a route northwards to China and the Indies had by this time become acute in Europe, and many bold navigators set out from England. Among the sailors who were maintaining her high record on the seas, Sir Martin Frobisher deserves especially to be mentioned. In 1576 he set out, cheered doubtless by knowing that Queen Elizabeth had "good liking of their doings," to find a northwest passage. On three occasions Frobisher voyaged northwards, and he reached Greenland and discovered the strait that was named after him.

In 1585 yet another distinguished explorer, John Davis, embarked upon his career, and during his voyages, he made discoveries that "converted the Arctic regions from a confused myth into a defined area." He found several passages towards the west, and thus strengthened the hope of finding a northwest passage; and he also reached "the farthest north," N 72°12", some 1,100 miles from the geographical North Pole.

As yet no one had turned his thoughts to the North Pole itself, but it may truly be said that Davis and men of his calibre were already beginning to prepare the way for the time when it would be reached. For his discoveries, like those of many of the earlier explorers, were both important in themselves and also acted as a guide and incentive to those who followed. In the meantime, Davis had obtained the record for the "farthest north," a record which Great Britain, except for a very few years, continued to hold until 1882.

Many English navigators did great work in maintaining this record, and among them was Henry Hudson, who set out in 1607 with the object of finding a northwest passage to the Indies. Hudson, in this voyage, reached N 80°, and did most valuable work in the Spitzbergen quadrant. It is also reported that two of his men saw a mermaid, which may at least be taken as evidence that they were more than ordinarily observant. Both geographically and commercially, Hudson's voyages were of the first importance. He not only made many discoveries, including that of the river which bears his name, but he also brought back the news that led directly to the establishment of the Spitzbergen whale fishery, an industry that was extremely lucrative to Holland.

In 1615 William Baffin discovered the land that is called after him; and then, for some time, English discovery in the Arctic regions ceased to be noteworthy. Baffin made no less than five voyages to the North, and, scientifically, his observations were permanently valuable to subsequent explorers.

Apart from geographical discovery, these Arctic voyages had so far been a great stimulant to trade. In Greenland, Davis Strait, and the Spitzbergen seas, trade had followed discovery, and what had happened in those parts of the Arctic also took place in Hudson Bay, after the Hudson's Bay Company was formed in 1668. In fact, for the time, the desire to make geographical discoveries was almost obliterated by the desire to trade.

It is, however, pleasant to note that during the eighteenth century some of our governments took an intelligent interest in geographical discovery. They offered a reward of £5,000 for reaching N 89°, and £20,000 was offered to anyone who could find the Northwest Passage. In the earlier part of the eighteenth century, the part that the Russians took in Arctic discovery must not be omitted. In 1728 Peter the Great sent out an expedition under the command of Vitus Bering, a Dane, in which the Bering Strait and other discoveries were made; and although it is impossible to mention them in detail, the contributions that the Russians made in revealing the New World to the Old were most creditable to them as a nation.

In 1773 Captain Phipps conducted an expedition, which now derives its chief interest from the fact that Horatio Nelson, then a young midshipman, took part in it. "Great," says Sir Clements Markham, "as are the commercial advantages obtained from Arctic discovery, and still greater as are its scientific results, the most important of all are its uses as a nursery for our seamen, as a school for our future Nelsons, and as affording the best opportunities for distinction to young naval officers in time of peace." And it is incontestably true that many of our finest sailors have learnt their trade in the severe school of geographical exploration.

With the advent of the nineteenth century many expeditions were sent to the Far North. The desire actually to reach the North Pole itself did not enter the thoughts of these courageous navigators, the main object of their voyages being either to find the Northwest Passage around North America to the Indies, or the Northeast Passage around Asia. Nevertheless, each one of these voyages added to the store of knowledge that was being accumulated, each expedition solved some of the mysteries of the North and prepared the way for the solution of what came to be considered the greatest mystery of all.

In 1819 Sir Edward Parry embarked upon the first of the Arctic voyages which have made his name famous in the annals of exploration. A sailor by profession, Parry was happy in possessing the qualities that fitted him to lead men. During his first expedition, the prize offered by the English government to the first navigator who passed the 110th meridian was won. Parry and his party spent a winter in the Arctic— a winter which, thanks to their leader's careful preparations, was passed without mishap; and then, when the winter was over, an expedition to explore the interior of Melville Island was made. Thus Arctic travelling was inaugurated by Parry.

Other successful voyages under the same leadership followed, and when, in 1827, our Admiralty began favourably to consider the idea of getting as near as possible to the Pole by way of Spitzbergen, Parry was naturally chosen to command the expedition. So, for the fourth time, Parry sailed northwards, and having reached the north coast of Spitzbergen, he found a good harbour for his ship, the *Hecla*, and left her there. The explorers had taken specially fitted boats with them, and they hoped to be able to haul over the ice in the boats. The summer, however, had begun to break up the floes, and in consequence, the travellers had constantly to take the steel runners off the boats so that the stretches of open water could be crossed. Moreover, the floes that they did find seemed to resent such treatment, for most of them were small and bestrewn with most obstructive hummocks. Not until they had been pulling and hauling for nearly a month did they meet with large floes, and by that time the southerly drift of the ice was in full swing.

However hard Parry and his men pulled, they found that the drift was as strong as they were—or stronger. After terrific labour Parry reached 82° 45", a higher latitude than any reached during the next fifty years. It was a great attempt by a man whose devotion to his duty is beyond all praise.

Before we come to the most tragic story in the history of Arctic exploration, reference must be made to the discoveries of Captain John Ross. In his first expedition to the North, Captain Ross was not successful; but in his second voyage, when he was accompanied by his nephew, James C. Ross (who afterwards gained distinction in the Antarctic), the magnetic North Pole was discovered, and the British flag fixed there in N 70°5'17", and W 76°16'4". Ross's expedition spent four consecutive winters in the Far North, discovered over 200 miles of coastline, and returned with a bountiful crop of scientific knowledge.

We may well admire the love of adventure and the desire to make geographical and scientific discoveries that induced these constant expeditions to parts of the world that cannot possibly be called inviting. Honour was, and is, due to the men who undertook them, but to John Franklin's memory special honour is paid, for his name is connected with both heroism and tragedy.

As a boy, Franklin, despite his father's opposition, was determined to be a sailor. At the age of fourteen he was on the *Polyphemus* at the battle of Copenhagen, and subsequently he was present at the battle of Trafalgar. Peace, then as always, brought unemployment for sailors with it, and at the age of twenty-nine Franklin found himself unwanted in the navy. When, however, the Admiralty decided, in 1818, to send expeditions to find the North Pole and the Northwest Passage, Franklin was chosen to command the *Trent*. This ship was unsuited for such a task, and owing to the official economy—not to say parsimony—Franklin had to return without achieving any success.

In the following year he was again sent out with orders to explore the northern coast of Arctic America, and "the trending of that coast from the mouth of the Coppermine eastwards." Not until 1822 did this expedition of discovery come to a close, after 5,550 miles had been covered by water and land.

The tale of its adventures, extraordinary as they were, is only the preface to Franklin's life as an explorer. So famous indeed was he, that when, in 1844, he returned from Tasmania, where he had been governor for seven years, he was offered the command of an important Arctic expedition. At this time he was nearly sixty years old, but he was anxious to resume his exploratory work, and in 1845 he sailed with the *Erebus* and the *Terror* (ships that had already won their laurels under Sir James Ross in the Antarctic).

In the hope of finding the Northwest Passage, so much coveted and so long concealed, Franklin was instructed to try a route by Wellington Channel, if ice did not block the way. The channel was found to be clear, and the explorers made their way up until they reached N 77°. Then their advance was blocked by ice, and they turned south and found winter quarters off Beechey Island. All, so far, had gone well, and when the ships were released from the ice at the end of the winter, hopes of further success must have run high. But presently a mistake was made that had fatal results—a mistake due to an error of the chart makers.

For some time the ships sailed gaily on, important discoveries being made from day to day. Then came the fatal decision. All were open to the south.

"If they had continued on their southerly course, the two ships would have reached Bering Strait. There was the navigable passage before them. But, alas! The chart-makers had drawn an isthmus (which only existed in their imagination) connecting Boothia with King William Land. They altered their course to the west, and were lost." Soon the ships were surrounded by a dense icepack and were dangerously imprisoned.

In the spring of 1847 travelling parties were sent out, and one of them, under Graham Gore's command, discovered a Northwest Passage and consequently proved the connection between the Atlantic and Pacific Oceans. When the parties returned Franklin was seriously ill, and he died on June 11, 1847.

A terrible winter for this gallant band of explorers followed. For months and months the ice remained impenetrable, and at last the ships had to be abandoned. Even if the *Erebus* and the *Terror* could have been freed from the ice, it was more than doubtful if they would float, so battered were they by their long, slow drift. Food was both inadequate in quantity and poisonous in quality. Twenty-two officers and men died during that winter of horror; the rest were so weak from privations that, although they knew their only chance was to retreat by Back's Fish River, none of them had the strength successfully to undertake such a march.

It is useless to dwell over the sufferings of these heroic men. Captain Crozier and Captain Fitzjames took every precaution and made all preparations that were under the circumstances possible, but the dice were too heavily loaded against them. With their two heavy boat sledges they started on April 22, 1848, to make their desperate effort. Not one of them survived. The *Erebus* sank when the ice released her. The *Terror* also sank, but not until she had drifted onto the American coast and been plundered by Eskimos.

It is pitiable to think that prompt action from England might have saved some, at least, of these valuable lives. But at first, although there was considerable anxiety about their fate, no effort was made to find them. Not until 1848 were expeditions sent out in search of Franklin's party, and neither of these was successful in finding any traces. One of these expeditions was, however, noteworthy, for Leopold McClintock, who subsequently became so renowned as a sledge traveller, took part in it.

By 1850 the whole country had become thoroughly aroused, and the government decided to send out strongly equipped expeditions. The *Enterprise* and the *Investigator*, under Captains Collinson and M'Clure, were sent out to search by way of Bering Strait; and four ships, under Captain Austin, were to seek for traces of the missing party by way of Lancaster Sound.

Austin's expedition failed to find the missing men, but it was excellently conducted and organized, and its sledge travellers (among whom was McClintock) covered over 7,000 miles, and discovered more than 1,200 miles of new land. When Captain Austin returned to England nothing had been heard of the *Enterprise* and the *Investigator*, and after some discussion and consequent delay, it was resolved again to send the four ships to the Arctic. Not only Franklin's men but also the *Enterprise* and the *Investigator* had now to be searched for. It was a case of search parties looking for search parties.

In their main objective—that of clearing up the mystery of Franklin and his companions—these expeditions were not successful, but in other ways they more than justified themselves. Both Collinson in the *Enterprise* and M'Clure in the *Investigator* succeeded in finding a Northwest Passage, and much-needed help was brought to M'Clure by the expedition sent out partly to aid him and Collinson. Further, the sledge journeys of McClintock and George Frederick Mecham during these expeditions were unrivalled in result and a real triumph of organization.

Owing to the outbreak of the Crimean War in 1854, popular interest in the fate of the Franklin expedition diminished, but Lady Franklin remained loyal to the object to which so many years of her life had been dedicated; and after the government had refused to assist her further, she decided to fit out a private expedition, of which Captain McClintock took command. In June 1857, the *Fox*, a steam yacht of 177 tons, started on her voyage to Greenland, but on reaching Melville Sound, McClintock found it extraordinarily packed with ice. The little vessel was firmly imprisoned and had to spend the winter in the drifting pack. During eight months she drifted southward for nearly 1,200 geographical miles, and she was not liberated from her prison until April 1858.

After such an experience many leaders would have made for a port in which to refit, but McClintock was of a different temper. No sooner had the *Fox* freed herself from her perilous position than he turned her head towards the north, and once more took up the work that he had been sent out to do. And this determination to concentrate, at all costs, on the definite object in hand ultimately met with its sad reward.

In June 1859, it was proved beyond any doubt that the report of the Eskimos (which had been received in England in 1854), to the effect that they had seen the dead bodies of several of Franklin's men, was true. "All the coastline along which the retreating crews performed their fearful march must," McClintock wrote, "be sacred to their names alone."

In 1853 an American expedition, under Elisha Kane, which was sent out in search of Franklin, to the north of Smith Sound, was fruitful in geographical discovery and outlined what has been called the American route to the Pole.

Interest in the Smith Sound route began to grow in England and was stimulated by another American expedition, led by Charles Hall in 1871. But although the desire to undertake more Arctic research was strongly felt by many Englishmen, it cannot be said that it was encouraged in official circles.

In November 1874, Lord Beaconsfield, who was at the time Prime Minister, announced that an Arctic expedition to encourage maritime enterprise and to explore the regions around the Pole would be sent out. Sir Clements Markham and other Arctic enthusiasts in England were delighted with this announcement, but their delight was short-lived.

These enthusiasts had for years been advocating that exploratory work should be undertaken in the region around the Pole, but they did not consider that a mere rush to the Pole should be undertaken until, at any rate, work of more value to mankind had been done. The conduct of the projected expedition was taken over by the Admiralty, and great was the consternation of Sir Clements and his friends when it was announced that "the main object of the expedition was to attain the highest latitude and, if possible, to reach the North Pole."

However displeasing such an object was to these enthusiasts, they could not but rejoice at the interest shown in the expedition, and in the fact that Captain Nares was appointed to command it. At the end of May 1875, the ships sailed from Portsmouth, and on arriving in the Arctic regions Nares had to bear in mind his definite instructions. In short, exploratory work was to give way to an effort to reach, if possible, the Pole itself. But anxious as he was to carry out his orders, one terrible scourge stood in his way. Scurvy, a deadly disease, attacked his party during the winter, and nearly half of his men suffered from it.

Under such conditions he was severely handicapped, but he decided to send out three sledge parties—eastward, westward, and to the north. Lieutenant Pelham Aldrich was in charge of the western party, and although most of the sledge crew were weakened by scurvy, they marched over 600 miles and succeeded in reaching N 82°48", a few miles farther north than Parry had reached some fifty years previously.

In 1882 an American expedition, under Lieutenant Greely, although terribly unfortunate in some respects, was successful in wresting the record for "farthest north" from the British.

North Polar Regions

Between 1892 and 1895 the American Lieutenant Peary, using dogs for purposes of traction, made two successful marches across Greenland, and so prepared himself for the attacks on the North Pole itself—attacks which he was eventually to bring to a successful conclusion.

Robert Peary had launched his first great attack upon the Pole. This expedition lasted for four years—1898 to 1902—but Peary encountered such dense packs of ice, which blocked his way to the polar ocean, that he failed in his main object.

Another attempt followed in 1906, and although this was not crowned with complete success, Peary made a world's record for "farthest north" by reaching 87°6". In this expedition he nearly lost his life, but he returned to America with the grim determination to make yet another attempt. Experience had been bought by Peary in abundance and at a great cost, and to this was added energy that was remarkable even among polar explorers. This third voyage to the polar regions had, in the nature of things, to be his last. He was, when he set out on it, fifty-three years old, and although, after spending over twenty years in Arctic work, he had an invaluable experience, and even experience cannot make an Arctic explorer forget that youth is also a great asset in the polar regions.

In May 1908, Peary published his programme, the main features of which are worthy of record. He decided to use the same ship, the *Roosevelt*, which had taken him to the north in his 1906 expedition. His route was to be by way of Smith Sound; his winter quarters were to be at Cape Sheridan, or even nearer to the Pole if the ship could proceed farther; he intended to use sledges and Eskimo dogs for traction; and, lastly, he placed his confidence in Eskimos, the Arctic Highlanders, as the rank-and-file of his sledge parties.

Most careful preparations were made for this expedition, and while Peary was making them he received much practical support, but also some suggestions that were not notably helpful. For instance, one cheerful crank invited him to become a "human cannonball"—some sort of machine was to be taken to the North, and then, when it was pointed towards the Pole, the inventor assured Peary that it would shoot him there in no time. The explorer did not see his way to accepting such an abrupt means of transit!

When the *Roosevelt* sailed on July 17, 1908, she had twenty-two men on board. The *Roosevelt* reached Cape York, Greenland, on August 1, and there she said a temporary goodbye to the civilized world. There also Peary met the Eskimos, whose friendship he had gained by many and continuous acts of kindness.

After leaving Cape York, Peary transferred himself for some days to the *Erik*, his auxiliary supply steamer, so that he could collect as many Eskimos and dogs as he required. By August 11 the *Erik* reached Etah and rejoined the *Roosevelt*. Finally, Peary selected 49 Eskimos and 246 dogs, and after having transferred them to the *Roosevelt*, the explorers set out to fight their way through the 350 miles of ice-blocked water that separated Etah from Cape Sheridan. And the ice during that journey was in no gentle mood. So great were the risks that the ship might at any time be crushed, that the boats, fully equipped and provisioned, were always ready to be lowered at a moment's notice.

A terrific battle with that uncompromising opponent, the ice, followed, but not until August 30 did the struggle reach its climax. On that day the ship was "kicked about by the floes as if she had been a football," and the pressure was so terrific that Peary decided to dynamite the ice. This operation was successful in relieving the situation, but some days passed before even the greatest optimist on the ship could consider her free from danger.

But on September 5 the *Roosevelt* managed to fight her way through to Cape Sheridan; and after a project to take her on to Porter Bay had been abandoned, the work of unloading her began, and with her lighter load Captain Bartlett proceeded to get her as near the shore as possible.

The first stage on the way to the Pole was behind the explorers, and if the next stage was shorter in distance, it was no less important than a part of the whole scheme. This second stage consisted of the transportation of supplies from Cape Sheridan to Cape Columbia, ninety miles northwest of the ship. Cape Columbia is the most northerly point of Grant Land, and from there Peary had determined to make his dash over the ice to the Pole.

By the end of the autumn season snow igloos had been built on the track to Cape Columbia. After leaving Cape Columbia, over 400 miles separated him from his goal, and these miles had to be travelled over the ice of the polar sea. "There is no land," he writes, "*between Cape Columbia and the North Pole, and no smooth and very little level ice.*" But even ice through which the traveller must sometimes pick-axe his way is not the most serious impediment to those who would reach the Pole.

The final attack on the Pole began on February 15, 1909, when Bartlett, with a pioneer party, left the Roosevelt, and a week later Peary started on his way. At this time seven members of the expedition, 19 Eskimos, 140 dogs, and 28 sledges, divided into various parties, were engaged in the great effort to reach the Pole. It was arranged that all of these parties should meet Peary at Cape Columbia on the last day of February; and on that day Bartlett and Borop started from the cape with advance parties. The duties of these advance parties were as onerous as they were important. For it was to Bartlett that Peary looked for a trail by which the main party could travel.

The explorers had advanced nearly fifty miles from Cape Columbia when they were held up by a big "lead," which refused most obstinately to cover itself with ice strong enough to bear the sledges. For a week this open water delayed the expedition, and Peary had good reason to wonder if his most careful preparation and organization were once more to miss the success that they deserved. On March 11, however, the parties managed to cross the "lead," and on the march that followed, they crossed the 84th parallel.

On April 5 the party reached N 89°25" and were within thirty-five miles of the Pole. So near, indeed, were they, that Peary writes: "By some strange shift of feeling the fear of the 'leads' had fallen from me completely. I now felt that success was certain."

And his confidence was justified. On April 6, 1909, Peary, with his assistant, Matthew Henson, and the four Eskimos, reached the Pole, and there the leader of this successful party wrote the following note;

-90° N. LAT. NORTH POLE
6th April 1909

I have to-day hoisted the national ensign of the United States of America at this place, which my observations indicate to be the North Pole axis of the earth, and have formally taken possession of the entire region and adjacent, for and in the name of the President of the United States of America. I leave this record and United States flag in possession.

ROBERT E. PEARY,
United States Navy

CHAPTER TWO

Across Barren Grounds, 1821

Sir John Franklin

Note: Organized by the British Navy, John Franklin's Coppermine expedition of 1819–1822 sought to chart the area from Hudson Bay to the north coast of Canada as part of its attempt to discover and map the Northwest Passage. It was the first of three Arctic expeditions by Franklin. He and his crew would die on his third voyage.

August 19

WE WERE ALMOST BEATEN OUT OF OUR COMFORTLESS ABODES BY RAIN during the night and this morning the gale continued without diminution. The thermometer fell to thirty-three degrees. Two men were sent with Junius to search for the deer which Augustus had killed. Junius returned in the evening, bringing part of the meat but, owing to the thickness of the weather, his companions parted from him and did not make their appearance. Divine service was read. On the 20th we were presented with the most chilling prospect, the small pools of water being frozen over, the ground covered with snow, and the thermometer at the freezing point at midday. Flights of geese were passing to the southward.

Considerable anxiety prevailing respecting Belanger and Michel, the two men who strayed from Junius yesterday, the rest were sent out to look for them. The search was successful and they all returned in the evening. The stragglers were much fatigued and had suffered severely from the cold, one of them having his thighs frozen and, what under our present circumstances was most grievous, they had thrown away all the meat.

The wind abated after midnight and the surf diminished rapidly, which caused us to be on the alert at a very early hour on the 22nd, but we had to wait until 6 a.m. for the return of Augustus who had continued out all night on an unsuccessful pursuit of deer. It appears that he had walked a few miles further along the coast than the party had done on the 18th and, from a sketch he drew on the sand, we were confirmed in our former opinion that the shore inclined more to the eastward beyond Point Turnagain. He also drew a river of considerable size that discharges its waters into Walker's Bay, on the banks of which stream he saw a piece of wood such as the Esquimaux use in producing fire, and other marks so fresh that he supposed they had recently visited the spot.

We therefore left several iron materials for them and, embarking without delay, prepared to retrace our steps. Our men, cheered by the prospect of returning, showed the utmost alacrity and, paddling with unusual vigour, carried us across Riley's and Walker's Bays, a distance of twenty miles before noon, when we landed on Slate-clay Point as the wind had freshened too much to permit us to continue the voyage.

We went dinnerless to bed.

August 25

Starting this morning with a fresh breeze in our favour we soon reached that part of Barry's Island where the canoes were detained on the 2nd and 3rd of this month and, contrary to what we then experienced, the deer were now plentiful. The hunters killed two and relieved us from all apprehension of immediate want of food.

The wind continued in the same direction until we had rounded Point Wollaston and then changed to a quarter which enabled us to steer for Hood's River, which we ascended as high as the first rapid and encamped. Here terminated our voyage on the Arctic Sea during which we had gone over 650 geographical miles. Our Canadian voyagers could not restrain their joy at having turned their backs on the sea, and passed the evening in talking over their past adventures with much humour and no little exaggeration. The consideration that the most painful, and certainly the most hazardous, part of the journey was yet to come did not depress their spirits at all. It is due to their character to mention that they displayed much courage in encountering the dangers of the sea, magnified to them by their novelty.

AUGUST 26

Previous to our departure this morning an assortment of iron materials, beads, looking glasses, and other articles were put up in a conspicuous situation for the Esquimaux and the English Union was planted on the loftiest sandhill where it might be seen by any ships passing in the offing. Here also was deposited in a tin box a letter containing an outline of our proceedings, the latitude and longitude of the principal places, and the course we intended to pursue towards Slave Lake.

Embarking at 8 a.m. we proceeded up the river which is full of sandy shoals but sufficiently deep for canoes in the channels. It is from one hundred to two hundred yards wide and is bounded by high and steep banks of clay. We encamped at a cascade of eighteen or twenty feet high which is produced by a ridge of rock crossing the river and the nets were set. A mile below this cascade Hood's River is joined by a stream half its own size which I have called James' Branch. Bear and deer tracks had been numerous on the banks of the river when we were here before but not a single recent one was to be seen at this time. Our distance made today was not more than six miles.

The next morning the net furnished us with ten white fish and trout. Having made a further deposit of ironwork for the Esquimaux we pursued our voyage up the river, but the shoals and rapids in this part were so frequent that we walked along the banks the whole day and the crews laboured hard in carrying the canoes thus lightened over the shoals or dragging them up the rapids, yet our journey in a direct line was only about seven miles

The summit of a hill above these falls, appeared so rapid and shallow that it seemed useless to attempt proceeding any farther in the large canoes. I therefore determined on constructing out of their materials two smaller ones of sufficient size to contain three persons for the purpose of crossing any river that might obstruct our progress. This operation was accordingly commenced and by the 31st, both the canoes being finished, we prepared for our departure on the following day.

The leather which had been preserved for making shoes was equally divided among the men, two pairs of flannel socks were given to each person, and such articles of warm clothing as remained were issued to those who most required them.

The next morning was warm and very fine. Everyone was on the alert at an early hour, being anxious to commence the journey. Our luggage consisted of ammunition, nets, hatchets, ice chisels, astronomical instruments, clothing, blankets, three kettles, and the two canoes, which were each carried by one man. The officers carried such a portion of their own things as their strength would permit; the weight carried by each man was about ninety pounds, and with this we advanced at the rate of about a mile an hour including rests. In the evening the hunters killed a lean cow out of a large drove of musk-oxen; but the men were too much laden to carry more than a small portion of its flesh.

On the morning of the 1st of September a fall of snow took place; the canoes became a cause of delay from the difficulty of carrying them in a high wind, and they sustained much damage through the falls of those who had charge of them. The face of the country was broken by hills of moderate elevation but the ground was plentifully strewed with small stones which, to men bearing heavy burdens and whose feet were protected only by soft moose-skin shoes, occasioned great pain.

At the end of eleven miles we encamped and sent for a musk-ox and a deer which St. Germain and Augustus had killed. The day was extremely cold, the thermometer varying between thirty-four and thirty-six degrees. In the afternoon a heavy fall of snow took place on the wind changing from northwest to southwest. We found no wood at the encampment but made a fire of moss to cook the supper and crept under our blankets for warmth.

At sunrise the thermometer was at thirty-one degrees and the wind fresh from northwest, but the weather became mild in the course of the forenoon and the snow disappeared from the gravel. The afternoon was remarkably fine and the thermometer rose to fifty degrees. One of the hunters killed a musk-ox.

Having ascertained from the summit of the highest hill near the tents that the river continued to preserve a west course and, fearing that by pursuing it farther we might lose much time and unnecessarily walk over a great deal of ground, I determined on quitting its banks the next day and making as directly as we could for Point Lake. We accordingly followed the river on the 3rd only to the place where the musk-ox had been killed last evening and, after the meat was procured, crossed the river in our two canoes lashed together. We now emerged from the valley of the river and entered a level but very barren country, varied only by small lakes and marshes, the ground being covered with small stones.

Having walked twelve miles and a half we encamped at 7 p.m. and distributed our last piece of pemmican and a little arrowroot for supper which afforded but a scanty meal. Our men now began to find their burdens very oppressive and were much fatigued by this day's march but did not complain.

One of them was lame from an inflammation in the knee. Heavy rain commenced at midnight and continued without intermission until five in the morning, when it was succeeded by snow on the wind changing to northwest, which soon increased to a violent gale. As we had nothing to eat and were destitute of the means of making a fire, we remained in our beds all the day, but the covering of our blankets was insufficient to prevent us from feeling the severity of the frost and suffering inconvenience from the drifting of the snow into our tents. There was no abatement of the storm the next day; our tents were completely frozen and the snow had drifted around them to a depth of three feet, and even in the inside there was a covering of several inches on our blankets.

Our suffering from cold in a comfortless canvas tent in such weather with the temperature at twenty degrees and without fire will easily be imagined; it was however less than that which we felt from hunger.

Just as we were about to commence our march I was seized with a fainting fit in consequence of exhaustion and sudden exposure to the wind but, after eating a morsel of portable soup, I recovered so far as to be able to move on. I was unwilling at first to take this morsel of soup, which was diminishing the small and only remaining meal for the party, but several of the men urged me to it with much kindness. The ground was covered a foot deep with snow, the margins of the lakes were encrusted with ice, and the swamps over which we had to pass were entirely frozen but the ice, not being sufficiently strong to bear us, we frequently plunged knee-deep in water.

Those who carried the canoes were repeatedly blown down by the violence of the wind and they often fell from making an insecure step on a slippery stone; on one of these occasions the largest canoe was so much broken as to be rendered utterly unserviceable. This we felt was a serious disaster as the remaining canoe having through mistake been made too small, it was doubtful whether it would be sufficient to carry us across a river. Indeed we had found it necessary in crossing Hood's River to lash the two canoes together.

In the afternoon we got into a more hilly country where the ground was strewed with large stones. The surface of these was covered with lichens of the genus *gyrophora*, which the Canadians term *tripe de roche*. We passed a comfortless night in our damp clothes but took the precaution of sleeping on our socks and shoes to prevent them from freezing. This plan was afterwards adopted throughout the journey.

At half-past five in the morning we proceeded and after walking about two miles came to Cracroft's River, flowing to the westward with a very rapid current over a rocky channel. We had much difficulty in crossing this, the canoe being useless, not only from the bottom of the channel being obstructed by large stones, but also from its requiring gumming, an operation which, owing to the want of wood and the frost, we were unable to perform. However after following the course of the river some distance we effected a passage by means of a range of large rocks that crossed a rapid. As the current was strong and many of the rocks were covered with water to the depth of two or three feet, the men were exposed to much danger in carrying their heavy burdens across, and several of them actually slipped into the stream but were immediately rescued by the others.

As several of the party were drenched from head to foot and we were all wet to the middle, our clothes became stiff with the frost and we walked with much pain for the remainder of the day. The march was continued to a late hour from our anxiety to rejoin the hunters who had gone before, but we were obliged to encamp at the end of ten miles and a quarter without seeing them.

Our only meal today consisted of a partridge each (which the hunters shot) mixed with *tripe de roche*. This repast, although scanty for men with appetites such as our daily fatigue created, proved a cheerful one and was received with thankfulness.

We started at six on the 9th and at the end of two miles regained our hunters who were halting on the borders of a lake amidst a clump of stunted willows. This lake stretched to the westward as far as we could see and its waters were discharged by a rapid stream 150 yards wide. Being entirely ignorant of where we might be led by pursuing the course of the lake, and dreading the idea of going a mile unnecessarily out of the way, we determined on crossing the river if possible, and the canoe was gummed for the purpose, the willows furnishing us with fire.

SEPTEMBER 10

We had a cold north wind and the atmosphere was foggy. The thermometer was eighteen degrees at 5 a.m. In the course of our march this morning we passed many small lakes and the ground, becoming higher and more hilly as we receded from the river, was covered to a much greater depth with snow. This rendered walking not only extremely laborious but also hazardous in the highest degree, for the sides of the hills, as is usual throughout the barren grounds, abounding in accumulations of large angular stones, it often happened that the men fell into the interstices with their loads on their backs, being deceived by the smooth appearance of the drifted snow. If anyone had broken a limb here his fate would have been melancholy indeed; we could neither have remained with him nor carried him on. We halted at ten to gather *tripe de roche* but it was so frozen that we were quite benumbed with cold before a sufficiency could be collected even for a scanty meal.

We set out on the 13th in thick hazy weather and, after an hour's march, had the extreme mortification to find ourselves on the borders of a large lake; neither of its extremities could be seen and, as the portion which lay to the east seemed the widest, we coasted along to the westward portion in search of a crossing-place. This lake being bounded by steep and lofty hills our march was very fatiguing. Those sides which were exposed to the sun were free from snow and we found upon them some excellent berries. We encamped at 6 p.m. having come only six miles and a half.

September 15

Soon after leaving the encampment we discerned a herd of deer and after a long chase a fine male was killed by Perrault, several others were wounded but they escaped. After this we passed round the north end of a branch of the lake and ascended the Willingham Mountains, keeping near the border of the lake. These hills were steep, craggy, and covered with snow. We encamped at seven and enjoyed a substantial meal. The party was in good spirits this evening at the recollection of having crossed the rapid and being in possession of provision for the next day. Besides we had taken the precaution of bringing away the skin of the deer to eat when the meat should fail. The temperature at 6 p.m. was thirty degrees. We started at seven the next morning and marched until ten when the appearance of a few willows peeping through the snow induced us to halt and breakfast.

Recommencing the journey at noon we passed over a more rugged country where the hills were separated by deep ravines whose steep sides were equally difficult to descend and to ascend, and the toil and suffering we experienced were greatly increased.

The party was quite fatigued when we encamped, having come ten miles and three-quarters. We observed many summer deer roads and some recent tracks. Some marks that had been put up by the Indians were also noticed. We have since learned that this is a regular deer pass and, on that account, annually frequented by the Copper Indians. The lake is called by them Contwoyto or Rum Lake in consequence of Mr. Hearne having here given the Indians who accompanied him some of that liquor. Fish is not found here.

September 21

We set out at seven this morning in dark foggy weather and changed our course two points to the westward. The party was very feeble and the men much dispirited; we made slow progress, having to march over a hilly and very rugged country.

Just before noon the sun beamed through the haze for the first time in six days and we obtained an observation in latitude 65°7'06" North, which was six miles to the southward of that part of Point Lake to the way our course was directed. By this observation we discovered that we had kept to the eastward of the proper course, which may be attributed partly to the difficulty of preserving a straight line through an unknown country, unassisted by celestial observations and in such thick weather that our view was often limited to a few hundred yards, but chiefly to our total ignorance of the amount of the variation of the compass.

We altered the course immediately to west-southwest and fired guns to apprise the hunters who were out of our view and ignorant of our having done so. After walking about two miles we waited to collect the stragglers. Two partridges were killed and these with some *tripe de roche* furnished our supper.

Notwithstanding a full explanation was given to the men of the reasons for altering the course, and they were assured that the observation had enabled us to discover our exact distance from Fort Enterprise, they could not divest themselves of the idea of our having lost our way, and a gloom was spread over every countenance. At this encampment Dr. Richardson was obliged to deposit his specimens of plants and minerals collected on the sea coast, being unable to carry them any farther. The way made today was five miles and a quarter.

SEPTEMBER 29

Strong southeast winds with fog in the morning, more moderate in the evening. Temperature of the rapid thirty-eight degrees. The men began at an early hour to bind the willows in fagots for the construction of the raft, and it was finished by seven but, as the willows were green, it proved to be very little buoyant, and was unable to support more than one man at a time. Even on this however we hoped the whole party might be transported by hauling it from one side to the other, provided a line could be carried to the other bank. Several attempts were made by Belanger and Benoit, the strongest men of the party, to convey the raft across the stream, but they failed for want of oars.

A pole constructed by tying the tent poles together was too short to reach the bottom at a short distance from the shore, and a paddle which had been carried from the sea coast by Dr. Richardson did not possess sufficient power to move the raft in opposition to a strong breeze which blew from the other side. All the men suffered extremely from the coldness of the water in which they were necessarily immersed up to the waists in their endeavours to aid Belanger and Benoit and, having witnessed repeated failures, they began to consider the scheme as hopeless.

At this time Dr. Richardson, prompted by a desire of relieving his suffering companions, proposed to swim across the stream with a line and to haul the raft over. He launched into the stream with the line round his middle but when he had got a short distance from the bank his arms became benumbed with cold and he lost the power of moving them; still he persevered and, turning on his back, had nearly gained the opposite bank when his legs also became powerless and, to our infinite alarm, we beheld him sink. We instantly hauled upon the line and he came again on the surface and was gradually drawn ashore in an almost lifeless state.

Being rolled up in blankets he was placed before a good fire of willows and fortunately was just able to speak sufficiently to give some slight directions respecting the manner of treating him. He recovered strength gradually and through the blessing of God was enabled in the course of a few hours to converse and by the evening was sufficiently recovered to remove into the tent.

We then regretted to learn that the skin of his whole left side was deprived of feeling in consequence of exposure to too great heat. He did not perfectly recover the sensation of that side until the following summer. I cannot describe what everyone felt at beholding the skeleton which the doctor's debilitated frame exhibited.

October 4

At length we reached Fort Enterprise and to our infinite disappointment and grief found it a perfectly desolate habitation. There was no deposit of provision, no trace of the Indians, no letter from Mr. Wentzel to point out where the Indians might be found. It would be impossible to describe our sensations after entering this miserable abode and discovering how we had been neglected; the whole party shed tears, not so much for our own fate as for that of our friends in the rear, whose lives depended entirely on our sending immediate relief from this place.

We now looked round for the means of subsistence and were gratified to find several deer skins which had been thrown away during our former residence. The bones were gathered from the heap of ashes; these with the skins and the addition of *tripe de roche* we considered would support us tolerably well for a time. As to the house, the parchment being torn from the windows, the apartment we selected for our abode was exposed to all the rigour of the season. We endeavoured to exclude the wind as much as possible by placing loose boards against the apertures. The temperature was now between fifteen and twenty degrees below zero. We procured fuel by pulling up the flooring of the other rooms, and water for cooking by melting the snow.

The unusual earliness of this winter became manifest to us from the state of things at this spot. Last year at the same season and still later there had been very little snow on the ground and we were surrounded by vast herds of reindeer; now there were but few recent tracks of these animals and the snow was upwards of two feet deep. Winter River was then open, now it was frozen two feet thick.

When I arose the following morning my body and limbs were so swollen that I was unable to walk more than a few yards. Adam was in a still worse condition, being absolutely incapable of rising without assistance. My other companions happily experienced this inconvenience in a less degree and went to collect bones and some *tripe de roche* which supplied us with two meals. The bones were quite acrid and the soup extracted from them excoriated the mouth if taken alone, but it was somewhat milder when boiled with *tripe de roche* and we even thought the mixture palatable with the addition of salt, of which a cask had been fortunately left here in the spring.

On the 13th the wind blew violently from southeast and the snow drifted so much that the party was confined to the house. Our conversation naturally turned upon the prospect of getting relief and upon the means which were best adapted for obtaining it. The absence of all traces of Indians on Winter River convinced me that they were at this time on the way to Fort Providence and that, by proceeding towards that post, we should overtake them as they move slowly when they have their families with them.

November 1

This day was fine and mild. Hepburn went hunting but was as usual unsuccessful. As his strength was rapidly declining we advised him to desist from the pursuit of deer, and only to go out for a short time and endeavour to kill a few partridges. The doctor obtained a little *tripe de roche* but Peltier could not eat any of it, and Samandre only a few spoonfuls, owing to the soreness of their throats. In the afternoon Peltier was so much exhausted that he sat up with difficulty and looked piteously; at length he slid from his stool upon his bed, as we supposed to sleep, and in this composed state he remained upwards of two hours without our apprehending any danger. We were then alarmed by hearing a rattling in his throat and on the doctor's examining him he was found to be speechless. He died in the course of the night. Samandre sat up the greater part of the day and even assisted in pounding some bones but, on witnessing the melancholy state of Peltier, he became very low and began to complain of cold and stiffness of the joints.

Being unable to keep up a sufficient fire to warm him we laid him down and covered him with several blankets. He did not however appear to get better and I deeply lament to add he also died before daylight. We removed the bodies of the deceased into the opposite part of the house but our united strength was inadequate to the task of interring them or even carrying them down to the river.

November 4

Calm and comparatively mild weather. The doctor and Hepburn, exclusive of their usual occupation, gathered some *tripe de roche*. I went a few yards from the house in search of bones and returned quite fatigued, having found but three. The doctor again made incisions in Adam's leg which discharged a considerable quantity of water and gave him great relief. We read prayers and a portion of the New Testament in the morning and evening, as had been our practice since Dr. Richardson's arrival, and I may remark that the performance of these duties always afforded us the greatest consolation, serving to reanimate our hope in the mercy of the Omnipotent, who alone could save and deliver us.

On the 5th the breezes were light with dark cloudy weather and some snow. The doctor and Hepburn were getting much weaker and the limbs of the latter were now greatly swelled. They came into the house frequently in the course of the day to rest themselves and when once seated were unable to rise without the help of one another, or of a stick. Adam was for the most part in the same low state as yesterday, but sometimes he surprised us by getting up and walking with an appearance of increased strength. His looks were now wild and ghastly and his conversation was often incoherent.

The next day was fine but very cold. The swellings in Adam's limbs having subsided he was free from pain and arose this morning in much better spirits, and spoke of cleaning his gun ready for shooting partridges or any animals that might appear near the house, but his tone entirely changed before the day was half over; he became again dejected and could scarcely be prevailed upon to eat. The doctor and Hepburn were almost exhausted. The cutting of one log of wood occupied the latter half an hour, and the other took as much time to drag it into the house, though the distance did not exceed thirty yards. I endeavoured to help the doctor but my assistance was very trifling. Yet it was evident that in a day or two if their strength should continue to decline at the same rate I should be the strongest of the party.

NOVEMBER 8

The Indians this morning requested us to remove to an encampment on the banks of the river as they were unwilling to remain in the house where the bodies of our deceased companions were lying exposed to view. We agreed but the day proved too stormy and Dr. Richardson and Hepburn, having dragged the bodies to a short distance and covered them with snow, the objections of the Indians to remain in the house were dissipated, and they began to clear our room of the accumulation of dirt and fragments of pounded bones. The improved state of our apartment and the large and cheerful fires they kept up produced in us a sensation of comfort to which we had long been strangers.

November 9

This morning was pleasantly fine. Crooked-Foot caught four large trout in Winter Lake which were very much prized, especially by the doctor and myself, who had taken a dislike to meat in consequence of our sufferings from repletion which rendered us almost incapable of moving. Adam and Hepburn in a good measure escaped this pain. Though the night was stormy and our apartment freely admitted the wind we felt no inconvenience, the Indians were so very careful in covering us up and in keeping a good fire, and our plentiful cheer gave such power of resisting the cold, that we could scarcely believe otherwise than that the season had become milder.

On the 13th the weather was stormy with constant snow. The Indians became desponding at the nonarrival of the supply and would neither go to hunt nor fish.

On the following day the doctor and Hepburn resumed their former occupation of collecting wood and I was able to assist a little in bringing it into the house. Adam, whose expectation of the arrival of the Indians had been raised by the fineness of the weather, became towards night very desponding and refused to eat the singed skin. The night was stormy and there was a heavy fall of snow. The next day he became still more dejected.

About eleven Hepburn, who had gone out for the wood, came in with the intelligence that a party appeared upon the river. The room was instantly swept and, in compliance with the prejudices of the Indians, every scrap of skin was carefully removed out of sight, for these simple people imagine that burning deer-skin renders them unsuccessful in hunting. The party proved to be Crooked-Foot, Thooeeyorre, and the Fop, with the wives of the two latter dragging provisions. They were accompanied by Benoit, one of our own men.

We made preparations for quitting Fort Enterprise the next day and accordingly, at an early hour on the 16th, having united in thanksgiving and prayer, the whole party left the house after breakfast. Our feelings on quitting the fort where we had formerly enjoyed much comfort, if not happiness, and latterly experienced a degree of misery scarcely to be paralleled, may be more easily conceived than described. The Indians treated us with the utmost tenderness, gave us their snowshoes, and walked without themselves, keeping by our sides that they might lift us when we fell. We descended Winter River and about noon crossed the head of Round-Rock Lake, distant about three miles from the house, where we were obliged to halt as Dr. Richardson was unable to proceed. The swellings in his limbs rendered him by much the weakest of the party. The Indians prepared our encampment, cooked for us, and fed us. The night was mild and fatigue made us sleep soundly.

From this period to the 26th of November we gradually improved through their kindness and attention, and on that day arrived in safety at the abode of our chief and companion Akaitcho. We were received by the party assembled in the leader's tent with looks of compassion and profound silence which lasted about a quarter of an hour and by which they meant to express their condolence for our sufferings. The conversation did not begin until we had tasted food.

The chief Akaitcho showed us the most friendly hospitality and all sorts of personal attention, even cooking for us with his own hands, an office which he never performs for himself. Annoethaiyazzeh and Humpy, the chief's two brothers, and several of our hunters, with their families, were encamped here together with a number of old men and women. In the course of the day we were visited by every person of the band, not merely from curiosity, but a desire to evince their tender sympathy in our late distress.

We found several of the Indian families in great affliction for the loss of three of their relatives who had been drowned in the August preceding by the upsetting of a canoe near Fort Enterprise. They bewailed the melancholy accident every morning and evening by repeating the names of the persons in a loud singing tone which was frequently interrupted by bursts of tears. One woman was so affected by the loss of her only son that she seemed deprived of reason and wandered about the tents the whole day, crying and singing out his name.

On the 1st of December we removed with the Indians to the southward.

On the 4th we again set off after the Indians about noon, and soon overtook them, as they had halted to drag from the water and cut up and share a moose-deer that had been drowned in a rapid part of the river, partially covered with ice. These operations detained us a long time which was the more disagreeable as the weather was extremely unpleasant from cold low fogs. We were all much fatigued at the hour of encampment, which was after dark, though the day's journey did not exceed four miles. At every halt the elderly men of the tribe made holes in the ice and put in their lines. One of them shared the produce of his fishery with us this evening.

In the afternoon of the 6th Belanger and another Canadian arrived from Fort Providence, sent by Mr. Weeks with two trains of dogs, some spirits and tobacco for the Indians, a change of dress for ourselves, and a little tea and sugar.

All the Indians flocked to our encampment to learn the news and to receive the articles brought for them. Having got some spirits and tobacco they withdrew to the tent of the chief and passed the greater part of the night in singing. We had now the indescribable gratification of changing our linen which had been worn ever since our departure from the sea coast.

DECEMBER 8

After a long conference with Akaitcho we took leave of him and his kind companions and set out with two sledges, heavily laden with provision and bedding, drawn by the dogs, and conducted by Belanger and the Canadian sent by Mr. Weeks. We encamped on the Grassy-Lake Portage, having walked about nine miles, principally on the Yellow Knife River. It was open at the rapids and in these places we had to ascend its banks and walk through the woods for some distance, which was very fatiguing, especially to Dr. Richardson whose feet were severely galled in consequence of some defect in his snowshoes.

On the 11th however we arrived at the fort which was still under the charge of Mr. Weeks. He welcomed us in the most kind manner, immediately gave us changes of dress, and did everything in his power to make us comfortable.

Our sensations on being once more in a comfortable dwelling after the series of hardships and miseries we had experienced may be imagined. Our first act was again to return our grateful praises to the Almighty for the manifold instances of His mercy towards us. Having found here some articles which Mr. Back had sent across from Moose-Deer Island I determined on awaiting the arrival of Akaitcho and his party in order to present these to them and to assure them of the promised reward as soon as it could possibly be procured.

We discovered at the commencement of his speech to us that he had been informed that our expected supplies had not come. He spoke of this circumstance as a disappointment indeed sufficiently severe to himself, to whom his band looked up for the protection of their interests, but without attaching any blame to us.

Mr. Weeks provided Dr. Richardson and me with a cariole each and we set out at 11 a.m. on the 15th for Moose-Deer Island. Our party consisted of Belanger who had charge of a sledge laden with the bedding and drawn by two dogs, our two cariole men, Benoit and Augustus. Previous to our departure we had another conference with Akaitcho who, as well as the rest of his party, bade us farewell with a warmth of manner rare among the Indians.

The badness of Belanger's dogs and the roughness of the ice impeded our progress very much and obliged us to encamp early. We had a good fire made of the driftwood which lines the shores of this lake in great quantities. The next day was very cold. We began the journey at 9 a.m. and encamped at the Big Cape, having made another short march in consequence of the roughness of the ice.

On the 17th we encamped on the most southerly of the Reindeer Islands. This night was very stormy but, the wind abating in the morning, we proceeded and by sunset reached the fishing huts of the company at Stony Point. Here we found Mr. Andrews, a clerk of the Hudson's Bay Company, who regaled us with a supper of excellent white fish for which this part of Slave Lake is particularly celebrated. Two men with sledges arrived soon afterwards, sent by Mr. McVicar, who expected us about this time.

We set off in the morning before daybreak with several companions and arrived at Moose-Deer Island about 1 p.m. Here we were received with the utmost hospitality by Mr. McVicar, the chief trader of the Hudson's Bay Company in this district, as well as by his assistant Mr. McAuley. We had also the happiness of joining our friend Mr. Back; our feelings on this occasion can be well imagined and we were deeply impressed with gratitude to him for his exertions in sending the supply of food to Fort Enterprise, to which under Divine Providence we felt the preservation of our lives to be owing.

CHAPTER THREE

In Search of John Franklin

Elisha Kent Kane

Note: In May 1845, Sir John Franklin sailed from England with the ships Erebus *and* Terror, *on what would be his final voyage to find the Northwest Passage. Nothing was heard from him a year after he departed. In 1853 Elisha Kent Kane set off on the Second Grinnell Expedition, to search for survivors of Franklin's lost expedition.*

IT WAS WITH MINGLED FEELINGS THAT WE NEARED THE BRIG. OUR little party had grown fat and strong upon the auks and eiders and scurvy-grass; and surmises were rife among us as to the condition of our comrades and the prospects of our ice-bound ship.

The tide-leads, which one year ago had afforded a precarious passage to the vessel, now barely admitted our whale-boat; and, as we forced her through the broken ice, she showed such signs of hard usage, that I had her hauled up upon the land-belt and housed under the cliffs at Six-mile Ravine. We crossed the rocks on foot, aided by our jumping-poles, and startled our shipmates by our sudden appearance.

In the midst of the greeting which always met our returning parties, and which gave to our little vessel the endearing associations of a homestead, our thoughts reverted to the feeble chances of our liberation, and the failure of our recent effort to secure the means of a retreat.

The brig had been imprisoned by closely-cementing ice for eleven months, during which period she had not budged an inch from her icy cradle.

August 8

This morning two saw-lines were passed from the open-water pools at the sides of our stern-post, and the ice was bored for blasting. In the course of our operations the brig surged and righted, rising two and a half feet. We are now trying to warp her a few yards toward Butler Island, where we again go to work with our powder-canisters. The blasting succeeded; one canister cracked and uplifted two hundred square yards of ice with but five pounds of powder. A prospect showed itself of getting inside the island at high water; and I determined to attempt it at the highest spring-tide, which takes place on the 12th.

August 12

The brig bore the strain of her new position very well. The tide fell fifteen feet, leaving her high and dry; but, as the water rose, everything was replaced, and the deck put in order for warping again. Everyone in the little vessel turned to; and after much excitement, at the very top of the tide, she passed "by the skin of her teeth." She was then warped in a bight of the floe, neat Fox-Trap Point, and there she now lies.

We congratulated ourselves upon effecting this crossing; Had we failed, we should have had to remain fast probably for the high tides a fortnight hence. The young ice is already forming, and our hopes rest mainly upon the late gales of August and September.

August 18

Reduced our allowance of wood to six pounds a meal. This, among eighteen mouths, is one-third of a pound of fuel for each. It allows us coffee twice a day, and soup once. Our fare besides this is cold pork boiled in quantity and eaten as required. This sort of thing works badly; but I must save coal for other emergencies. I see "darkness ahead."

My attempt to reach Beechy Island had disclosed, as I thought it would, the impossibility of reaching the settlements of Greenland.

Everything before us was now involved in gloomy doubt. Hopeful as I had been, it was impossible not to feel that we were near the climax of the expedition.

I determined to place upon Observatory Island a large signal-beacon or cairn, and to bury under it documents which, in case of disaster to our party, would convey to any who might seek us intelligence of our proceedings and our fate. The memory of the first winter-quarters of Sir John Franklin, and the painful feelings with which, while standing by the graves of his dead, I had five years before Sought for written signs pointing to the fate of the living, me careful to avoid a similar neglect.

A conspicuous spot was selected upon a cliff looking out upon the icy desert, and on a broad face of rock the words—

ADVANCE,
A.D. 1853–54

were painted in letters which could be read at a distance. A pyramid of heavy stones, perched above it, was marked with the Christian symbol of the cross. It was not without a holier sentiment than that of mere utility that I placed under this the coffins of our two poor comrades. It was our beacon, and their gravestone.

Near this a hole was worked into the rock, and a paper, enclosed in glass, sealed in with melted lead. It read as follows:—

BRIG "ADVANCE," AUGUST 14, 1854

E. K. Kane, with his comrades, members of the Second Grinnell Expedition in search of Sir John Franklin and the missing crews of the Erebus and Terror, were forced into this harbour while endeavouring to bore the ice to the north and east.

They were frozen in on the 8th of September 1853, and liberated——.

During this period the labours of the expedition have delineated 960 miles of coast-line, without developing any traces of the missing ships or the slightest information bearing upon their fate. The amount of travel to effect this exploration exceeded 2000 miles, all of which was upon foot or by the aid of dogs.

(Signed) E. K. KANE
Commanding Expedition. Fox-Trap Point, August 14, 1854

The following note was added some hours later:—

> The young ice having formed between the brig and this island, and
> prospects of a gale showing themselves, the date of departure is left
> unfilled. If possible, a second visit will be made to insert our dates,
> our final escape being still dependent upon the course of the season.
>
> E. K. Kane

And now came the question of the second winter—how to look
our enemy in the face, and how to meet him. Anything was better than
inaction; and, in spite of the uncertainty which yet attended our plans,
a host of expedients were to be resorted to, and much Robinson Crusoe
labour ahead. Moss was to be gathered for eking out our winter fuel, and
willow-stems, and stonecrops, and sorrel, as anti-scorbutics, collected and
buried in the snow. But while all these were in progress came other and
graver questions.

Some of my party had entertained the idea that an escape to
the south was still practicable; and this opinion was supported by
Mr. Petersen, our Danish interpreter, who had accompanied the
Searching Expedition of Captain Penny, and had a matured experience in
the changes of Arctic ice. They even thought that the safety of all would
be promoted by a withdrawal from the brig.

August 21

The question of detaching a party was in my mind some time ago; but the
more I thought it over, the more I was convinced that it would be neither
right in itself nor practically safe. For myself personally, it is a simple duty
of honour to remain by the brig: I could not think of leaving her till I
had proved the effect of the later tides; and after that, as I have known all
along, it would be too late. Come what may, I share her fortunes."

I know all this as a medical man and an officer; and I feel that we
might be wearing away the hearts and energies, if not the lives of all, by
forcing those who were reluctant to remain. With half a dozen confiding,
resolute men, I have no fears of ultimate safety.

I will make a thorough inspection of the ice tomorrow, and decide finally the prospects of our liberation.

August 23

The brig cannot escape. I got an eligible position with my sledge to review the floes, and returned this morning at two o'clock. There is no possibility of our release, unless by some extreme intervention of the coming tides. I doubt whether a boat could be forced as far as the Southern Water. When I think of the extraordinary way in which the ice was impacted last winter, how very little it has yielded through the summer, and how early another winter is making its onset upon us, I am very doubtful, indeed, whether our brig can get away at all. It would be inexpedient to attempt leaving her now in boats—the water-streams closing, the pack nearly fast again, and the young ice almost impenetrable.

I shall call the officers and crew together, and make known to them very fully how things look, and what hazards must attend such an effort as has been proposed among them. They shall have my view unequivocally expressed. I will then give them twenty-four hours to deliberate; and at the end of that time all who determine to go shall say so in writing, with a full exposition of the circumstances of the case. They shall have the best outfit I can give, an abundant share of our remaining stores, and my goodbye blessing.

August 24

At noon today I had all hands called, and explained to them frankly the considerations which have determined me to remain where we are. I endeavoured to show them that an escape to open water could not succeed, and that the effort must be exceedingly hazardous: I alluded to our duties to the ship; in a word, I advised them strenuously to forego the project. I then told them that I should freely give my permission to such as were desirous of making the attempt, but that I should require them to place themselves under the command of officers selected by them before setting out, and to renounce in writing all claims upon myself and the rest who were resolved to stay by the vessel. Having done this, I directed the roll to be called, and each man to answer for himself.

In the result, eight out of the seventeen survivors of my party resolved to stand by the brig.

I divided to the others their portion of our resources justly and even liberally; and they left us on Monday, the 28th, with every appliance our narrow circumstances could furnish to speed and guard them. One of them, George Riley, returned a few days afterward; but weary months went by before we saw the rest again. They carried with them a written assurance of a brother's welcome should they be driven back; and this assurance was redeemed when hard trials had prepared them to share again our fortunes.

The party moved off with the elastic step of men confident in their purpose, and were out of sight in a few hours. As we lost them among the hummocks, the stern realities of our condition pressed themselves upon us anew. The reduced numbers of our party, the helplessness of many, the waning efficiency of all, the impending winter, with its cold dark night, our penury of resources, the dreary sense of increased isolation—these made the staple of our thoughts.

For a time Sir John Franklin and his party, our daily topic through so many months, gave place to the question of our own fortunes—how we were to escape, how to live. The summer had gone, the harvest was ended, and—. We did not care to finish the sentence.

We were like men driven to the wall, quickened, not depressed. Our plans were formed at once: there is nothing like emergency to speed, if not to instruct, the energies.

My resolve was to practise on the lessons we had learned from the Esquimaux. I had studied them carefully, and determined that their form of habitation and their peculiarities of diet, without their unthrift and filth, were the safest and best to which the necessity of our circumstances invited us.

My journal tells how these resolves were carried out:—

SEPTEMBER 6

We are at it, all hands, sick and well, each man according to his measure, working at our winter's home. We are none of us in condition to brave the frost, and our fuel is nearly out.

The sledge is to bring us moss and turf from wherever the men can scrape it. This is an excellent non-conductor; and when we get the quarter-deck well padded with it, we shall have a nearly cold-proof covering. Down below we will enclose a space some eighteen feet square, and pack it from floor to ceiling with inner walls of the same material. The floor itself we are calking carefully with plaster of Paris and common paste, and will cover it, when we have done, with Manilla oakum a couple of inches deep, and a canvas carpet. The entrance is to be from the hold, by a low, moss-lined tunnel, the *tossut* of the native huts, with as many doors and curtains to close it up as our ingenuity can devise. This is to be our apartment of all uses—not a very large one; but we are only ten to stow away, and the closer the warmer.

SEPTEMBER 10

The work goes bravely on. We have got moss enough for our roof, and something to spare for below. Tomorrow we begin to strip off the outer-deck planking of the brig, and to stack it for firewood. It is cold work, hatches open and no fires going; but we saved time enough for our Sunday exercises, though we forego its rest.

I determined to try a novel expedient for catching seal. Not more than ten miles to seaward the icebergs keep up a rude stream of broken ice and water, and the seals resort there in scanty numbers to breathe. I drove out with my dogs, taking Hans along; but we found the spot so hemmed in by loose and fragile ice that there was no approaching it. The thermometer was eight degrees, and a light breeze increased my difficulties.

Deo volente, I will be more lucky tomorrow. I am going to take my long Kentucky rifle, the kayack, an Esquimaux harpoon with its attached line and bladder, *naligeit* and *awahtok*, and a pair of large snow-shoes to boot. My plan this time is to kneel where the ice is unsafe, resting my weight on the broad surface of the snow-shoes, Hans following astride of his kayack, as a sort of life-preserver in case of breaking in. If I am fortunate enough to stalk within gun-range, Hans will take to the water and secure the game before it sinks. We will be gone for some days probably, tenting it in the open air; but our sick men—that is to say, all of us—are languishing for fresh meat.

I started with Hans and five dogs, and in a couple of hours we emerged upon a plain unlimited to the eye and smooth as a billiard-table. Feathers of young frosting gave a plush-like nap to its surface, and toward the horizon dark columns of frost-smoke pointed clearly to the open water. This ice was firm enough; our experience satisfied us that it was not a very recent freezing.

We pushed on without hesitation, cheering ourselves with the expectation of coming every minute to the seals. We passed a second ice-growth; it was not so strong as the one we had just come over, but still safe for a party like ours. On we went at a brisker gallop, maybe for another mile, when Hans sang out, at the top of his voice, "Pusey! puseymut! seal, seal!" At the same instant the dogs bounded forward, and, as I looked up, I saw crowds of grey netsik, the rough or hispid seal of the whalers, disporting in an open sea of water.

I had hardly welcomed the spectacle when I saw that we had passed upon a new belt of ice that was obviously unsafe. To turn was impossible; we had to keep up our gait. We urged on the dogs with whip and voice, the ice rolling like leather beneath the sledge-runners; it was more than a mile to the lump of solid ice. Fear gave to the poor beasts their utmost speed, and our voices were soon hushed to silence.

This desperate race against fate could not last: the rolling of the tough salt-water ice terrified our dogs; and when within fifty paces from the floe they paused. The left-hand runner went through; our leader "Toodlamick" followed, and in one second the entire left of the sledge was submerged. My first thought was to liberate the dogs. I leaned forward to cut poor Tood's traces, and the next minute was swimming in a little circle of pasty ice and water alongside him. Hans, dear good fellow, drew near to help me, uttering piteous expressions in broken English; but I ordered him to throw himself on his belly, with his hands and legs extended, and to make for the island by cogging himself forward with his jack-knife. In the meantime—a mere instant—I was floundering about with sledge, dogs, and lines, in a confused puddle around me.

I succeeded in cutting poor Tood's lines and letting him scramble to the ice, for the poor fellow was drowning me with his piteous caresses, and made my way for the sledge; but I found that it would not buoy me, and that I had no resource but to try the circumference of the hole.

Around this I paddled faithfully, the miserable ice always yielding when my hopes of a lodgment were greatest. During this process I enlarged my circle of operations to a very uncomfortable diameter, and was beginning to feel weaker after every effort. Hans meanwhile had reached the firm ice, and was on his knees, like a good Moravian, praying incoherently in English and Esquimaux; at every fresh crushing-in of the ice he would ejaculate "God!" and when I recommenced my paddling he recommenced his prayers.

I was nearly gone. My knife had been lost in cutting out the dogs; and a spare one which I carried in my trouser-pocket was so enveloped in the wet skins that I could not reach it. I owed my extrication at last to a newly broken team dog, who was still fast to the sledge, and in struggling carried one of the runners choke against the edge of the circle. All my previous attempts to use the sledge as a bridge had failed, for it broke through, to the much greater injury of the ice. I felt that it was a last chance. I threw myself on my back, so as to lessen as much as possible my weight, and placed the nape of my neck against the rim or edge of the ice; then with caution slowly bent my leg, and, placing the ball of my mocassined foot against the sledge, I pressed steadily against the runner, listening to the half-yielding crunch of the ice beneath.

Presently I felt that my head was pillowed by the ice, and that my wet fur jumper was sliding up the surface. Next came my shoulders; they were fairly on. One more decided push, and I was launched up on the ice and safe. I reached the ice-floe, and was rubbed by Hans with frightful zeal. We saved all the dogs; but the sledge, kayack, tent, gun, snow-shoes, and everything besides, were left behind.

On reaching the ship, after a twelve-mile trot, I found so much of comfort and warm welcome that I forgot my failure. The fire was lit up, and one of our few birds slaughtered forthwith. It is with real gratitude that I look back upon my escape, and bless the great presiding Goodness for the very many resources which remain to us.

September 17

Writing by this miserable flicker of my pork-fat lamp, I can hardly steady pen, paper, or thought. All hands have rested after a heavy week's work, which has advanced us nobly in our arrangements for the winter. The season is by our tables at least three weeks earlier than the last, and everything indicates a severe ordeal ahead of us.

Just as we were finishing our chapter this morning in the "Book of Ruth," M'Gary and Morton, who had been to Anoatok, came in triumphantly, pretty well worn down by their fifty miles' travel, but with good news, and a flipper of walrus that must weigh some forty pounds. Ohlsen and Hans are in too. They arrived as we were sitting down to celebrate the Anoatok ratification of our treaty of the 6th.

It is a strange life we are leading. We are absolutely nomads, so far as there can be anything of pastoral life in this region; and our wild encounter with the elements seems to agree with us all. Our table-talk at supper was as merry as a marriage bell. One party was just in from a seventy-four miles' trip with the dogs; another from a journey of a 160, with five nights on the floe. Each had his story to tell.

September 30

We have been clearing up on the ice.

Thanks to our allies the Esquimaux, our beef-house is now a pile of barrels holding our water-soaked beef and pork. Flour, beans, and dried apples make a quadrangular blockhouse on the floe; from one corner of it rises our flagstaff, lighting up the dusky grey with its red and white ensign, only on Sunday giving place to the Henry Grinnell flag, of happy memories.

From this, along an avenue that opens abeam of the brig,— *New London Avenue*, named after M'Gary's town at home—are our boats and square cordage. Outside of all these is a magnificent hut of barrel-frames and snow, to accommodate our Esquimaux visitors—the only thing about it exposed to hazard being the tempting woodwork. What remains to complete our camp-plot is the rope barrier that is to mark out our little curtilage around the vessel; this, when finished, is to be the dividing-line between us and the rest of mankind.

There is something in the simplicity of all this *simplex munditiis,* which might commend itself to the most rigorous taste. Nothing is wasted on ornament.

October 4

I sent Hans and Hickey two days ago out to the hunting-ice, to see if the natives have had any luck with the walrus. They are back tonight with bad news—no meat, no Esquimaux. These strange children of the snow have made a mysterious flitting—where or how it is hard to guess, for they have no sledges. They cannot have travelled very far; and yet they have such unquiet impulses, that, once on the track, no civilised man can say where they will bring up.

October 5

We are nearly out of fresh meat again, one rabbit and three ducks being our sum total. We have been on short allowance for several days. What vegetables we have—the dried apples and peaches, and pickled cabbage—have lost much of their anti-scorbutic virtue by constant use. Our spices are all gone. Except four small bottles of horse-radish, our *carte* is comprised in three lines—bread, beef, pork.

I must be off after these Esquimaux. They certainly have meat, and wherever they have gone we can follow. Once upon their trail, our hungry instincts will not risk being baffled. I will stay only long enough to complete my latest root-beer brewage. Its basis is the big crawling willow, the miniature giant of our Arctic forests, of which we laid in a stock some weeks ago. It is quite pleasantly bitter, and I hope to get it fermenting in the deck-house without extra fuel, by heat from below.

October 7

Lively sensation, as they say in the land of olives and champagne. "Nannook, nannook!"—"A bear, a bear!"—Hans and Morton in a breath!

To the scandal of our domestic regulations, the guns were all impracticable. While the men were loading and capping anew, I seized my pillow-companion six-shooter, and ran on deck. A medium-sized bear, with a four months' cub, was in active warfare with our dogs. They were hanging on her skirts, and she with wonderful alertness was picking out one victim after another, snatching him by the nape of the neck, and flinging him many feet, or rather yards, by a barely perceptible movement of her head.

I lodged a pistol-ball in the side of the cub. Ohlsen wounded the mother as she went, but she scarcely noticed it. She tore down, by single efforts of her forearms, the barrels of frozen beef which made the triple walls of the storehouse, mounted the rubbish, and snatching up a half barrel of herrings, carried it down by her teeth, and was making off. It was time to close, I thought. Going up within half-pistol range, I gave her six buckshot. She dropped, but instantly rose, and, getting her cub into its former position, moved off once more.

This time she would really have escaped but for the admirable tactics of our new recruits from the Esquimaux. The dogs of Smith's Sound are educated more thoroughly than any of their southern brethren. Next to the walrus, the bear is the staple of diet to the north, and except for the fox, supplies the most important element of the wardrobe. Unlike the dogs we had brought with us from Baffin's Bay, these were trained, not to attack, but to embarrass. They ran in circles round the bear, and when pursued would keep ahead with regulated gait, their comrades effecting a diversion at the critical moment by a nip at her hind-quarters. This was done so systematically, and with so little seeming excitement, as to strike everyone on board. I have seen bear-dogs elsewhere that had been drilled to relieve each other in the *melée* and avoid the direct assault but here, two dogs without even a demonstration of attack, would put themselves before the path of the animal, and retreating right and left, lead him into a profitless pursuit that checked his advance completely.

The poor animal was still backing out, yet still fighting, carrying along her wounded cub, embarrassed by the dogs, yet gaining distance from the brig, when Hans and myself threw in the odds in the shape of a couple of rifle-balls. She staggered in front of her young one, faced us in death-like defiance, and only sank when pierced by six more bullets.

The little cub sprang upon the corpse of her mother, and raised a woeful lamentation over her wounds. She repelled my efforts to noose her with great ferocity; but at last, completely muzzled with a line fastened by a running knot between her jaws and the back of her head, she moved off to the brig amid the clamour of the dogs. We have her now chained alongside, but snarling and snapping constantly, evidently suffering from her wound.

October 10

If I was asked what, after darkness and cold and scurvy, are the three besetting curses of our Arctic sojourn, I should say, "Rats, Rats, Rats." A mother-rat bit my finger to the bone last Friday, as I was intruding my hand into a bear-skin mitten which she had chosen as a homestead for her little family. I withdrew it of course with instinctive courtesy; but among them they carried off the mitten before I could suck the finger.

October 14

Wilson and Hickey reported last night a wolf at the meat-house. Now, the meat-house is a thing of too much worth to be left to casualty, and a wolf might incidentally add some freshness of flavour to its contents. So I went out in all haste with the Marston rifle, but without my mittens, and with only a single cartridge. The metal burnt my hands, as metal is apt to do at fifty degrees below the point of freezing; but I got a somewhat rapid shot. I hit one of our dogs, a truant from Morton's team; luckily a flesh wound only, for he is too good a beast to lose. I could have sworn he was a wolf.

October 19

Our black dog Erebus has come back to the brig. Morton has perhaps released him, but he has more probably broken loose.

October 21

Hard at it still, slinging chains and planting shores. The thermometer is too near zero for work like this. We swaddle our feet in old cloth, and guard our hands with fur mits; but the cold iron bites through them all.

6:30 p.m.—Morton and Hans are in, after tracking the Esquimaux to the lower settlement of Etah. I cannot give their report tonight: the poor fellows are completely knocked up by the hardships of their march. Hans, who is always careless of powder and firearms exploded his powder-flask while attempting to kindle a tinder fire. The explosion has risked his hand. I have dressed it, extracting several pieces of foreign matter, and poulticing it in yeast and charcoal. Morton has frost-bitten both his heels; I hope not too severely, for the indurated skin of the heel makes it a bad region for suppuration. But they bring us 270 pounds of walrus-meat, and a couple of foxes. This supply, with what we have remaining of our two bears, must last us till the return of daylight allows us to join the natives in their hunts.

The light is fast leaving us. The sun has ceased to reach the vessel. The northeastern headlands, or their southern faces up the fiords, have still a warm yellow tint, and the pinnacles of the icebergs far out on the floes are lighted up at noonday; but all else is dark shadow.

The Coming Winter

October 26

The thermometer at thirty-four degrees below zero, but fortunately no wind blowing. We go on with the outdoor work. We burn but seventy pounds of fuel a day, most of it in the galley—the fire being allowed to go out between meals. We go without fire altogether for four hours of the night; yet such is the excellence of our moss-walls and the air-proof of our *tossut*, that, when our housing is arranged, and the main hatch secured with a proper weather-tight screen of canvas, we shall be able, I hope, to meet the extreme cold of February and March without fear.

Darkness is the worst enemy we have to face; but we will strive against the scurvy in spite of him, till the light days of sun and vegetation.

Wilson and Brooks are my principal subjects of anxiety; for although Morton and Hans are on their backs, making four of our ten, I can see strength of system in their cheerfulness of heart. The best prophylactic is a hopeful, sanguine temperament; the best cure, moral resistance— that spirit of combat against every trial, which is alone true bravery.

October 27

The work is going on; we are ripping off the extra planking of our deck for fuel during the winter. The cold increases fast, and in spite of all my efforts we will have to burn largely into the brig. I prepared for this two months ago, and satisfied myself, after a consultation with the carpenter, that we may cut away some seven or eight tons of fuel without absolutely destroying her sea-worthiness.

Yet some of these are topics of interest. The intense beauty of the Arctic firmament can hardly be imagined. It looks close above our heads, with its stars magnified in glory, and the very planets twinkling so much as to baffle the observations of our astronomer. I am afraid to speak of some of these night-scenes. I have trodden the deck and the floes, when the life of earth seemed suspended—its movements, its sounds, its colouring, its companionships; and as I looked on the radiant hemisphere, circling above me as if rendering worship to the unseen centre of light, I have ejaculated in humility of spirit, "Lord, what is man that Thou art mindful of him?" And then I have thought of the kindly world we had left, with its revolving sunshine and shadow, and the other stars that gladden it in their changes, and the hearts that warmed to us there, till I lost myself in memories of those who are not—and they bore me back to the stars again.

The winter is now upon us, and little or nothing can be done either to effect the liberation of the brig from her icy fetters, or to further our explorations.

On board the brig the mode of life is the same as last winter, except that we are subject to greater privations, consequent on the great demands which have been made upon the stores. We have little to amuse ourselves, and we go through the monotonous round of the day's duties with as much celerity and ready will, as our drooping circumstances will admit of.

I cannot hide from myself the fact that the main object of our expedition must now be finally abandoned; and our duty, in the next instance, is toward ourselves: to wait the return of light in order to accomplish our escape from the ice—with the brig if possible, if impossible, without it—before the frail appliances and stores which are now left are entirely exhausted. Of course, it would be both impolitic and unwise to apprise the crew of my thoughts on this painful subject, so I will keep my own counsel in the meantime. I can see, however, that I am not alone in my convictions.

During November, I observed a few of my best men getting nervous and depressed—M'Gary paced the deck all one Sunday in a fit of home-sickness, without eating a meal—I do my best to cheer them; but it is hard work to hide one's own trials for the sake of others who have not as many. I am glad of my professional drill and its companion influence over the sick and toil worn. I could not get along at all unless I combined the offices of physician and commander. You cannot punish sick men.

December saw the brig fitted up for the winter; and, all things considered, very comfortably we made it. Tom Hickey, our good-humoured, blundering cabin-boy, decorated since poor Schubert's death with the dignities of cook, is in that little dirty cot on the starboard-side; the rest are bedded in rows, Mr. Brooks and myself choke aft. Our bunks are close against the frozen moss-wall, where we can take in the entire family at a glance. The apartment measures twenty feet by eighteen; its height six feet four inches at one place, but diversified elsewhere by beams crossing at different distances from the floor. The avenue by which it is approached is barely to be seen in the moss-wall forward. The avenue—Ben-Djerback is our poetic name for it—closes on the inside with a door well patched with flannel, from which, stooping upon all-fours, you back down a descent of four feet in twelve, through a tunnel three feet high and two feet six inches broad. It would have been a tight squeeze for a man like Mr. Brooks, when he was better fed and fatter.

Arrived at the bottom, you straighten yourself, and a second door admits you into the dark and sorrowing hold, empty of stores, and stripped to its naked ceiling for firewood. From this we grope our way to the main hatch, and mount by a rude stairway of boxes into the open air.

December 2

Many of the men are down with sickness and scurvy, and this adds greatly to my anxiety. M'Gary, Riley, Wilson, and Brooks, are all on the sick-list, and as for poor Morton, I am afraid I will lose him. Poor fellows, I can ill afford to lose any of them; but if Morton dies, it will be a great loss indeed. He is not only one of my most intelligent men, but he is daring, cool, and every way trustworthy.

On the 7th we had an agreeable surprise. I was asleep in the forenoon, after the fatigue of an extra night-watch, when I was called to the deck by the report of "Esquimaux sledges." They came on rapidly, five sledges, with teams of six dogs each, most of the drivers strangers to us; and in a few minutes were at the brig. Their errand was of charity: they were bringing back to us Bonsall and Petersen, two of the party that left us on the 28th of August.

The party had many adventures and much suffering to tell of. They had verified by painful and perilous experience all I had anticipated for them. But the most stirring of their announcements was the condition they had left their associates in, 200 miles off, divided in their counsels, their energies broken, and their provisions nearly gone. Space and opportunity will not permit of my giving an account of their wanderings and privations, but they were very severe. My first thought was of the means of rescuing them. After a little necessary delay I despatched a party to relieve them.

On the morning of the 12th Brooks awoke me with the cry of "Esquimaux again!" I dressed hastily, and groping my way over the pile of boxes that leads up from the hold into the darkness above, made out a group of human figures, masked by the hooded jumpers of the natives. They stopped at the gangway, and, as I was about to challenge, one of them sprang forward and grasped my hand. It was Doctor Hayes. A few words, dictated by suffering, certainly not by any anxiety as to his reception, and at his bidding the whole party came upon deck. Poor fellows! I could only grasp their hands and give them a brother's welcome.

One by one they all came in and were housed. Poor fellows! As they threw open their Esquimaux garments by the stove, how they relished the scanty luxuries which we had to offer them! The coffee and the meat-biscuit soup, and the molasses and wheat bread, even the salt pork which our scurvy forbade the rest of us to touch—how they relished it all! For more than two months they had lived on frozen seal and walrus-meat.

December 23

A very serious occurrence took place today, which might have resulted in disastrous consequences. A watch had been stationed in charge of the lamp, with the usual order of "No uncovered lights." He deserted his post. Soon afterward Hans found the cooking-room on fire. It was a horrible crisis; for no less than eight of our party were absolutely nailed to their beds, and there was nothing but a bulkhead between them and the fire. I gave short but instant orders, stationing a line between the tide-hole and the main hatch, detailing two men to work with me, and ordering all the rest who could move to their quarters. Dr. Hayes with his maimed foot, Mr. Brooks with his contracted legs, and poor Morton, otherwise among our best men, could do nothing.

Before we reached the fire the entire bulkhead was in a blaze as well as the dry timbers and skin of the brig. Our moss walls, with their own tinder-like material and their light casing of inflammable wood, were entirely hidden by the flames. Fortunately the furs of the recently-returned party were at hand, and with them I succeeded in smothering the fire. But I was obliged to push through the blaze of our sailcloth bulkhead in order to defend the wall; and in my anxiety to save time, I had left the cabin without either cap or mittens. I got through somehow or other, and tore down the canvas which hung against that dangerous locality. Our rifles were in this corner, and their muzzles pointing in all directions.

The water now began to pass down; but with the discharge of the first bucketful the smoke overcame me. As I found myself going I pushed for the hatchway, knowing that the bucket-line would *feel* me. Seeing was impossible; but, striking Ohlsen's legs as I fell, I was passed up to the deck, *minus* beard, eyebrows, and forelock, *plus* two burns on the forehead and one on each palm.

In about three minutes after making way with the canvas the fire was got under, and in less than half an hour all was safe again. But the transition, for even the shortest time, from the fiery Shadrachin furnace-temperature below, to forty-six degrees below zero above, was intolerably trying. Every man suffered, and few escaped without frost-bitten fingers.

The remembrance of the danger and its horrible results almost miraculously averted, shocks us all. Had we lost our brig, not a man could have survived. Without shelter, clothing, or food, what help could we have on the open ice field?

DECEMBER 25, CHRISTMAS DAY

All together again, the returned and the steadfast, we sat down to our Christmas dinner. There was more love than with the "stalled ox" of former times; but of herbs none. We forgot our discomforts in the blessings which adhered to us still; and when we thought of the long road ahead of us, we thought of it hopefully. I pledged myself to give them their next Christmas with their homes; and each of us drank to his "absent friends" with ferocious zest over one-eighteenth part of a bottle of sillery—the last of its hamper."

We entered upon the New Year 1851 with mingled feelings of hope and dismay. The long, dull, dreary months of January and February "dragged their slow length along" without much variety or incidents worth noting. We devised plans by which we hoped to be able to get away from our frozen fortress, but could do nothing in the way of execution until the much-longed-for light reappeared.

FEBRUARY 10

At length we have prognostications of the return of the blessed sun. The day is beginning to glow with its rays. The south at noon has almost an orange tinge. In ten days his direct rays will reach our hill tops, and in a week after he will be dispensing his blessed medicine among our sufferers.

FEBRUARY 21

Today the crests of the northeast headland were gilded by true sunshine, and all who were able assembled on deck to greet it. For the past ten days we have been watching the growing warmth of our landscape, as it emerged from buried shadow, through all the stages of distinctness of an India-ink washing, step by step, into the sharp, bold definition of our desolate harbour scene. We have marked every dash of colour which the great Painter in his benevolence vouchsafed to us; and now the empurpled blues, clear, unmistakable, the spreading lake, the flickering yellow; peering at all these, poor wretches! Everything seemed superlative lustre and unsurpassable glory. We had so grovelled in darkness that we oversaw the light.

My journal for March is little else than a chronicle of sufferings. Our little party was quite broken down. Every man on board was tainted with scurvy, and it was not common to find more than three who could assist in caring for the rest. The greater number were in their bunks, absolutely unable to stir.

The advent of April brings with it a better state of matters. Petersen has so far recovered that he is able to go hunting, and he has met with some success; and never was blessing more welcome than the fresh meat with which his gun supplied our long starved table. Several of the crew are on their legs again, and things generally begin to assume a healthier aspect. Business, as far as our shattered constitutions will permit, is now the order of the day.

April 20

A relief-watch, of Riley, Morton, and Bonsall, are preparing to saw out sledge runners from the cross-beams of the brig. It is slow work. They are very weak, and the thermometer sinks at night to minus twenty-six degrees. Nearly all our beams have been used up for fuel; but I have saved enough to construct two sledges. I want a sledge sufficiently long to bring the weight of the whale-boat and her stowage within the line of the runner; this will prevent her rocking and pitching when crossing hummocked ice, and enable us to cradle her firmly to the sledge.

April 21

The beam was too long to be carried through our hatches; we therefore have sawed it as it stands, and will carry up the slabs separately. These slabs are but one and a half inch wide, and must be strengthened by iron bolts and cross-pieces; still they are all that we have. I made the bolts out of our cabin curtain-rods, long disused. Mr. Petersen aids Ohlsen in grinding his tools. They will complete the job tomorrow—for we must work on Sunday now—and by Monday be able to begin at other things. Petersen undertakes to manufacture our cooking and mess-gear. I have a sad-looking assortment of battered rusty tins to offer him; but with the stove-pipe much may be done.

APRIL 22

Gave rest for all but the sawyers, who keep manfully at the beam. Some notion of our weakness may be formed from the fact of these five poor follows averaging among them but one foot per hour.

FAREWELL TO THE *ADVANCE*

Our last farewell to the brig on May 20 was made with more solemnity. The entire ship's company was collected in our dismantled winter-chamber to take part in the ceremonial. It was Sunday. Our moss walls had been torn down, and the wood that supported them burned. Our beds were off at the boats. The galley was unfurnished and cold. Everything about the little den of refuge was desolate.

We read prayers and a chapter of the Bible; and then, all standing silently round, I took Sir John Franklin's portrait from its frame and cased it in an India-rubber scroll. I next read the reports of inspection and survey which had been made by the several commissions organized for the purpose, all of them testifying to the necessities under which I was about to act.

I then addressed the party: I did not affect to disguise the difficulties that were before us; but I assured them that they could all be overcome by energy and subordination to command; and that the 1,300 miles of ice and water that lay between us and North Greenland could be traversed with safety for most of us, and hope for all. I added, that as men and messmates, it was the duty of us all, enjoined by gallantry as well as religion, to postpone every consideration of self to the protection of the wounded and sick; and that this must be regarded by every man, and under all circumstances, as a paramount order. In conclusion, I told them to think over the trials we had all of us gone through, and to remember each man for himself how often an unseen Power had rescued him in peril; and I admonished them still to place reliance on Him who could not change.

I was met with a right spirit. After a short conference, an engagement was drawn up by one of the officers, and brought to me with the signatures of all the company, without an exception. It read as follows:—

Being convinced of the impossibility of the liberation of the brig, and equally convinced of the impossibility of remaining in the ice a third winter, do fervently concur with the commander in his attempt to reach the south by means of boats.

Knowing the trials and hardships which are before us, and feeling the necessity of union, harmony, and discipline, we have determined to abide faithfully by the expedition and our sick comrades, and to do all that we can, as true men, to advance the objects in view.

I had prepared a brief memorial of the considerations which justified our abandonment of the vessel, and had read it as part of my address. I now fixed it to a stanchion near the gangway, where it must attract the notice of any who might seek us hereafter, and stand with them as my vindication for the step, in case we should be overtaken by disaster. It closed with these words:—

I regard the abandonment of the brig as inevitable. We have by actual inspection but thirty-six days' provisions, and a careful survey shows that we cannot cut more firewood without rendering our craft unseaworthy. A third winter would force us, as the only means of escaping starvation, to resort to Esquimaux habits and give up all hope of remaining by the vessel and her resources. It would therefore in no manner advance the search after Sir John Franklin.

Under any circumstances, to remain longer would be destructive to those of our little party who have already suffered from the extreme severity of the climate and its tendencies to disease. Scurvy has enfeebled more or less every man in the expedition; and an anomalous spasmodic disorder, allied to tetanus, has cost us the life of two of our most prized comrades.

I hope, speaking on the part of my companions and myself, that we have done all that we ought to do to prove our tenacity of purpose and devotion to the cause which we have undertaken. This attempt to escape by crossing the southern ice on sledges is regarded by me as an imperative duty,—the only means of saving ourselves and preserving the laboriously-earned results of the expedition.

E. K. KANE
Commander, Grinnell Expedition
"ADVANCE," RENSSELAER BAY, May 20, 1855

We then went upon deck: the flags were hoisted and hauled down again, and our party walked once or twice around the brig, looking at her timbers and exchanging comments upon the scars which reminded them of every stage of her dismantling. Our figure-head—the fair Augusta, the little blue girl with pink cheeks, who had lost her breast by an iceberg and her nose by a nip off Bedevilled Reach—was taken from our bows and placed aboard the "Hope." "She is at any rate wood," said the men, when I hesitated about giving them the additional burden; "and if we cannot carry her far we can burn her."

No one thought of the mockery of cheers: we had no festival-liquor to mislead our perception of the real state of things. When all hands were quite ready, we scrambled off over the ice together, much like a gang of stevedores going to work over a quayful of broken cargo.

Excluding four sick men, who were unable to move, and myself, who had to drive the dog-team and serve as common carrier and courier, we numbered but twelve men—which would have given six to a sledge, or too few to move it. It was therefore necessary to concentrate our entire force upon one sledge at a time. On the other hand, however, it was important to the efficiency of our organization that matters of cooking, sleeping baggage, and rations, should be regulated by separate messes.

The routine I established was the most precise:—Daily prayers both morning and evening, all hands gathering round in a circle and standing uncovered during the short exercise; regulated hours; fixed duties and positions at the track-lines and on the halt; the cooking to be taken by turns, the captains of the boats alone being excused. The charge of the log was confided to Dr. Hayes, and the running survey to Mr. Sontag. Though little could be expected from either of these gentlemen at this time, I deemed it best to keep up the appearance of ordinary voyaging;

and after we left the first ices of Smith's Straits I was indebted to them for valuable results. The thermometer was observed every three hours.

To my faithful friend and first officer, boatswain Brooks, I assigned the command of the boats and sledges. I knew how well he was fitted for it; and when forced, as I was afterward during the descent, to be in constant motion between the sick-station, the Esquimaux settlements, and the deserted brig, I felt safe in the assurance of his tried fidelity and indomitable resolution. The party under him was marshalled at the rue-raddies as a single gang; but the messes were arranged with reference to the two whale-boats, and when we came afterward to the open water the crews distributed in the same way:

Up to the evening of the 23rd, the progress was little more than a mile a day for one sledge; on the 24th, both sledges reached First Ravine, a distance of seven miles, when we found that the dog-sledge had brought on to this station the buffalo bags and other sleeping appliances which we had prepared during the winter. The condition of the party was such that it was essential they should sleep in comfort; and it was a rule, therefore, during the whole journey, never departed from unless in extreme emergency, never to begin a new day's labour till the party was refreshed from the exertions of the day before. Our halts were regulated by the condition of the men rather than by arbitrary hours, and sleep was meted out in proportion to the trials of the march. We slept by day when the sun was warmest, and travelled when we could avoid his greatest glare.

Mr. Morton, Ohlsen, and Petersen, during this time performed a double duty. They took their turn at the sledges with the rest, but they were also engaged in preparing the *Red Eric* as a comrade boat. She was mounted on our good old sledge, the *Faith*—a sledge that, like her namesake, our most reliable whale-boat, had been our very present help in many times of trouble. I believe every man felt, when he saw her brought out, that stout work was to be done, and under auspices of good.

In the meantime I had carried Mr. Goodfellow, with my dog-sledge, to a sick-station, which I had arranged at Anoatok; and had managed to convey the rest one by one to the same spot. Mr. Wilson who suffered from scurvy; George Whipple, whose tendons were so contracted that he could not extend his legs, and poor Stephenson, just able to keep the lamps burning and warm up food for the rest, were the other invalids, all incapable of moving without assistance. It is just that I should speak of the manly fortitude with which they bore up during this painful imprisonment. Dr. Hayes, though still disabled from his frozen foot, adhered manfully to the sledges.

As I review my notes of the first few days of our ice-journey, I find them full of incidents, interesting and even momentous when they occurred, but which cannot claim a place in this narrative. The sledges were advancing slowly, the men often discouraged, and now and then one giving way under the unaccustomed labour.

The *Red Boat* was completed for service in a few days, and joined the sledge-party on the floes,—an additional burden, but a necessary one, for our weary rue-raddies; and I set out for the sick-station with Mr. Goodfellow, our last remaining invalid. As my team reached the entrance of Force Bay, I saw that poor Nessark, the Esquimaux, who had carried Mr. Wilson and some stores to Anoatok, finding his sledge-load too heavy, had thrown out a portion of it upon the ice.

He had naturally enough selected the bread for his jettison, an article of diet unknown among the Esquimaux, but precisely that of which our sick were most in need. I lost some time in collecting such parts of his rejected cargo as I could find, and, when I reached the huts after a twelve hours' drive, the condition of our sick men made it imperative that I should return at once to the brig. The strength of the dogs began to fail while crossing the reach of Force Bay, and I was forced to camp out with them on the ice-belt, but early in the morning I came upon the fires of the sledge-party.

The men were at prayers when I first saw them; but, as they passed to the drag-ropes, I was pained to see how wearily they moved. Poor Brooks' legs were so swollen that he could not brace them in his blanket coverings, and Dr. Hayes could hardly keep his place. The men generally showed symptoms of increasing scurvy. It was plain that they could not hold their own without an increased allowance, if not of meat, at least of fresh bread and hot tea.

Taking with me Morton, my faithful adjutant always, I hurried on to the brig.

We lighted fires in the galley, melted pork, baked a large batch of bread, gathered together a quantity of beans and dried apples, somewhat damaged, but still eatable, and by the time our dogs had fed and rested, we were ready for the return. Distributing our supplies as we passed the squads on the floe, I hastened to Anoatok. I had taken Godfrey with us from his party, and, as it was painfully evident that the men could not continue to work without more generous food, I sent him on to Etah with the dogs, in the hope of procuring a stock of walrus-meat.

The little company at the hut welcomed my return. They had exhausted their provisions; their lamp had gone out; the snow-drift had forced its way in at the door, so that they could not close it; it was blowing a northeaster; and the thermometer, which hung against the blanketed walls, stood only sixteen degrees above zero. The poor fellows had all the will to protect themselves, but they were lame, and weak, and hungry, and disheartened. We built a fire for them of tarred rope, dried their bedding, cooked them a porridge of meat-biscuit and pea-soup, fastened up their desolate doorway, hung a dripping-slab of pork-fat over their lamp-wick, and, first joining in a prayer of thankfulness, and then a round of merry gossip, all hands forgot sickness, and privation, and distance in the contentment of our sleeping-bags. I cannot tell how long we slept, for all our watches ran down before we awoke.

The gale had risen, and it was snowing hard when I replenished the fires of our heartstone. But we went on burning rope and fat, in a regular tea-drinking frolic, till not an icicle or even a frost-mark was to be seen on the roof. After a time Godfrey rejoined us; Metek came with him; and between their two sledges they brought an ample supply of meat. With part of this I hastened to the sledge-party. They were now off Ten-mile Ravine, struggling through the accumulated snows, and much exhausted, though not out of heart. In spite of their swollen feet, they had worked fourteen hours a day, passing in that time over some twelve miles of surface, and advancing a mile and a half on their way.

Once more leaving the party on the floe, Morton and myself, with Metek and his sledge in company, revisited the brig, and set ourselves to work baking bread. The brig was dreary enough, and Metek was glad to bid it good-bye, with one hundred and fifty pounds on his dog-sledge, consigned to Mr. Brooks. But he carried besides a letter, safely trusted to his inspection, which directed that he should be sent back forthwith for another load. It was something like a breach of faith, perhaps; but his services were indispensable, and his dogs still more so. He returned, of course, for there was no escaping us; his village lay in the opposite direction, and he could not deviate from the track after once setting out. In the time we had cooked about a hundred pounds of flour pudding, and tried out a couple of bagfuls of pork-fat—a good days work—and we were quite ready, before the subdued brightness of midnight came, to turn in to our beds. Our beds!—there was not an article of covering left on board. We ripped open the old mattresses, and, all three crawling down among the curled hair, Morton, Metek, and the Nalegak, slept as sound as vagrants on a haystack.

On Monday, the 28th, we all set out for the boats and Anoatok. Both Metek and myself had all our sledges heavily laden. We carried the last of our provision-bags, completing now our full complement of fifteen hundred pounds, the limit of capacity of our otherwise crowded boats.

It caused me a bitter pang to abandon our collection of objects of natural history, the cherished fruit of so much exposure and toil; and it was hardly easier to leave some other things behind—several of my well-tested instruments, for instance, and those silent friends, my books. They had all been packed up, hoping for a chance of saving them; and, to the credit of my comrades, let me say gratefully that they offered to exclude both clothes and food in favour of a full freight of these treasures.

But the thing was not to be thought of. I gave a last look at the desolate galley-stove, the representative of our long winter's fireside, at the still bright coppers now full of frozen water, the theodolite, the chart-box, and poor Wilson's guitar—one more at the remnant of the old moss-walls, the useless daguerreotypes, and the skeletons of dog, and deer, and bear, and musk-ox—stoppered in the rigging.

CHAPTER FOUR

The Last Voyage of the *Polaris*, 1871

Reverend Z. A. Mudge

Note: Charles Francis Hall died under what many felt were circumstances while leading the American-sponsored and ill-fated Polaris *expedition to reach the North Pole in 1871. Nearly one hundred years later, in 1968, an autopsy found he had consumed a lethal amount of arsenic in the last two weeks of his life.*

THE *POLARIS* WAS A CRAFT OF ABOUT FOUR HUNDRED TONS. SHE WAS A screw-propeller, and rigged as a fore-topsail schooner. Her sides were covered with a six-inch white oak planking, nearly doubling their strength. Her bows were nearly solid white oak, made sharp, and sheathed with iron. One of her boilers was fitted for the use of whale or seal oil, by which steam could be raised if the coal was exhausted. She was supplied with five extraordinary boats.

One of these must have been the last Yankee invention in the boat line. It is represented as having a capacity to carry twenty-five men, yet weighing only 250 pounds; when not in use it could be folded up and packed snugly away. The *Polaris* was, of course, amply equipped and ably manned, and great and useful results were expected from her.

President Grant is said to have entered with interest into this enterprise of Captain Hall, and the nation said, "God bless him and his perilous undertaking!" though many doubted the wisdom of Arctic expeditions.

A few days before his departure Mr. Hall received from the hand of his friend, Henry Grinnell, a flag of historic note. It had fluttered in the wind near the South Pole with Lieutenant Wilkes in 1838. It had been borne by De Haven far northward; it had gone beyond De Haven's highest in the Kane voyage and was planted still farther North Poleward by Hayes.

"I believe," exclaimed Captain Hall, on receiving it, "that this flag, in the spring of 1872, will float over a new world, in which the North Pole star is its crowning jewel."

The *Polaris* left New York June 29, 1871, tarried for a few days at New London, and was last heard from as she was ready to steam northward, the last of August, from Tussuissak, the most northern of the Greenland outposts.

As our voyagers are now about to enter upon the terribly earnest conflicts of North Pole explorers, and as their complement of men *and women* are complete, we will further introduce them to our readers.

The commander, Hall, is well-proportioned, muscular, of medium height, quiet, but completely enthusiastic in his chosen line of duty, believing thoroughly in himself and his enterprise, yet believing well too easily of others, especially of the rough men of his command, some of whom have grown up under the harsh discipline of the whale-ship or the naval service.

The next in command is the sailing-master, Captain S. O. Buddington. Captain Tyson, commissioned was commissioned assistant navigator to the expedition. William Morton, who sailed with Elisha Kent Kane, is second mate.

On the 24th of August the *Polaris* left Tussuissak and fairly began her Arctic fight in the ice, current, and wind encounters of Melville Bay. But on she steamed, passing in a few days through the Bay into the North Water, into Smith Sound, passing Hayes's winter-quarters, yet steaming on by Dr. Kane's winter-quarters.

The *Polaris* finally brings up in the ice barriers of north latitude 82°16". The highest points of previous voyages in this direction are far south. That new world of which the North Pole star is "the crowning jewel" is less than 600 miles farther. If that open sea located in this latitude by confident explorers was only a fact, how easily and how soon would the brave *Polaris* be there! But the ice-floe, strong and defiant, and the southern current, were facts, and the open sea nowhere visible. The *Polaris* was taken in hand by the ice and current in the historic, Arctic fashion, and set back about fifty miles. The Ice King had said, "Thus far and no farther," and pointed with his frosty fingers southward.

The *Polaris* early in September was glad to steam in under the land, anchor to an iceberg, and make her winter-quarters. Captain Hall called the harbor "Thank-God Harbor," and the friendly anchorage "Providence Berg." A little farther north, at a place he called "Repulse Harbor," he went ashore, threw the stripes and stars to the breeze, and took possession of the land "in the name of God and the President of the United States."

Now commenced in earnest preparations for an Arctic winter. Hall and some, at least, some of his officers knew how to do it. The hunters were abroad at once, and an early prize was a musk-ox weighing three hundred pounds. His meat was tender and good, having no musky odor. This was but the beginning of the good gunning afforded by this far northern region. Two seals were soon after shot. The country was found to abound in these, and in geese, ducks, rabbits, wolves, foxes, partridges, and bears. The scurvy was not likely to venture near our explorers.

A pleasant incident occurred on shipboard about this time which the reader will better appreciate as our story progresses. It was September 24th. The Sabbath religious service of the preceding day had been conducted by Chaplain Bryant in his usual happy manner. At its close Commander Hall made some kind, earnest remarks to the men by which their rough natures were made tender, and they sent a letter from the forecastle to the cabin expressing to him their thanks. To this he replied in the following note:—

Sirs: The reception of your letter of thanks to me of this date I acknowledge with a heart that deeply feels and fully appreciates the kindly feeling that has prompted you to this act. I need not assure you that your commander has, and ever will have, a lively interest in your welfare. You have left your homes, friends, and country; indeed, you have bid farewell for a time to the whole civilized world, for the purpose of aiding me in discovering the mysterious, hidden parts of the earth. I therefore must and shall care for you as a prudent father cares for his faithful children.

October 10, after careful preparation, Captain Hall started northward on an experiment in the way of sledging. He purposed more extended sledge journeys in the spring, until the Pole itself should be reached. He took two sledges, drawn by seven dogs each. Deep snows, treacherous ice, which was in a state of change by the action of winds and currents, intense cold, and vexed and vicious dogs, all put in their appearance. But Captain Hall says, "These drawbacks are nothing new to an Arctic traveler. We laugh at them, and plod on determined to execute the service faithfully to the end."

The sledge expedition was gone two weeks, and traveled north fifty miles. They discovered a lake and a river. They came to the southern cape of a bay which they had seen from the *Polaris* in her drift from above. They named the bay Newman Bay, and attached Senator Sumner's name to the cape. From the top of an iceberg they surveyed the bay and believed it extended inland thirty miles. Crossing the mouth of the bay they clambered up its high northern cape, which they called Brevoort.

Here they looked westward over the waters up which a good distance past this point the *Polaris* had sailed, and which they had named Robeson Strait. They peered longingly into the misty distance, and fondly hoped to penetrate it with sledge or steamer in the spring. They built here their sixth snow-hut. It was warmer than at Thank-God Harbor, and birds, musk-oxen, foxes, and rabbits, were seen, and bear and wolf tracks were in the vicinity.

Captain Hall was joyous at the future prospect. He wrote a dispatch from this high latitude in which he says, "We have all been well up to this time." A copy of it was placed in a copper cylinder and buried under a pile of stones. The party turned their faces homeward; Captain Hall's Arctic explorations were ended.

Disaster

About noon of October 24 Captain Hall and his party were seen in the distance approaching the ship. Captain Tyson, the assistant navigator, went out to meet them. Not even a dog had been lost, and Captain Hall was jubilant over his trip and the future of the expedition. While he was absent the work of banking up the *Polaris* with snow as an increased defense against the cold, the building of a house on shore for the stores, and their removal to it from the ship, had gone forward nearly to completion.

He looked at the work, greeted all cheerfully, and entered the cabin. He obtained water, and washed and put on clean underclothes. The steward, Mr. Herron, asked him what he would have to eat, expressing at the same time a wish to get him "something nice."

He thanked him, but said he wanted only a cup of coffee, and complained of the heat of the cabin. He drank a part of the cup of coffee and set it aside. Soon after he complained of sickness at the stomach, and threw himself into his berth. Chester, the mate, and Morton, second mate, watched with him all night, during which he was at times delirious. It was thought he was partially paralyzed.

The surgeon, Dr. Bessel, was in constant attendance, but after temporary improvement he became wildly delirious, imagining someone had poisoned him, and accused first one, then another. He thought he saw blue gas coming from the mouths of persons about him. He refused clean stockings, thinking they were poisoned, and he made others taste the food tendered him before taking it himself, even that from sealed cans opened in his cabin.

During the night of November 7 he was clear in his mind, and as Surgeon Bessel was putting him to bed and tucking him in, he said in his own kind tone, "Doctor, you have been very kind to me, and I am obliged to you." Early in the morning of November 8 he died, and with his death the American North Polar Expedition was ended.

The grave of their beloved commander was dug by the men under Captain Tyson, inland, southeast, about a half mile from the *Polaris*. The frozen ground yielded reluctantly to the picks, and the grave was of necessity very shallow.

On the 11th a mournful procession moved from the *Polaris* to the place of burial. Though not quite noon it was Arctic night. A weird, electric light filled the air, through which the stars shone brilliantly. Captain Tyson walked ahead with a lantern, followed by Commander Buddington and his officers, and then by the scientific corps, which included the chaplain, Mr. Bryan; the men followed, drawing the coffin on a sled, one of their number bearing another lantern.

The fitting pall thrown over the coffin was the American flag. Following the sled were the Esquimo—last in the procession but not the least in the depth and genuineness of their sorrow. At the grave, Tyson held the light for the chaplain to read the burial service. As the solemn, yet comforting words were uttered, "I am the resurrection and the life, saith the Lord," all were subdued to tears.

Only from the spirit of the Gospel, breathing its tender influence through these words, was there any cheerful inspiration. The day was cold and dismal, and the wind howled mournfully. Inland over a narrow snow-covered plain, and in the shadowy distance, were huge masses of slate-rock, the ghostly looking sentinels of the barren land beyond. Seaward was the extended ice of Polaris Bay, and the intervening shore strewn with great ice-blocks in wild confusion. About five hundred paces away was the little hut called an observatory, and from its flag-staff drooped at half-mast the stars and stripes.

Far away were his loved family and friends, whose prayers had followed him during his adventures in the icy north, who even now hoped for his complete success and safe return; and far away the Christian burial place where it would have been to them mournfully pleasant to have laid him. But he who had declared that he loved the Arctic regions, and to whose ears there was music in its wailing winds, and to whose eyes there was beauty in its rugged, icy barrenness, had found his earthly resting-place where nature was clothed in its wildest Arctic features. A board was erected over his grave in which was cut:—

TO THE MEMORY OF C. F. HALL,
Late Commander of the North Polar Expedition.
Died November 8, 1871,
Aged fifty years.

When the funeral procession had returned to the ship, all moved about in the performance of their duty in gloomy silence. It is sad to record that the great affliction caused by the death of Hall was rendered more intense by the moral condition of the surviving party.

Two hideous specters had early in the expedition made their appearance on board the *Polaris*. They were the spirits of Rum and Discord! Commander Hall had forbidden the admission of liquor on shipboard, but it had come *with* the medicines whether *of* them or not. It was put under the key of the locker, but it broke out—no, we will not do injustice even to this foulest of demons: *an officer*, selected to guard the safety and comfort of the ship's company, broke open the locker and let it out.

This brought upon him a reprimand from Captain Hall, and later a letter of stricture upon his conduct. The doctor's alcohol could not be safely kept for professional purposes, which raised "altercations" on board. So Rum and Discord, always so closely allied, went stalking through the ship, with their horrid train. Insubordination, of course, was from the first in attendance. Hall had, it would seem, in part *persuaded* into submission this ghastly specter.

On the Sunday following the burial of Hall it was announced that from that time the Sunday service would be omitted. "Each one can pray for himself just as well," it was remarked. The faithful chaplain, however, seems to have held religious service afterward for such as pleased to attend. Hall had taken great pleasure in it, and it had, we think, attended every Arctic expedition through which we have carried the reader.

After such a purpose to dismiss public worship from the vessel we are not surprised to learn that "the men made night hideous by their carousings." Nature without had ceased to distinguish night from day, and our explorers did not follow the example of their predecessors in this region, and *make* day and night below decks by requiring the light to be put out at a stated hour. So the noise and card-playing had all hours for their own.

Under these circumstances, as if to make the *Polaris* forecastle the counterpart of one of our city "hells," pistols were put into the hands of the men. Discord was now armed, and Alcohol was at the chief place of command.

Then Christmas came, but no religious service with it. New Year's day brought nothing special. The winter dragged along but not the wind, which roared in tempests, and rushed over the floe in currents traveling fifty-three miles an hour. It played wild and free with the little bark which had intruded upon its domains, breaking up the ice around it, and straining at its moorings attached to the friendly berg.

Spring came at last. Hunting became lively and successful. His majesty, the bear, became meat for the hunters after a plucky fight, in which two dogs had their zeal for bear combat fairly subdued. Musk-oxen stood in stupid groups to be shot. White foxes would not be hit at any rate. Birds, trusting to their spread wings, were brought low, plucked and eaten. Seals coming out of their holes, and stretching themselves on the ice to enjoy dreamily a little sunshine, to which they innocently thought they had a right as natives of the country, were suddenly startled by the crack of the rifles, and often under such circumstances died instantly of lead.

It seemed hardly fair. In fact we are confident that the animals about Polaris Bay contracted a prejudice against the strangers, except the white foxes, who could not see what *hurt* these hunters did—at least to foxes—and they were of a mind that it was decided fun to be hunted by them.

The Esquimo have been in this high latitude in the not distant past, as a piece of one of their sledges was found.

Soon after Hall's death the chief officers had mutually pledged in writing that, "It is our honest intention to honor our flag, and to hoist it upon the most northern point of the earth." During the spring and summer some journeys northward were made, but were not extended beyond regions already visited. The eye which would have even now looked with hope and faith to the region of the star which is the "crowning jewel" of the central north, was dim in death. Captain Buddington, now in chief command, had faith and hope in the homeward voyage only.

On the 12th of August 1872, the *Polaris* was ready, with steam up, for the return trip. The *Polaris* had made a tolerably straight course up, but now made a zig-zag one back. On she went, steaming, drifting, banging against broken floes, through the waters over which we have voyaged with Kane and Hayes, until they came into the familiar regions of Hayes's winter-quarters.

On the afternoon of the 15th of October the wind blew a terrific gale from the northwest. The floe, in an angry mood, *nipped* the ship terribly. She groaned and shrieked, in pain but not in terror, for with her white oak coat of mail she still defied her icy foe, now rising out of his grasp, and then falling back and breaking for herself an easier position. The hawsers were attached to the floe, and the men stood waiting for the result of the combat on which their lives depended.

At this moment the engineer rushed to the deck with the startling announcement that the *Polaris* had sprung a leak, and that the water was gaining on the pumps. "The captain threw up his arms, and yelled the order to throw everything on the ice."

No examination into the condition of the leak seems to have been made. A panic followed, and overboard went everything in reckless confusion, many valuable articles falling near the vessel, and, of course, were drawn under by her restless throes and lost. Overboard went boats, provisions, ammunition, men, women, and children, nobody knew what nor who.

It was night—an intensely dark, snowy, tempestuous night.

It was in this state of things, when the ship's stores and people were divided between the floe and her deck, that the anchors planted in the floe tore away, and the mooring lines snapped like pack-thread, and away went the *Polaris* in the darkness, striking against huge ice-cakes, and drifting none knew where. "Does God care for sparrows?" and will he not surely care for these imperiled explorers, both those in the drifting steamer, and those on the floe whom he alone can save, unhoused in an Arctic night on which no sun will rise for many weeks, exposed to the caprice of winds, currents, and the ever untrustworthy ice-raft on which they are cast?

We will leave the floe party awhile in His care, and follow the fortunes of the brave little vessel and her men.

THE LAST OF THE *POLARIS*

Those left on board of the *Polaris* were oppressed with fears both for themselves and those on the floe. The leak in the ship was serious, and the water was gaining in the hold, and threatened to reach and put out the fires, and thus render the engine useless. Besides, the deck pumps were frozen up, and only two lower ones could be used.

But "just before it was too late," hot water was procured from the boiler and poured in buckets-full into the deck-pumps, and they were thawed out. The men then worked at the pumps with an energy inspired by imminent danger of death. They had already been desperately at work for six unbroken hours, and ere long the fight for life was on the verge of failure. Just then came to the fainting men the shout "steam's up," and tireless steam came to the rescue of weary muscles.

As the dim light of the morning of October 16 dawned on the anxious watchers, they saw that they had been forced by the violent wind out of Baffin Bay into Smith Sound.

Not until now, since the hour of separation, had they counted their divided company. The assistant navigator, the meteorologist, all the Esquimo, and six seamen were missing; part of the dogs had also gone with the floe party. Fourteen men remained, including the commander and the mate, the surgeon, and the chaplain.

Men were sent to the mast-head to look for the missing ones, but the most careful gaze with the best glass failed to discern them. Hope of their safety was inspired by the fact that they had all the boats, even to the little scow; yet it was not certainly known that the boats had not been sunk or drifted off in the darkness, and thus lost to them. So all was tantalizing uncertainty.

An examination revealed the encouraging fact that a good supply of fuel and provisions remained on board. A breeze sprung up at noon by whose aid the *Polaris* was run eastward, through a fortunate lead, as near to the land as possible. Here lines were carried out on the floe and made fast to the hummocks, all the anchors having been lost. She lay near the shore, and grounded at low water. An examination showed that the vessel was so battered and leaky, that surprise was excited that she had not gone down before reaching the shore. It was decided at once that she could not be made to float longer. The steam-pumps were stopped, the water filled her hold, and decided her fate.

The sheltered place into which the *Polaris* had by Divine guidance entered was Life-Boat Cove, only a little north of Etah Bay, every mile of which we have surveyed in former visits. The famous city of Etah with its two huts was not far away, but out of it and its vicinity had come timely blessings to other winter-bound explorers.

Our party at once commenced to carry ashore the provisions, clothing, ammunition, and all such articles from the vessel as might make them comfortable. The spars, sails, and some of the heavy wood-work of the cabin, were used in erecting a house. When done their building was quite commodious, being twenty-two feet by fourteen. The sails aided in making the roof, which proved to be water-tight, and the snow thrown up against the sides made it warm. Within, it was one room for all, and for all purposes. "Bunks" were made against the sides for each of the fourteen men. A stove with cooking utensils was brought from the ship and set up; lamps were suspended about the room, and a table with other conveniences from the cabin were put in order.

But before this was done a party of Esquimo with five sledges made their appearance. They stopped at a distance, and signified their friendly purpose by their customary wild gesticulations and antics. The white men at first took them for the floe party, and raised three rousing cheers of welcome.

The whole party went to work with a will, having pleasant visions before them of a new stock of needles, knives, and other white-man treasures. They clambered over the hummocky floe, bringing loads of coal from the ship, and with their sleds brought fresh-water ice for the melting apparatus. Several families finally came, built their huts near the vessel, and spent the winter. The ship-wrecked whites had nearly worn out their fur suits, and their supply had been greatly reduced by the losses on the floe. So the Esquimo replenished their stock, and their women repaired the worn ones.

The winter wore off. There was no starvation, nor even short rations. The coal burned cheerfully in the stove until February, and then fuel torn from the *Polaris* supplied its place. The friendly natives brought fresh walrus meat, and scurvy was kept away. For all their valuable services the Esquimo felt well repaid in the coveted treasures which were given them.

The time during the sunless days was passed in reading, writing, amusements, and discussions, according to the taste and inclination of each. Of course there were some daily domestic duties to be done. The scientific men pursued their inquiries so far as circumstances allowed.

The spring came, and with it successful hunting. One deer was shot, and some hares caught. Chester, the mate, who seems to have been *the* Yankee of the party, planned and assisted the carpenter in building two boats. The material was wrenched from the *Polaris*. They were each twenty-five feet long and five feet wide, square fore and aft, capable of carrying, equally divided between them, the fourteen men, two months' provisions, and other indispensable articles. When these were done they made a smaller boat, and presented it to the Esquimo; it would aid them in getting eggs and young birds about the shore.

Clear water did not reach Life-Boat Cove until the last of May. On its appearance in the immediate vicinity the waiting explorers put everything in readiness for their departure. The boats were laden, and each man assigned his place. Bags were made of the canvas sails in which to carry the provisions. What remained of the *Polaris* was given to the Esquimo chief as an acknowledgment of favors received. On the 3rd of June, in fine spirits and good health, the explorers launched their boats and sailed southward. At first the boats leaked badly, but they sailed and rowed easily, and proved very serviceable. It was a continuous day, and the weather favorable.

Seals could be had for the pains of hunting them, and the sea-fowl were so plenty that ten were at times brought down at a shot. On the downward trip old localities were touched, such as Etah, Hakluyt Island, and Northumberland Island. The average amount of Arctic storms were encountered, the drift ice behaved in its usual manner, though not as badly as it has been known to do.

The little crafts had their hair-breadth escapes and were battered not a little. Every night, when the toils of the day were over, the boats were drawn upon the floe, everything taken out, and the only hot meal of the day was prepared. Each boat carried pieces of rope from the *Polaris*, and a can of oil. With these a fire was made in the bottom of an iron pot. Over this fire they made their steaming pots of tea.

The party halted a while at Fitz Clarence Rock in Booth Bay, about sixteen miles south of Cape Parry, and within sight of the high, bleak plain on which Dr. Hayes's boat-party spent their fearful winter. On the tenth day of their voyaging they had reached Cape York. In comparison to Dr. Kane's trip over the same waters, theirs was as a summer holiday excursion. But Melville Bay was now before them with its defiant bergs, hummocks, currents, stormy winds, and blinding snows—a horrid crew!

No wonder that the fear prevailed among them that if not rescued they could never reach any settlement. But the rescuers were not far off. For another ten days they were made to feel that their battle for life was to be a hard-fought one. On the 23rd they saw, away in the distance, what appeared to be a whaler.

They dared scarcely trust their eyes, for the object was ten miles away. Yes, it was a steamer, and beset, too, so she could not get away. New courage was inspired, and they toiled on. But for this timely spur to their zeal they would have lost heart, for one of the boats in being lifted over the hummocks was badly stove, and their provisions were giving out, though they had calculated that they had two months' supply. Soon after they saw the steamer they were seen by the watch from the masthead.

They were taken for Esquimo, but a sharp lookout was kept upon their movement, which soon showed them to be white men. Signals of recognition were immediately given, and eighteen picked men were sent to their relief. Seeing this, Captain Buddington sent forward two men, and the rescuers soon met and returned with them. With even this addition to their strength, it took six hours to drag the boats the twelve miles which intervened between them and the whaler. They were received with a kind-hearted welcome by the noble Scotchman, Captain Allen, of the *Ravenscraig*, of Dundee. Their toils were over, and their safety insured.

THE FEARFUL SITUATION

On the floe, one of the anchors of the *Polaris*, in starting on the night of the separation, tore off a large piece of the floe with three men upon it. As the *Polaris* swept past them they cried out in agony, "What shall we do?" Captain Buddington shouted back, "We can do nothing for you. You have boats and provisions; you must shift for yourselves."

This was the last word from the *Polaris*.

Seeing the sad plight of these men, Captain Tyson, who from the first had been upon the floe, took "the donkey," a little scow which had been tossed upon the ice, and attempted to rescue them. But the donkey almost at once sunk, and he jumped back upon the floe and launched one of the boats. Some of the other men started in the other boat at the same time, and the three men were soon united to the rest of the floe party.

One of the last things Tyson drew out of the way of the vessel as its heel was grinding against the parting floe were some musk-ox skins. They lay across a widening crack, and in a moment more would have been sunk in the deep, or crushed between colliding hummocks.

Our darkness and storm-beset party did not dare to move about much, for they could not tell the size of the ice on which they stood, nor at what moment they might step off into the surging waters. So they rolled themselves up in the musk-ox skins and *slept*! Captain Tyson alone did not lie down, but walked cautiously about during the night. The morning came, and with it a revelation of their surroundings. Huge bergs were in sight which had in the storm and darkness charged upon the floe, and caused the breaking up of the preceding night. It had been a genuine Arctic assault.

Their own raft was nearly round, and about four miles in circumference, and immovably locked between several grounded bergs. It was snow-covered, and full of hillocks and intervening ponds of water which the brief summer sun had melted from their sides. Those who had laid down were covered with snow, and looked like little mounds. When the party roused, the first thing they thought of was the ship. But she was nowhere to be seen. A lead opened to the shore inviting their escape to the land. Captain Tyson ordered the men to get the boats in immediate readiness, reminding them of the uncertainty of the continued opening of the water, and of the absolute necessity of instant escape from the floe in order to regain the ship and save their lives. But the men were in no hurry, and obedience to orders had long been out of their line.

They were hungry and tired, and were determined to eat first; and they didn't want a cold meal, and so they made tea and chocolate, and cooked canned meat. This done they must change their wet clothes for dry ones.

In the meantime the drifting ice *was* in a hurry and had shut up in part the lead. But Tyson was determined to try to reach the shore though the difficulties had so greatly increased during the delay. The boats were laden and launched, but when they were about half way to the shore the lead closed, and they returned to the floe and hauled up the boats.

Just then the *Polaris* was seen under both steam and sail. She was eight or ten miles away, but signals were set to attract her attention, and she was watched with a glass with intense interest until she disappeared behind an island. Soon after, Captain Tyson sent two men to a distant part of the floe to a house made of poles, which he had erected for the stores soon after they began to be thrown from the vessel.

In going for these poles the steamer was again seen, apparently fast in the ice behind the island. She could not then come to the floe party, being beset and without boats, and so Tyson ordered the men to get the boats ready for another attempt to reach the land, and thus in time connect with the vessel. He lightened the boats of all articles not absolutely necessary, that they might be drawn to the water safely and with speed. He then went ahead to find the nearest and best route for embarking. The grounded bergs in the meanwhile, relaxed their grasp upon the explorers' ice-raft, and they began to drift southward.

With malicious intent, on came a terrific snow-storm at the same time. Tyson hurried back to hasten up the men. They were in no hurry, but, with grumbling and trifling, finally made ready as they pretended, one boat crowded with everything both needful and worthless. When at last it was dragged to the water's edge, it was ascertained that the larger part of the oars and the rudder had been left at the camp far in the rear.

In this crippled condition the boat was launched. But not only oars and rudder, but *will* on the part of the men was wanting. So the boat was drawn upon the floe, and left with all its valuables near the water. The night was approaching, the storm was high, and the men were weary, so no attempt was made to return it to the old camp. All went back to the middle of the floe. Tyson, Mr. Meyers, one of the scientific corps, and the Esquimo, made a canvas shelter, using the poles as a frame, and the others camped near them. Captain Tyson, after eating a cold supper, rolled himself in a musk-ox skin, and lay down for the first sleep he had sought for forty-eight hours. His condition seemed to be a specially hard one.

While, on the night of the great disaster, he was striving to save the general stores, the saving of which proved the salvation of the company, others were looking after their personal property, so they had their full supply of furs and fire-arms, while his were left in the ship.

He, however, slept soundly until the morning, when he was startled by a shriek from the Esquimo. The floe had played them an Arctic trick;

it had broken and set the whole party adrift on an ice-raft not more than 150 yards square. What remained of their old floe of four miles' circumference contained the house made of poles, in which remained six bags of bread, and the loaded boat, in which were the greater part of their valuables.

Yet one boat remained with which they might have gone after the other one, but the men seemed infatuated and refused to go. Away the little raft sailed, crumbling as it went, assuring its passengers that they must all stow away in their one boat or soon be dropped in the sea. For four days they thus drifted, during which the Esquimo shot several seals. On the 21st a crewman using the spy-glass suddenly shouted for joy. He had spied the lost boat lodged on a part of the old floe which had swung against the little raft of our party. He and Captain Tyson, with a dog-team, instantly started for it, and after a hard pull returned with boat and cargo. Soon after, their old floe, in an accommodating mood, thrust itself against the one they were on, the boats were passed over, and everything was again together—boats and provisions.

As there was only faint hope now of again seeing the *Polaris*, and as their ice-boat seemed to sail farther and farther from the shore, they began to make the best winter-quarters their circumstances allowed. Several snow houses were put up.

The huts erected, their next pressing need was sledges. The men, with great difficulty, dragged some lumber from the old storehouse, and a passable one was made.

Though the quantity of provisions was quite large, yet with nineteen persons to consume it, and with possibly no addition for six months, it was alarmingly small. Besides, in their unprincipled greed, some of the party broke into the storeroom and took more than a fair allowance. So the party agreed upon two meals a day, and a weighed allowance at each meal.

It was now the last of October. The sun had ceased to show his pleasant face, and the long night was setting in. To add to their discomfort, the question of light and fuel assumed a serious aspect. The men, either from want of skill or patience, or both, did not succeed well in using seal fat for these purposes, in the Esquimo fashion; so they began, with a reckless disregard to their future safety, to break up and burn one of the boats.

Hans, with a true Esquimo instinct, when the short allowance pinched him, began to kill and eat the dogs. He might be excused, however. Four children, with their faces growing haggard, looked to him for food.

Thus situated, our floe party drifted far away from the land—drifting on and on, whether they slept or woke—drifting they knew not to what end.

THE WONDERFUL DRIFT

Early in November Captain Tyson saw through his glass, about twelve miles off to the southeast, the Cary Islands, so they were in the "North water" of Baffin Bay, and southwest from Cape Parry, where we have been so many times. From this cape, or a little south of it, it would not be a great sledge trip to where they last saw the *Polaris*, and where they had reason to think she now was. So our party made one more effort to reach the shore. The boats being in readiness the night before, they started early in the morning. Of course their day was now only a noon twilight, and the *morning* was almost midday. But the floe was not in a favoring mood. The hummocks were as hard in their usage of the boats and men as usual. The deceitful cracks in the ice at one time put the lives of the dogs and men in great peril; and, as if these obstacles were not enough, a storm brought up its forces against them. They had dragged the boats halfway to the shore when they retreated "before superior forces."

Their huts being of perishable material were reconstructed. A little later the men built a large snow hut as "a reserve." All were weak through insufficient food. Mr. Meyers was nearly prostrate, and went to live with the men; Captain Not the least of the trial in the Esquimo huts were the piteous cries of the children for food. Nearly two weeks passed before any further success attended the hunters; then several were shot, and Captain Tyson, who was ready to perish, had one full meal—a meal of uncooked seal meat, skin, hair, and all, washed down with seal blood. *Some* others had not been so long without a full meal, as the bread continued to be stolen.

Thanksgiving Day came. A little extra amount of the canned meat was allowed each one, and all had a taste of mock-turtle soup and canned green corn, kept for this occasion, to which was added a few pieces of dried apple. How far it all fell short of the *home* feast may be judged by the fact that Captain Tyson, to satisfy the fierce hunger which remained after dinner, finished "with eating strips of frozen seals' entrails, and lastly seal skin, hair and all."

The hunters had seen tracks of bears, so they were on the lookout for them while they hunted seal. One day Joe and Hans went out as usual with their guns. They lost sight of each other and of the camp. Joe returned quite late, expecting to find Hans already in his hut. When he learned that he had not returned, he, as well as others, felt concerned about him. Accompanied by one of the men, he went in search of him. As the two, guns in hand, were stumbling over the hummocks, they saw in the very dim twilight, as they thought, a bear. Their guns were instantly leveled and brought to the sight, and their mouths almost tasted a bear-meat supper. "Hold on there! That's not a bear! what is it?" "Why, it's Hans!" Well, he *did* look in the darkness like a bear, as in his shaggy coat he clambered, on all-fours, over the ice-hills.

December came in with its continuous night. Seals could not be successfully hunted in the darkness, and where seals could not be seen bears would not make their appearance. The rations became smaller than ever, and ghastly, horrid starvation seemed encamped among our drifting, forlorn party. Under these circumstances a specter even *worse* than starvation appeared to Joe. To him, at least, it was a terrifying reality. It was the demon form of cannibalism! He had looked into the eyes of the men in the big hut, and they spoke to him of an intention to save themselves by first killing and eating Hans and family, and then taking him and his. He and Hannah were greatly terrified, and he handed his pistol to Captain Tyson, which he was not willing to part with before. He was assured that the least child should not be touched for so horrid a purpose without such a defense as the pistol could give.

Christmas came. The last ham had been kept for this occasion, and it was divided among all, with a few other dainties, in addition to the usual morsel.

The shore occasionally appeared in the far away distance. They were drifting through Baffin Bay toward the *western* side, so that their craft evidently did not intend to land them at any of the familiar ports of Greenland. It seemed to have an ambition to drop them nearer home.

As the year was going out, and Joe's family were gnawing away at some *dried* seal skin, submitted, to be sure, to a process Hannah called cooking, a shout was heard from him. "Kayak! kayak!" he cried. He had shot a seal, and it was floating away. Fortunately the kayak was at hand, and the game was bagged. As usual, it was divided among all. The *eyes* were given to Charlie Polaris, and they were nice in his eyes, and mouth, too.

New Year's came, and Captain Tyson dined on two feet of frozen seal entrails, and a little seal fat. There was now nothing to burn except what little seal blubber they could spare for that purpose. One boat had been burned, their only sled had gone the same way, and the reckless, desperate men could hardly be restrained from burning the only one now remaining, and thus cut off all good hope of final escape. To be sure, their provocation to this act was very great; the temperature was thirty-six below zero! In their strait, the desperate expedient was entertained of trying to get to land. The emaciated men would have to drag the loaded boat over the hummocky ice without a sledge. The women and children must be added to the load or abandoned. It would be a struggle for life against odds more fearful than that which now oppressed them.

But what *should* they do!

God knew! Hark! What shout is that! "Kayak! kayak!" The kayak was at hand, but it had to be carried a mile. Yet it paid, for a seal shot by Joe was secured just in time to keep the men from utter desperation. To this item of comfort another was added a few days later. The sun reappeared January 19, after an absence of eighty-three days, and remained shining upon them two hours. He brought hope to fainting hearts. Through January there was a seal taken at long intervals, but one always came just before it was too late! The men continued to grumble and deceive themselves with the idea of soon getting to Disco, "where rum and tobacco were plenty." How sad that man can sink *below* the brute, which, however hungry, never cries out for "rum and tobacco!"

February was a dreadful month on board the floe. The huts were buried under the snow. It was with difficulty that Joe and Hans, almost the entire dependence of the party, could go abroad for game, and when they did they secured a few seals only, very small, and now and then a dovekie, a wee bit of a pensive sea-bird. Narwhal, the sea unicorn, were shot in several instances, but they sunk in every case and were lost. Hunger and fear seemed to possess the men in the large tent, and Joe and Hannah began to be again terrified by the thought that these hunger-mad men would kill and eat them.

Now, will not God appear to help those in so helpless a condition? Yes, his hand has ever been wonderfully apparent in all Arctic perils. On the second of March, just when the dark cloud of these drifting sufferers was never darker, it parted, and a flood of light burst upon their camp. Joe shot an *oogjook*, belonging to the largest species of seal. He was secured and dragged by all hands to the huts. He measured nine feet, weighed about seven hundred pounds, and contained, by estimation, thirty gallons of oil. There was a shout of seal in the camp! The warm blood was relished like new milk, and drank freely. All eat and slept, and woke to eat again, and hunger departed for the time from the miserable huts it had so long haunted. Joe and Hannah dismissed their horrid visions of cannibalism.

THE ESCAPE

Our voyagers needed all the strength and courage which the timely capture of the great seal had given them. They had drifted into a warmer sea, and windy March was well upon them. Their floe began to herald its fast approaching dissolution. The weary and anxious drifters were startled by day, and awakened suddenly by night, by a rumbling, mingled with fearful grindings and crashes underneath them. Heavy ice-cakes, over-rode by the heavier floe, ground along its under surface, and when finding an opening of thin ice, rushed with a thundering sound to the upper surface. The din was at times so great that it seemed to combine all alarming sounds:—

Through all its scale the horrid discord ran;
Now mocked the beast—now took the groan of man.

On the 11th a storm commenced. Whole fleets of icebergs, having broken away from the icy bands in which the floe had held them, hovered round to charge upon the helpless campers. The vast area of ice on which they had been riding for so many months was lifted in places by mighty seas beneath, causing it to crack with a succession of loud reports and dismal sounds, some of which seemed to be directly under them. The wind drove before it a dense cloud of snow, so that one could scarcely see a yard. Night came with a darkness that could be felt. The icy foundation of their camp might separate at any moment, and tumble their huts about their ears, or plunge them in the sea.

They gathered their few treasures together, and stood ready to fly—but where? Death seemed to guard every avenue of escape. Suddenly, soon after the night set in, the disruption came. Their floe was shattered, with a fearful uproar, into hundreds of pieces, and they went surging off among the fragments on a piece less than a hundred yards square. They were within twenty yards of its edge, but God had kindly forbid the separation to run through their camp and sever them from their boat or from each other.

After raging sixty hours the storm abated, and their little ice-ship drifted rapidly in the pack. A goodly number of seals were shot, and they began to breathe more freely. After a short time another *oogjook* was captured, so food was plenty.

March wore away, seals were plenty, and readily taken; and though the bergs ground together and made fierce onsets into the pack, our ice-ship held gallantly on her way. One night the inmates of Joe's hut were about retiring, when a noise was heard outside. "What is it, Joe? Is the ice breaking up?" Joe does not stop to answer, but rushes out. But in ten seconds he comes back in a greater hurry, pale and breathless.

"There's a bear close to my kayak," he exclaims in an excited tone. Now the situation was this: The kayak was within ten paces of the entrance to the hut, and the loaded guns, which can never be kept in an Esquimo hut on account of the moisture, were in and leaning against the kayak. If the bear should take a notion to put his nose at the hut door, and, liking the odor, knock down the snow wall with his strong paw, and commence a supper on one of its inmates, what was to hinder him? But bears, like many young people, often fail to improve their golden opportunities. He found some seal fat and skins in the kayak, and these he pulled out, and walked off with them a rod or two to enjoy the feast. Joe crept out of the hut, and ran to alarm the men. Captain Tyson followed, slipped softly up to the kayak and seized his gun, but in taking it he knocked down another one and alarmed the bear, who looked up and growled his objections to having his supper disturbed.

Tyson leveled his rifle, snapped it, but it missed fire. He tried a second and third time, and it did not go—but *he* did, for his bearship was taking the offensive. Content to see his enemy flee, the bear returned to his supper. How many foolish bears have we seen on our explorations lose their lives by an untimely eating.

The captain returned to the field with a new charge in his gun. This time it sent a ball *through* the bear; the ball entering the left shoulder and passing through the heart, came out at the other side. He staggered, but before he fell Joe had sent another ball into his vitals. He dropped dead instantly. This affair occurred when it was too dark to see many yards, and was much pleasanter in its results than in its duration.

The seal hunting was successful, and with bear meat and blubber, a full store, there was no hunger unappeased; but the wind blew a gale, and the sailless, rudderless, oarless little ice-ship, now banging against a berg, and now in danger of being run down by one, all the while growing alarmingly smaller, finally shot out into the open sea away from the floe.

This would not do. So, feeling that they might soon be dropped into the sea, they loaded the boat with such things as was strictly necessary, and all hands getting aboard, sailed away. A part of their ammunition, their fresh meat, a full month's supply, and many other desirable things, were abandoned. The boat, only intended to carry eight persons, was so overloaded with its twenty, including children, that it was in danger of being swamped at any moment. The frightened children cried, and the men looked sober. They sailed about twenty miles west and landed on the first tolerably safe piece of ice which they met. Hans and family nestled down in the boat, and the rest, spreading on the floe what skins they had, set up a tent, and all, after eating a dry supper of bread and pemmican, lay down to rest.

Thus, boating by day, and camping on the ice at night for several days, they drew up on the 4th of April upon a solid looking floe. Snow-huts were built, seals were taken, and hope revived. But what is hope, resting on Arctic promises? The gale was abroad again, the sea boisterous, and their floe was thrown into a panic. Fearful noises were heard beneath and around them, and their icy foundations quaked with fear. Joe's snow-hut was shaken down. He built it again, and then lot and house fell off into the sea and disappeared. Thus warned, the camp was pushed farther back from the water. But they did not know where the crack and separation would next come. Thus they lived in anxious watchings through weary days, the gale unabated. Finally, one night, the feared separation came.

All hands except Mr. Meyers were in the tent; near them, so near a man could scarcely walk between, was the boat, containing Meyers and the kayak; but with mischievous intent, the crack run so as to send the boat drifting among the breaking and overlapping ice. Mr. Meyers could not manage it, of course, under such circumstances, and the kayak was of no use to any but an Esquimo, so he set it afloat, hoping it would drift to the floe-party. Here was a fearful situation!

The floe-party, as well as Mr. Meyers, was sure to perish miserably if the boat was not returned. There was only a dim light, and objects at a short distance looked hazy. It was a time for instant and desperate action. Joe and Hans took their paddles and ice-spears and started for the boat, jumping from one piece of floating, slippery ice to another. They were watched in breathless suspense until they *seemed*, in the shadowy distance, to have reached the boat, and then all was shut out in the darkness.

The morning came, and the floe party was glad to see that the boat had three men in it. It was a half mile off, and the kayak was as far away in another direction. It was soon clear that the boat could not be brought back without a stronger force. Tyson led the way, and finally all but two of the men made the desperate passage of the floating ice to the imperiled craft. It was with difficulty that, with their combined force, the boat was returned to the floe. The kayak was also recovered.

For a brief time there was quiet all around. The aurora gleamed and displayed its wonderful beauty of form and motion; while the majestic icebergs, in every varied shape, reflected its sparkling light. The grandeur of sea and sky seemed a mockery to the danger-beset voyagers. The elements might be grand, but they had combined to destroy them, for a new form of peril now appeared. The sea came aboard of their icy craft.

They were sitting one evening under their frail tent, the boat near, when a wave swept over their floe, carrying away tent, clothing, provisions—everything except what was on their persons or in the boat. The women and children had been put on board in fear of such an occurrence, and the men had just time to save themselves by clinging to the gunwale. The boat itself was borne into the middle of the floe. When the wave subsided, the boat was dragged back, lest another push by a succeeding one might launch it into the sea from the other side. It was well they did this, for another wave bore it to the opposite edge and partly slipped it into the water. This game of surging the boat from one side to the other of the floe was kept up from nine o'clock in the evening to seven in the morning. All this time the men were in the water, fighting the desperate battle for its safety, and the preservation of their own lives; the conflict being made more terrible by the fact that every wave bore with it ice-blocks from a foot square to those measuring many yards, having sharp edges and jagged corners, with which it battered their legs until they were black and blue. It was the severest test of their courage and endurance yet experienced. But God was their helper. Not one perished, and when the defeated sea was by his voice commanded to retire, and the day appeared, they were not seriously harmed. But they were cold and wet, without a change of clothes and utterly provisionless.

It is not surprising that after their rough handling on the floe they should seek a larger and safer one. This they did, launching their crowded boat into the turbulent sea, and, working carefully along, succeeded in landing safely on one stronger looking; nothing worse happening than the tumbling overboard of the cook, who was quickly rescued. Here, cold, half-drowned, hungry, and weary to faintness, they tried to dry and warm themselves in the feeble rays of the sun, and wait for their food at the hand of the great Provider in the use of such means as were yet left to them. They had preserved their guns and a small supply of powder and shot. Snow and rain came on, and continued until noon of the next day, April 22. Their hunger was fearful. Mr. Meyers had been slightly frost-bitten when drifting away alone in the boat, his health seemed broken, and he was actually starving.

In the afternoon of this day Joe went as usual with his gun. He had caught nothing on this floe, and now there were no signs of seals, though it was his fourth time out that day. What should they do? God had their relief all arranged. Joe saw what he did not expect to see, and what was seldom seen so far south—a bear! He ran back to the boat, called Hans with his trusty rifle, and the two lay down behind the hummocks.

All were ordered to lie down, keep perfectly quiet, and feign themselves seals, the Esquimo helping out the deception by imitating the seal bark. Bruin came on cautiously. He, too, was hungry. What are those black objects, and what is that noise, he seemed to say? They don't look *quite* like seals! The noise is not *just* like the seal cry! But hunger is a weighty reason with men and bears, on the side of what they desire to believe, so the bear came on. When fairly within an easy range both rifles cracked, and he fell dead. The whole party arose with a shout. Polar was dragged to the boat and skinned. His warm blood slaked their raging thirst. His meat, tender and good, satisfied their gnawing hunger. They were saved from a terrible death! Seals were secured soon after, and hope again revived.

It was not long before their ice-craft crumbled away, so they were obliged to repeat the experiment, always full of danger, of launching into the sea and making for a larger and safer one. April 28 they were beset by a fleet of bergs, which were crashing against each other with a thundering noise, and occasionally turning a threatening look toward the frail craft of our drifters. So angrily at last did one come down upon them that they abandoned their floe and rowed away. Surely there is no peace for them by night or day, on the floe or afloat in their boat. They dare not lie down a moment without keeping one-half of their number on the watch.

But what is that in the distance? A steamer! A thrill of joy goes through the boat's company. Every possible signal is given, but she does not see them, and another night is spent on the floe. The next morning every eye was straining to see a whaler. Soon one appears. They shout, raise their signals, and fire every gun at once. But she passes out of sight. April 13, as the night was setting in foggy and dark, the shout from the watch of "steamer" brought all to their feet. She was right upon them in the fog before she was seen. Hans was soon alongside of her in his kayak, telling their story as best he could. In a few moments the whaler was alongside of their piece of ice. Captain Tyson removed his old well-worn cap, called upon his men, and three cheers were given, ending with a "tiger" such as the poor fellows had not had a heart to give for many long months. The cheers were returned by a hundred men from the rigging and deck of the vessel. It was the sealer *Tigress*, Captain Bartlett, of Conception Bay, Newfoundland. They soon had the planks of a good ship beneath them instead of a treacherous floe; curious but kind friends beset them, instead of threatening bergs; and every comfort succeeded to utter destitution. They had been on the floe six months and floated more than 1,600 miles.

They were speedily conveyed, by the way of Conception Bay and St. John's, to their own homes, the telegraph having flashed throughout the length and breadth of the land their coming, and the nation rejoiced. But there were tears mingled with the joy, that one, the noble, the true, the Christian commander of the expedition, Charles Francis Hall, lay in his icy grave in the far north.

As speedily as possible the *Tigress* was purchased and fitted out by the United States government in search of the *Polaris* party. Captain Tyson and Joe were among her men. She reached Life-boat Cove about two months after Captain Buddington and his men had left. They learned that, much to the grief of the natives, the *Polaris* had floated off and sunk. The Buddington party arrived home in the fall, by the way of England.

Thus ended the last American North Pole Expedition. The last from other governments have not been more successful. Yet, while we write, England and Austria are reported as getting ready further North Polar expeditions to start in the spring of 1875. It must be allowed that the icy sceptered guardian of the North has made a good fight against the invaders into his dominions. But the nations of the earth are determined to send men to sit on his throne, though they find it a barren and worthless, as well as a cold domain.

CHAPTER FIVE

Reaching the Pole

Robert E. Peary

BY AN ODD COINCIDENCE, SOON AFTER MARVIN LEFT US ON HIS FATAL journey from 86°38" back to land, the sun was obscured and a dull, lead-colored haze spread over all the sky. This grayness, in contrast to the dead white surface of the ice and snow and the strangely diffused quality of the light, gave an indescribable effect. It was a shadowless light and one in which it was impossible to see for any considerable distance.

That shadowless light is not unusual on the ice-fields of the polar sea; but this was the first occasion on which we had encountered it since leaving the land. One looking for the most perfect illustration of the arctic inferno would find it in that gray light. A more ghastly atmosphere could not have been imagined even by Dante himself— sky and ice seeming utterly wan and unreal.

Notwithstanding the fact that I had now passed the "farthest north" of all my predecessors and was approaching my own best record, with my eight companions, sixty dogs, and seven fully loaded sledges in far better condition than I had even dared to hope, the strange and melancholy light in which we traveled on this day of parting from Marvin gave me an indescribably uneasy feeling. Man in his egotism, from the most primitive ages to our own, has always imagined a sympathetic relationship between nature and the events and feelings of human life. So—in the light of later events—admitting that I felt a peculiar awe in contemplating the ghastly grayness of that day, I am expressing only an ineradicable instinct of the race to which I belong.

The first three-quarters of the march after Marvin turned back, on March 26, the trail was fortunately in a straight line, over large level snow-covered floes of varying height, surrounded by medium-rough old rafters of ice; and the last quarter was almost entirely over young ice averaging about one foot thick, broken and rafered, presenting a rugged and trying surface to travel over in the uncertain light. Without Bartlett's trail to follow, the march would have been even more difficult.

Near the end of the day we were again deflected to the west some distance by an open lead. Whenever the temperature rose as high as minus fifteen degrees, where it had stood at the beginning of the day, we were sure of encountering open water. But just before we reached the camp of Bartlett's pioneer division, the gray haze in which we had traveled all day lifted, and the sun came out clear and brilliant. The temperature had also dropped to minus twenty degrees. Bartlett was just starting out again when I arrived, and we agreed that we had made a good fifteen miles in the last march.

The next day, March 27, was a brilliant dazzling day of arctic sunshine, the sky a glittering blue, and the ice a glittering white, which, but for the smoked goggles worn by every member of the party, would certainly have given some of us an attack of snow blindness. From the time when the reappearing sun of the arctic spring got well above the horizon, these goggles had been worn continuously.

The temperature during this march dropped from minus thirty degrees to minus forty degrees, there was a biting northeasterly breeze, and the dogs traveled forward in their own white cloud of steam. On the polar ice we gladly hail the extreme cold, as higher temperatures and light snow always mean open water, danger, and delay. Of course, such minor incidents as frosted and bleeding cheeks and noses we reckon as part of the great game. Frosted heels and toes are far more serious, because they lessen a man's ability to travel, and traveling is what we are there for. Mere pain and inconvenience are inevitable, but, on the whole, inconsiderable.

This march was by far the hardest for some days. At first there was a continuation of the broken and rafered ice, sharp and jagged, that at times seemed almost to cut through our sealskin kamiks and hareskin stockings, to pierce our feet. Then we struck heavy rubble ice covered with deep snow, through which we had literally to plow our way, lifting and steadying the sledges until our muscles ached.

During the day we saw the tracks of two foxes in this remote and icy wilderness, nearly 240 nautical miles beyond the northern coast of Grant Land.

Finally we came upon Bartlett's camp in a maze of small pieces of very heavy old floes raftered in every direction. He had been in his igloo but a short time, and his men and dogs were tired out and temporarily discouraged by the heart-racking work of making a road.

I told him to take a good long sleep before getting under way again; and while my men were building the igloos, I lightened the loads of Bartlett's sledges about 100 pounds, to put them in better trim for pioneering in this rough going. The added weight would be less burdensome on our own sledges than on his. Notwithstanding the crazy road over which we had traveled, this march netted us twelve good miles toward the goal.

We were now across the 87th parallel and into the region of perpetual daylight, as the sun had not set during the last march. The knowledge that we had crossed the 87th parallel with men and dogs in good condition, and plenty of supplies upon the sledges, sent me to sleep that night with a light heart. Only about six miles beyond this point, at 87°6", I had been obliged to turn back nearly three years before, with exhausted dogs, depleted supplies, and a heavy and discouraged heart. It seemed to me then that the story of my life was told and that the word failure was stamped across it.

Now, three years older, with three more years of the inevitable wear and tear of this inexorable game behind me, I stood again beyond the 87th parallel still reaching forward to that goal which had beckoned to me for so many years. Even now, on reaching my highest record with every prospect good, I dared not build too much on the chances of the white and treacherous ice which stretched 180 nautical miles northward between me and the end. I had believed for years that this thing could be done and that it was my destiny to do it, but I always reminded myself that many a man had felt thus about some dearly wished achievement, only to fail in the end.

When I awoke the following day, March 28, the sky was brilliantly clear; but ahead of us there was a thick, smoky, ominous haze drifting low over the ice, and a bitter northeast wind, which, in the orthography of the Arctic, plainly spelled open water. Did this mean failure again? No man could say. Bartlett had, of course, left camp and taken to the trail again long before I and the men of my division were awake. This was in accordance with my general plan, previously outlined, that the pioneer division should be traveling while the main division slept, and *vice versa*, so that the two divisions might be in communication every day.

After traveling at a good rate for six hours along Bartlett's trail, we came upon his camp beside a wide lead, with a dense, black, watery sky to the northwest, north, and northeast, and beneath it the smoky fog which we had been facing all day long. In order not to disturb Bartlett, we camped a hundred yards distant, put up our igloos as quietly as possible, and turned in, after our usual supper of pemmican, biscuit, and tea. We had made some twelve miles over much better going than that of the last few marches and on a nearly direct line over large floes and young ice.

I was just dropping off to sleep when I heard the ice creaking and groaning close by the igloo, but as the commotion was not excessive, nor of long duration, I attributed it to the pressure from the closing of the lead which was just ahead of us; and after satisfying myself that my mittens were where I could get them instantly, in an emergency, I rolled over on my bed of deerskins and settled myself to sleep. I was just drowsing again when I heard someone yelling excitedly outside.

Leaping to my feet and looking through the peep-hole of our igloo, I was startled to see a broad lead of black water between our two igloos and Bartlett's, the nearer edge of water being close to our entrance; and on the opposite side of the lead stood one of Bartlett's men yelling and gesticulating with all the abandon of an excited and thoroughly frightened Eskimo.

Awakening my men, I kicked our snow door into fragments and was outside in a moment. The break in the ice had occurred within a foot of the fastening of one of my dog teams, the team escaping by just those few inches from being dragged into the water. Another team had just escaped being buried under a pressure ridge, the movement of the ice having providentially stopped after burying the bight which held their traces to the ice. Bartlett's igloo was moving east on the ice raft which had broken off, and beyond it, as far as the belching fog from the lead would let us see, there was nothing but black water. It looked as if the ice raft which carried Bartlett's division would impinge against our side a little farther on, and I shouted to his men to break camp and hitch up their dogs in a hurry, in readiness to rush across to us should the opportunity present itself.

Then I turned to consider our own position. Our two igloos, Henson's and mine, were on a small piece of old floe, separated by a crack and a low-pressure ridge, a few yards away, from a large floe lying to the west of us. It was clear that it would take very little strain or pressure to detach us and set us afloat also like Bartlett's division.

I routed Henson and his men out of their igloo, gave orders to everybody to pack and hitch up immediately, and, while this was being done, leveled a path across the crack to the big floe at the west of us. This was done with a pickax, leveling the ice down into the crack, so as to make a continuous surface over which the sledges could pass. As soon as the loads were across and we were safe on the floe, we all went to the edge of the lead and stood ready to assist Bartlett's men in rushing their sledges across the moment their ice raft should touch our side.

Slowly the raft drifted nearer and nearer, until the side of it crunched against the floe. The two edges being fairly even, the raft lay alongside us as a boat lies against a wharf, and we had no trouble in getting Bartlett's men and sledges across and onto the floe with us.

Though there is always a possibility that a lead may open directly across a floe as large as this one, we could not waste our sleeping hours in sitting up to watch for it. Our former igloos being lost to us, there was nothing to do but to build another set and turn in immediately. It goes without saying that this extra work was not particularly agreeable. That night we slept with our mittens on, ready at a moment's notice for anything that might happen. Had a new lead formed directly across the sleeping platform of our igloo, precipitating us into the icy water, we should not have been surprised after the first shock of the cold bath, but should have clambered out, scraping the water off our fur garments, and made ready for the next move on the part of our treacherous antagonist—the ice.

Notwithstanding the extra fatigue and the precarious position of our camp, this last march had put us well beyond my record of three years before, probably 87°12", so that I went to sleep with the satisfaction of having at last beaten my own record, no matter what the morrow might bring forth.

The following day, March 29, was not a happy one for us. Though we were all tired enough to rest, we did not enjoy picnicking beside this arctic Phlegethon, which, hour after hour, to the north, northeast, and northwest, seemed to belch black smoke like a prairie fire. So dense was this cloud caused by the condensation of the vapor and the reflection in it of the black water below that we could not see the other shore of the lead—if, indeed, it had a northern shore. As far as the evidence of our senses went, we might be encamped on the edge of that open polar sea which myth-makers have imagined as forever barring the way of man to the northern end of the earth's axis. It was heartbreaking, but there was nothing to do but wait. After breakfast we overhauled the sledges and made a few repairs, dried out some of our garments over the little oil lamps which we carried for that purpose, and Bartlett made a sounding of 1,260 fathoms, but found no bottom. He did not let all the line go out, fearing there might be a defect in the wire which would lose us more of it, as we were desirous of keeping all that we had for a sounding at our "farthest north," which we hoped would be at the Pole itself. I had only one sounding lead now left, and I would not let Bartlett risk it at this point, but had him use a pair of sledge shoes (brought along for this very purpose from the last broken up sledge) to carry the line down.

When our watches told us that it was bedtime—for we were now in the period of perpetual sunlight—we again turned into the igloos which had been hurriedly built after our exciting experience the night before. A low murmur as of distant surf was issuing from the blackness ahead of us, and steadily growing in volume. To the inexperienced it might have seemed an ominous sound, but to us it was a cheering thing because we knew it meant the narrowing, and perhaps the closing, of the stretch of open water that barred our way. So we slept happily in our frosty huts that "night."

BARTLETT REACHES 87°47"

Our hopes were soon realized, for at one o'clock in the morning, March 30, when I awoke and looked at my watch, the murmur from the closing lead had increased to a hoarse roar, punctuated with groans and with reports like those of rifles, dying away to the east and west like the sounds from a mighty firing line. Looking through the peephole, I saw that the black curtain had thinned so that I could see through it to another similar, though blacker, curtain behind, indicating still another lead further on.

At eight o'clock in the morning the temperature was down to minus thirty degrees, with a bitter northwest breeze. The grinding and groaning of the ice had ceased, and the smoke and haze had disappeared, as is usual when a lead closes up or freezes over. We rushed across before the ice should open again. All this day we traveled together, Bartlett's division, Henson's, and mine, constantly crossing narrow lanes of young ice, which had only recently been open water. During this march we had to cross a lake of young ice some six or seven miles across—so thin that the ice buckled under us as we rushed on at full speed for the other side. We did our best to make up for the previous day's delay, and when we finally camped on a heavy old floe we had made a good twenty miles.

The entire region through which we had come during the last four marches was full of unpleasant possibilities for the future. Only too well we knew that violent winds for even a few hours would set the ice all abroad in every direction. Crossing such a zone on a journey north, is only half the problem, for there is always the return to be figured on. Though the motto of the Arctic must be, "Sufficient unto the day is the evil thereof," we ardently hoped there might not be violent winds until we were south of this zone again on the return.

The next march was to be Bartlett's last, and he let himself out to do his best. The going was fairly good, but the weather was thick. There was a strong northerly wind blowing full in our faces, bitter and insistent, and the temperature was in the minus thirties. But this northerly wind, though hard to struggle against, was better than an easterly or westerly one, either of which would have set us adrift in open water, while, as it was, the wind was closing up every lead behind us and thus making things easier for Bartlett's supporting party on its return. True, the wind pressure was forcing to the south the ice over which we traveled, and thus losing us miles of distance; but the advantage of frozen leads was more than compensation for this loss.

So good was Bartlett's pace during the last half of the march that if I stopped an instant for any purpose I had to jump on a sledge or run, to catch up, and during the last few miles I walked beside Bartlett in advance. He was very sober and anxious to go further; but the program was for him to go back from here in command of the fourth supporting party, and we did not have supplies enough for an increase in the main party. The food which he and his two Eskimos and dog teams would have consumed between this point and the Pole, on the upward and return journeys, might mean that we would all starve before we could reach the land again.

Had it been clear we should undoubtedly have covered twenty-five miles in this march; but it is difficult to break a trail in thick weather as rapidly as in clear, and this day netted us only twenty miles. We knew that if we were not on or close to the 88th parallel at the end of this march, it would be because the northern winds of the past two days had set the ice south, crushing up the young ice in the leads between us and the land.

The sun came out just as we were preparing to camp, and it looked as if we should have clear weather the next day for Bartlett's meridian observations at his "farthest north."

When our igloos were built, I told the two Eskimos, Keshungwah and Karko, that they were to go back with the captain the next day; so they could get their clothes as dry as possible, as they probably would not have time to dry them on the forced march home. Bartlett was to return with these two Eskimos, one sledge, and eighteen dogs.

After about four hours' sleep, I turned everyone out at five o'clock in the morning. The wind had blown violently from the north all night, and still continued.

After breakfast Bartlett started to walk five or six miles to the north in order to make sure of reaching the 88th parallel. On his return he was to take a meridian observation to determine our position. While he was gone I culled the best dogs from his teams, replacing them with the poorer dogs from the teams of the main party. The dogs were on the whole in very good condition, far better than on any of my previous expeditions. I had been throwing the brunt of the dragging on the poorest dogs, those that I judged were going to fail, so as to keep the best dogs fresh for the final spurt.

My theory was to work the supporting parties to the limit, in order to keep the main party fresh; and those men who I expected from the beginning would form the main party at the last had things made as easy as possible for them all the way up. Ootah, Henson, and Egingwah were in this group. Whenever I could do so I had eased their loads for them, giving them the best dogs, and keeping the poorest dogs with the teams of those Eskimos who I knew were going back. It was a part of the deliberate plan to work the supporting parties as hard as possible, in order to keep the main party fresh up to the farthest possible point.

From the beginning there were certain Eskimos who, I knew, barring some unforeseen accident, would go to the Pole with me. There were others who were assigned not to go anywhere near there, and others who were available for either course. If any accidents occurred to those men whom I had originally chosen, I planned to fill their places with the next best ones who were all willing to go.

On Bartlett's return the Eskimos built the usual wind shelter already described, and Bartlett took a latitude observation, getting 87°46'49".

Bartlett was naturally much disappointed to find that even with his five-mile northward march of the morning he was still short of the 88th parallel. Our latitude was the direct result of the northerly wind of the last two days, which had crowded the ice southward as we traveled over it northward. We had traveled fully twelve miles more than his observation showed in the last five marches, but had lost them by the crushing up of the young ice in our rear and the closing of the leads.

Bartlett took the observations here, as had Marvin five camps back partly to save my eyes and partly to have independent observations by different members of the expedition. When the calculations were completed, two copies were made, one for Bartlett and one for me, and he got ready to start south on the back trail in command of my fourth supporting party, with his two Eskimos, one sledge, and eighteen dogs.

I felt a keen regret as I saw the captain's broad shoulders grow smaller in the distance and finally disappear behind the ice hummocks of the white and glittering expanse toward the south. But it was no time for reverie, and I turned abruptly away and gave my attention to the work which was before me. I had no anxiety about Bartlett. I knew that I should see him again at the ship. My work was still ahead, not in the rear. Bartlett had been invaluable to me, and circumstances had thrust upon him the brunt of the pioneering instead of its being divided among several, as I had originally planned.

Though he was naturally disappointed at not having reached the 88th parallel, he had every reason to be proud, not only of his work in general, but that he had surpassed the Italian record by a degree and a quarter. I had given him the post of honor in command of my last supporting party for three reasons: first, because of his magnificent handling of the *Roosevelt*; second, because he had cheerfully and gladly stood between me and every possible minor annoyance from the start of the expedition to that day; third, because it seemed to me right that, in view of the noble work of Great Britain in arctic exploration, a British subject should, next to an American, be able to say that he had stood nearest the North Pole.

With the departure of Bartlett, the main party now consisted of my own division and Henson's. My men were Egingwah and Seegloo; Henson's men were Ootah and Ooqueah. We had 5 sledges and 40 dogs, the pick of 140 with which we had left the ship. With these we were ready now for the final lap of the journey.

We were now 133 nautical miles from the Pole. Pacing back and forth in the lee of the pressure ridge near which our igloos were built, I made out my program. Every nerve must be strained to make five marches of at least twenty-five miles each, crowding these marches in such a way as to bring us to the end of the fifth march by noon, to permit an immediate latitude observation. Weather and leads permitting, I believed that I could do this. From the improving character of the ice, and in view of the recent northerly winds, I hoped that I should have no serious trouble with the going.

If for any reason I fell short of these proposed distances, I had two methods in reserve for making up the deficit. One was to double the last march—that is, make a good march, have tea and a hearty lunch, rest the dogs a little, and then go on again, without sleep. The other was, at the conclusion of my fifth march, to push on with one light sledge, a double team of dogs, and one or two of the party, leaving the rest in camp. Even should the going be worse than was then anticipated, eight marches like the three from 85°48" to 86°38", or six similar to our last one, would do the trick.

Underlying all these calculations was the ever-present knowledge that a twenty-fours' gale would open leads of water which might be impassable, and that all these plans would be negated.

As I paced to and fro, making out my plans, I remembered that three years ago that day we had crossed the "big lead" on our way north, April 1, 1906. A comparison of conditions now and then filled me with hope for the future.

This was the time for which I had reserved all my energies, the time for which I had worked for twenty-two years, for which I had lived the simple life and trained myself as for a race. In spite of my years, I felt fit for the demands of the coming days and was eager to be on the trail. As for my party, my equipment, and my supplies, they were perfect beyond my most sanguine dreams of earlier years. My party might be regarded as an ideal which had now come to realization—as loyal and responsive to my will as the fingers of my right hand.

My four Eskimos carried the technic of dogs, sledges, ice, and cold as their racial heritage. Henson and Ootah had been my companions at the farthest point on the expedition three years before. Egingwah and Seegloo had been in Clark's division, which had such a narrow escape at that time, having been obliged for several days to subsist upon their sealskin boots, all their other food being gone.

And the fifth was young Ooqueah, who had never before served in any expedition; but who was, if possible, even more willing and eager than the others to go with me wherever I should elect. For he was always thinking of the great treasures which I had promised each of the men who should go to the farthest point with me—whale-boat, rifle, shotgun, ammunition, knives, et cetera—wealth beyond the wildest dreams of Eskimos, which should win for him the daughter of old Ikwah of Cape York, on whom he had set his heart.

All these men had a blind confidence that I would somehow get them back to land. But I recognized fully that all the impetus of the party centered in me. Whatever pace I set, the others would make good; but if I played out, they would stop like a car with a punctured tire. I had no fault to find with the conditions, and I faced them with confidence.

The Final Spurt Begun

Henson, with his years of arctic experience, was skilful at this work. He could handle dogs and sledges. He was a part of the traveling machine. Had I taken another member of the expedition also, he would have been a passenger, necessitating the carrying of extra rations and other impediments. It would have amounted to an additional load on the sledges, while the taking of Henson was in the interest of economy of weight.

As to the dogs, most of them were powerful males, as hard as iron, in good condition, but without an ounce of superfluous fat; and, by reason of the care which I had taken of them up to this point, they were all in good spirits, like the men. The sledges, which were being repaired that day, were also in good condition. My food and fuel supplies were ample for forty days, and by the gradual utilization of the dogs themselves for reserve food, might be made to last for fifty days if it came to a pinch.

As the Eskimos worked away at repairing the sledges while we rested there on the first day of April, they stopped from time to time to eat some of the boiled dog which the surplus numbers in Bartlett's returning team had enabled them to have. They had killed one of the poorest dogs and boiled it, using the splinters of an extra broken sledge for fuel under their cooker. It was a change for them from the pemmican diet. It was fresh meat, it was hot, and they seemed thoroughly to enjoy it. But though I remembered many times when from sheer starvation I had been glad to eat dog meat raw, I did not feel inclined to join in the feast of my dusky friends.

A little after midnight, on the morning of April 2, after a few hours of sound, warm, and refreshing sleep, and a hearty breakfast, I started to lift the trail to the north, leaving the others to pack, hitch up, and follow. As I climbed the pressure ridge back of our igloo, I took up another hole in my belt, the third since I left the land—thirty-two days before. Every man and dog of us was as lean and flat-bellied as a board, and as hard.

Up to this time I had intentionally kept in the rear, to straighten out any little hitch or to encourage a man with a broken sledge, and to see that everything was in good marching order. Now I took my proper place in the lead. Though I held myself in check, I felt the keenest exhilaration, and even exultation, as I climbed over the pressure ridge and breasted the keen air sweeping over the mighty ice, pure and straight from the Pole itself.

These feelings were not in any way dampened when I plunged off the pressure ridge into water mid-thigh deep, where the pressure had forced down the edge of the floe north of us and had allowed the water to flow in under the surface snow. My boots and trousers were tight, so that no water could get inside, and as the water froze on the fur of my trousers I scraped it off with the blade of the ice lance which I carried, and was no worse for my involuntary morning plunge. I thought of my unused bathtub on the *Roosevelt*, 330 nautical miles to the south, and smiled.

It was a fine marching morning, clear and sunlit, with a temperature of minus twenty-five degrees, and the wind of the past few days had subsided to a gentle breeze. The going was the best we had had since leaving the land. The floes were large and old, hard and level, with patches of sapphire blue ice (the pools of the preceding summer). While the pressure ridges surrounding them were stupendous, some of them fifty feet high, they were not especially hard to negotiate, either through some gap or up the gradual slope of a huge drift of snow. The brilliant sunlight, the good going save for the pressure ridges, the consciousness that we were now well started on the last lap of our journey, and the joy of again being in the lead affected me like wine.

The years seemed to drop from me, and I felt as I had felt in those days fifteen years before, when I headed my little party across the great ice-cap of Greenland, leaving twenty and twenty-five miles behind my snowshoes day after day, and on a spurt stretching it to thirty or forty.

Perhaps a man always thinks of the very beginning of his work when he feels it is nearing its end. The appearance of the ice-fields to the north this day, large and level, the brilliant blue of the sky, the biting character of the wind—everything excepting the surface of the ice, which on the great cap is absolutely dead level with a straight line for a horizon— reminded me of those marches of the long ago.

The most marked difference was the shadows, which on the ice-cap are absent entirely, but on the polar ice, where the great pressure ridges stand out in bold relief, are deep and dark. Then, too, there are on the polar ice those little patches of sapphire blue already mentioned, made from the water pools of the preceding summer. On the Greenland ice-cap years ago I had been spurred on by the necessity of reaching the musk-oxen of Independence Bay before my supplies gave out. Now I was spurred on by the necessity of making my goal, if possible, before the round face of the coming full moon should stir the tides with unrest and open a network of leads across our path.

After some hours the sledges caught up with me. The dogs were so active that morning, after their day's rest, that I was frequently obliged to sit on a sledge for a few minutes or else run to keep up with them, which I did not care to do just yet. Our course was nearly, as the crow flies, due north, across floe after floe, pressure ridge after pressure ridge, headed straight for some hummock or pinnacle of ice which I had lined in with my compass.

In this way we traveled for ten hours without stopping, covering, I felt sure, thirty miles, though, to be conservative, I called it twenty-five. My Eskimos said that we had come as far as from the *Roosevelt* to Porter Bay, which by our winter route scales thirty-five miles on the chart. Anyway, we were well over the 88th parallel, in a region where no human being had ever been before. And whatever distance we made, we were likely to retain it now that the wind had ceased to blow from the north. It was even possible that with the release of the wind pressure the ice might rebound more or less and return us some of the hard-earned miles which it had stolen from us during the previous three days.

Near the end of the march I came upon a lead which was just opening. It was ten yards wide directly in front of me, but a few hundred yards to the east was an apparently practicable crossing where the single crack was divided into several. I signaled to the sledges to hurry; then, running to the place, I had time to pick a road across the moving ice cakes and return to help the teams across before the lead widened so as to be impassable. This passage was affected by my jumping from one cake to another, picking the way, and making sure that the cake would not tilt under the weight of the dogs and the sledge, returning to the former cake where the dogs were, encouraging the dogs ahead while the driver steered the sledge across from cake to cake, and threw his weight from one side to the other so that it could not overturn. We got the sledges across several cracks so wide that while the dogs had no trouble in jumping, the men had to be pretty active in order to follow the long sledges. Fortunately the sledges were of the new Peary type, twelve feet long. Had they been of the old Eskimo type, seven feet long, we might have had to use ropes and pull them across hand over hand on an ice cake.

It is always hard to make the dogs leap a widening crack, though some of the best dog drivers can do it instantly, using the whip and the voice. A poor dog driver would be likely to get everything into the water in the attempt. It is sometimes necessary to go ahead of the dogs, holding the hand low and shaking it as though it contained some dainty morsel of food, thus inspiring them with courage for the leap.

Perhaps a mile beyond this, the breaking of the ice at the edge of a narrow lead as I landed from a jump sent me into the water nearly to my hips; but as the water did not come above the waistband of my trousers, which were water-tight, it was soon scraped and beaten off before it had time to freeze.

This lead was not wide enough to bother the sledges.

As we stopped to make our camp near a huge pressure ridge, the sun, which was gradually getting higher, seemed almost to have some warmth. While we were building our igloos, we could see, by the water clouds lying to the east and southeast of us some miles distant, that a wide lead was opening in that direction. The approaching full moon was evidently getting in its work.

As we had traveled on, the moon had circled round and round the heavens opposite the sun, a disk of silver opposite a disk of gold. Looking at its pallid and spectral face, from which the brighter light of the sun had stolen the color, it seemed hard to realize that its presence there had power to stir the great ice-fields around us with restlessness—power even now, when we were so near our goal, to interrupt our pathway with an impassable lead.

The moon had been our friend during the long winter, giving us light to hunt by for a week or two each month. Now it seemed no longer a friend, but a dangerous presence to be regarded with fear. Its power, which had before been beneficent, was now malevolent and incalculably potent for evil.

When we awoke early in the morning of April 3, after a few hours' sleep, we found the weather still clear and calm. There were some broad heavy pressure ridges in the beginning of this march, and we had to use pickaxes quite freely. This delayed us a little, but as soon as we struck the level old floes we tried to make up for lost time. As the daylight was now continuous we could travel as long as we pleased and sleep as little as we must. We hustled along for ten hours again, as we had before, making only twenty miles, because of the early delay with the pickaxes and another brief delay at a narrow lead. We were now halfway to the 89th parallel, and I had been obliged to take up another hole in my belt.

Some gigantic rafters were seen during this march, but they were not in our path. All day long we had heard the ice grinding and groaning on all sides of us, but no motion was visible to our eyes. Either the ice was slacking back into equilibrium, sagging northward after its release from the wind pressure, or else it was feeling the influence of the spring tides of the full moon. On, on we pushed, and I am not ashamed to confess that my pulse beat high, for the breath of success seemed already in my nostrils.

ONLY ONE DAY FROM THE POLE

With every passing day even the Eskimos were becoming more eager and interested, notwithstanding the fatigue of the long marches. As we stopped to make camp, they would climb to some pinnacle of ice and strain their eyes to the north, wondering if the Pole was in sight, for they were now certain that we should get there this time.

We slept only a few hours the next night, hitting the trail again a little before midnight between the 3rd and 4th of April. The weather and the going were even better than the day before. The surface of the ice, except as interrupted by infrequent pressure ridges, was as level as the glacial fringe from Hecla to Cape Columbia, and harder. I rejoiced at the thought that if the weather held good I should be able to get in my five marches before noon of the 6th.

Again we traveled for ten hours straight ahead, the dogs often on the trot and occasionally on the run, and in those ten hours we reeled off at least twenty-five miles. I had a slight accident that day, a sledge runner having passed over the side of my right foot as I stumbled while running beside a team; but the hurt was not severe enough to keep me from traveling.

Near the end of the day we crossed a lead about one hundred yards wide, on young ice so thin that, as I ran ahead to guide the dogs, I was obliged to slide my feet and travel wide, bear style, in order to distribute my weight, while the men let the sledges and dogs come over by themselves, gliding across where they could. The last two men came over on all fours.

I watched them from the other side with my heart in my mouth—watched the ice bending under the weight of the sledges and the men. As one of the sledges neared the north side, a runner cut clear through the ice, and I expected every moment that the whole thing, dogs and all, would go through the ice and down to the bottom. But it did not.

This dash reminded me of that day, nearly three years before, when in order to save our lives we had taken desperate chances in recrossing the "Big Lead" on ice similar to this—ice that buckled under us and through which my toe cut several times as I slid my long snowshoes over it. A man who should wait for the ice to be really safe would stand small chance of getting far in these latitudes. Traveling on the polar ice, one takes all kinds of chances. Often a man has the choice between the possibility of drowning by going on or starving to death by standing still, and challenges fate with the briefer and less painful chance.

That night we were all pretty tired, but satisfied with our progress so far. We were almost inside of the 89th parallel, and I wrote in my diary: "Give me three more days of this weather!" The temperature at the beginning of the march had been minus forty degrees. That night I put all the poorest dogs in one team and began to eliminate and feed them to the others, as it became necessary.

We stopped for only a short sleep, and early in the evening of the same day, the 4th, we struck on again. The temperature was then minus thirty-five degrees, the going was the same, but the sledges always haul more easily when the temperature rises, and the dogs were on the trot much of the time. Toward the end of the march we came upon a lead running north and south, and as the young ice was thick enough to support the teams, we traveled on it for two hours, the dogs galloping along and reeling off the miles in a way that delighted my heart. The light air which had blown from the south during the first few hours of the march veered to the east and grew keener as the hours wore on.

I had not dared to hope for such progress as we were making. Still the biting cold would have been impossible to face by anyone not fortified by an inflexible purpose. The bitter wind burned our faces so that they cracked, and long after we got into camp each day they pained us so that we could hardly go to sleep. The Eskimos complained much, and at every camp fixed their fur clothing about their faces, waists, knees, and wrists. They also complained of their noses, which I had never known them to do before. The air was as keen and bitter as frozen steel.

At the next camp I had another of the dogs killed. It was now exactly six weeks since we left the *Roosevelt*, and I felt as if the goal were in sight. I intended the next day, weather and ice permitting, to make a long march, "boil the kettle" midway, and then go on again without sleep, trying to make up the five miles which we had lost on the 3rd of April.

During the daily march my mind and body were too busy with the problem of covering as many miles of distance as possible to permit me to enjoy the beauty of the frozen wilderness through which we tramped. But at the end of the day's march, while the igloos were being built, I usually had a few minutes in which to look about me and to realize the picturesqueness of our situation—we, the only living things in a trackless, colorless, inhospitable desert of ice. Nothing but the hostile ice, and far more hostile icy water, lay between our remote place on the world's map and the utmost tips of the lands of Mother Earth.

I knew of course that there was always a *possibility* that we might still end our lives up there, and that our conquest of the unknown spaces and silences of the polar void might remain forever unknown to the world which we had left behind. But it was hard to realize this. That hope which is said to spring eternal in the human breast always buoyed me up with the belief that, as a matter of course, we should be able to return along the white road by which we had come.

Sometimes I would climb to the top of a pinnacle of ice to the north of our camp and strain my eyes into the whiteness which lay beyond, trying to imagine myself already at the Pole. We had come so far, and the capricious ice had placed so few obstructions in our path, that now I dared to loose my fancy, to entertain the image which my will had heretofore forbidden to my imagination—the image of ourselves at the goal.

We had been very fortunate with the leads so far, but I was in constant and increasing dread lest we should encounter an impassable one toward the very end. With every successive march, my fear of such impassable leads had increased. At every pressure ridge I found myself hurrying breathlessly forward, fearing there might be a lead just beyond it, and when I arrived at the summit I would catch my breath with relief—only to find myself hurrying on in the same way at the next ridge.

At our camp on the 5th of April I gave the party a little more sleep than at the previous ones, as we were all pretty well played out and in need of rest. I took a latitude sight, and this indicated our position to be 89°25", or thirty-five miles from the Pole; but I determined to make the next camp in time for a noon observation, if the sun should be visible.

Before midnight on the 5th we were again on the trail. The weather was overcast, and there was the same gray and shadowless light as on the march after Marvin had turned back. The sky was a colorless pall gradually deepening to almost black at the horizon, and the ice was a ghastly and chalky white, like that of the Greenland ice-cap—just the colors which an imaginative artist would paint as a polar ice-scape. How different it seemed from the glittering fields, canopied with blue and lit by the sun and full moon, over which we had been traveling for the last four days.

The going was even better than before. There was hardly any snow on the hard granular surface of the old floes, and the sapphire blue lakes were larger than ever. The temperature had risen to minus fifteen degrees, which, reducing the friction of the sledges, gave the dogs the appearance of having caught the high spirits of the party. Some of them even tossed their heads and barked and yelped as they traveled.

Notwithstanding the grayness of the day, and the melancholy aspect of the surrounding world, by some strange shift of feeling the fear of the leads had fallen from me completely. I now felt that success was certain, and, notwithstanding the physical exhaustion of the forced marches of the last five days, I went tirelessly on and on, the Eskimos following almost automatically, though I knew that they must feel the weariness which my excited brain made me incapable of feeling.

When we had covered, as I estimated, a good fifteen miles, we halted, made tea, ate lunch, and rested the dogs. Then we went on for another estimated fifteen miles. In twelve hours' actual traveling time we made thirty miles. Many laymen have wondered why we were able to travel faster after the sending back of each of the supporting parties, especially after the last one. To any man experienced in the handling of troops this will need no explanation. The larger the party and the greater the number of sledges, the greater is the chance of breakages or delay for one reason or another. A large party cannot be forced as rapidly as a small party.

With my party reduced to five picked men, every man, dog, and sledge under my individual eye, myself in the lead, and all recognizing that the moment had now come to let ourselves out for all there was in us, we naturally bettered our previous speed.

When Bartlett left us the sledges had been practically rebuilt, all the best dogs were in our pack, and we all understood that we must attain our object and get back as quickly as we possibly could. The weather was in our favor. The average march for the whole journey from the land to the Pole was over fifteen miles. We had repeatedly made marches of twenty miles. Our average for five marches from the point where the last supporting party turned back was about twenty-six miles.

WE REACH THE POLE

The last march northward ended at ten o'clock on the forenoon of April 6. I had now made the five marches planned from the point at which Bartlett turned back, and my reckoning showed that we were in the immediate neighborhood of the goal of all our striving. After the usual arrangements for going into camp, at approximate local noon, of the Columbia meridian, I made the first observation at our polar camp. It indicated our position as 89°57".

We were now at the end of the last long march of the upward journey. Yet with the Pole actually in sight I was too weary to take the last few steps. The accumulated weariness of all those days and nights of forced marches and insufficient sleep, constant peril and anxiety, seemed to roll across me all at once. I was actually too exhausted to realize at the moment that my life's purpose had been achieved. As soon as our igloos had been completed and we had eaten our dinner and double-rationed the dogs, I turned in for a few hours of absolutely necessary sleep, Henson and the Eskimos having unloaded the sledges and got them in readiness for such repairs as were necessary. But, weary though I was, I could not sleep long. It was, therefore, only a few hours later when I woke. The first thing I did after awaking was to write these words in my diary:

> The Pole at last. The prize of three centuries. My dream and goal
> for twenty years. Mine at last! I cannot bring myself to realize it.
> It seems all so simple and commonplace.

Everything was in readiness for an observation at 6 p.m., Columbia meridian time, in case the sky should be clear, but at that hour it was, unfortunately, still overcast. But as there were indications that it would clear before long, two of the Eskimos and myself made ready a light sledge carrying only the instruments, a tin of pemmican, and one or two skins; and drawn by a double team of dogs, we pushed on an estimated distance of ten miles. While we traveled, the sky cleared, and at the end of the journey, I was able to get a satisfactory series of observations at Columbia meridian midnight. These observations indicated that our position was then beyond the Pole.

Nearly everything in the circumstances which then surrounded us seemed too strange to be thoroughly realized; but one of the strangest of those circumstances seemed to me to be the fact that, in a march of only a few hours, I had passed from the western to the eastern hemisphere and had verified my position at the summit of the world. It was hard to realize that, in the first miles of this brief march, we had been traveling due north, while, on the last few miles of the same march, we had been traveling south, although we had all the time been traveling precisely in the same direction. It would be difficult to imagine a better illustration of the fact that most things are relative. Again, please consider the uncommon circumstance that, in order to return to our camp, it now became necessary to turn and go north again for a few miles and then to go directly south, all the time traveling in the same direction.

As we passed back along that trail which none had ever seen before or would ever see again, certain reflections intruded themselves which, I think, may fairly be called unique. East, west, and north had disappeared for us. Only one direction remained and that was south. Every breeze which could possibly blow upon us, no matter from what point of the horizon, must be a south wind. Where we were, one day and one night constituted a year, a hundred such days and nights constituted a century. Had we stood in that spot during the six months of the arctic winter night, we should have seen every star of the northern hemisphere circling the sky at the same distance from the horizon, with Polaris (the North Star) practically in the zenith.

All during our march back to camp the sun was swinging around in its ever-moving circle. At six o'clock on the morning of April 7, having again arrived at Camp Jesup, I took another series of observations. These indicated our position as being four or five miles from the Pole, towards Bering Strait. Therefore, with a double team of dogs and a light sledge, I traveled directly towards the sun an estimated distance of eight miles. Again, I returned to the camp in time for a final and completely satisfactory series of observations on April 7 at noon, Columbia meridian time. These observations gave results essentially the same as those made at the same spot twenty-four hours before.

I had now taken in all thirteen single, or six and one-half double, altitudes of the sun, at two different stations, in three different directions, at four different times. All were under satisfactory conditions, except for the first single altitude on the sixth. The temperature during these observations had been from minus eleven degrees Fahrenheit to minus thirty degrees Fahrenheit, with clear sky and calm weather.

In traversing the ice in these various directions as I had done, I had allowed approximately ten miles for possible errors in my observations, and at some moment during these marches and countermarches, I had passed over or very near the point where north and south and east and west blend into one.

Of course there were some more or less informal ceremonies connected with our arrival at our difficult destination, but they were not of a very elaborate character. We planted five flags at the top of the world. The first one was a silk American flag which Mrs. Peary gave me fifteen years ago. That flag has done more traveling in high latitudes than any other ever made. I carried it wrapped about my body on every one of my expeditions northward after it came into my possession, and I left a fragment of it at each of my successive "farthest norths": Cape Morris K. Jesup, the northernmost point of land in the known world; Cape Thomas Hubbard, the northernmost known point of Jesup Land, west of Grant Land; Cape Columbia, the northernmost point of North American lands; and my farthest north in 1906, latitude 87°6" in the ice of the polar sea. By the time it actually reached the Pole, therefore, it was somewhat worn and discolored.

A broad diagonal section of this ensign would now mark the farthest goal of earth—the place where I and my dusky companions stood.

It was also considered appropriate to raise the colors of the Delta Kappa Epsilon fraternity, in which I was initiated a member while an undergraduate student at Bowdoin College, the "World's Ensign of Liberty and Peace," with its red, white, and blue in a field of white, the Navy League flag, and the Red Cross flag.

After I had planted the American flag in the ice, I told Henson to time the Eskimos for three rousing cheers, which they gave with the greatest enthusiasm. Thereupon, I shook hands with each member of the party—surely a sufficiently unceremonious affair to meet with the approval of the most democratic.

Then, in a space between the ice blocks of a pressure ridge, I deposited a glass bottle containing a diagonal strip of my flag and records of which the following is a copy:

90 N. LAT., NORTH POLE
April 6, 1909

Arrived here to-day, 27 marches from C. Columbia.

I have with me 5 men, Matthew Henson, colored, Ootah, Egingwah, Seegloo, and Ookeah, Eskimos; 5 sledges and 38 dogs. My ship, the S. S. Roosevelt, is in winter quarters at C. Sheridan, 90 miles east of Columbia.

The expedition under my command which has succeeded in reaching the Pole is under the auspices of the Peary Arctic Club of New York City, and has been fitted out and sent north by the members and friends of the club for the purpose of securing this geographical prize, if possible, for the honor and prestige of the United States of America.

The officers of the club are Thomas H. Hubbard, of New York, President; Zenas Crane, of Mass., Vice-president; Herbert L. Bridgman, of New York, Secretary and Treasurer.

I start back for Cape Columbia to-morrow.

ROBERT E. PEARY
United States Navy

90 N. LAT., NORTH POLE
April 6, 1909

I have to-day hoisted the national ensign of the United States of America at this place, which my observations indicate to be the North Polar axis of the earth, and have formally taken possession of the entire region, and adjacent, for and in the name of the President of the United States of America.

I leave this record and United States flag in possession.

ROBERT E. PEARY
United States Navy

If it were possible for a man to arrive at ninety degrees north latitude without being utterly exhausted, body and brain, he would doubtless enjoy a series of unique sensations and reflections. But the attainment of the Pole was the culmination of days and weeks of forced marches, physical discomfort, insufficient sleep, and racking anxiety. It is a wise provision of nature that the human consciousness can grasp only such degree of intense feeling as the brain can endure, and the grim guardians of earth's remotest spot will accept no man as guest until he has been tried and tested by the severest ordeal.

Perhaps it ought not to have been so, but when I knew for a certainty that we had reached the goal, there was not a thing in the world I wanted but sleep. But after I had a few hours of it, there succeeded a condition of mental exaltation which made further rest impossible. For more than a score of years that point on the earth's surface had been the object of my every effort. To its attainment my whole being, physical, mental, and moral, had been dedicated. Many times my own life and the lives of those with me had been risked. My own material and forces and those of my friends had been devoted to this object. This journey was my eighth into the arctic wilderness. In that wilderness I had spent nearly twelve years out of the twenty-three between my thirtieth and my fifty-third year, and the intervening time spent in civilized communities during that period had been mainly occupied with preparations for returning to the wilderness. The determination to reach the Pole had become so much a part of my being that, strange as it may seem, I long ago ceased to think of myself save as an instrument for the attainment of that end. To the layman this may seem strange, but an inventor can understand it, or an artist, or anyone who has devoted himself for years upon years to the service of an idea.

But though my mind was busy at intervals during those thirty hours spent at the Pole with the exhilarating thought that my dream had come true, there was one recollection of other times that, now and then, intruded itself with startling distinctness. It was the recollection of a day three years before, April 21, 1906, when after making a fight with ice, open water, and storms, the expedition which I commanded had been forced to turn back from 87°6" north latitude because our supply of food would carry us no further. And the contrast between the terrible depression of that day and the exaltation of the present moment was not the least pleasant feature of our brief stay at the Pole.

During the dark moments of that return journey in 1906, I had told myself that I was only one in a long list of arctic explorers, dating back through the centuries, all the way from Henry Hudson to the Duke of the Abruzzi, and including Franklin, Kane, and Melville—a long list of valiant men who had striven and failed. I told myself that I had only succeeded, at the price of the best years of my life, in adding a few links to the chain that led from the parallels of civilization towards the polar center, but that, after all, at the end the only word I had to write was failure.

But now, while quartering the ice in various directions from our camp, I tried to realize that, after twenty-three years of struggles and discouragement, I had at last succeeded in placing the flag of my country at the goal of the world's desire. It is not easy to write about such a thing, but I knew that we were going back to civilization with the last of the great adventure stories—a story the world had been waiting to hear for nearly four hundred years, a story which was to be told at last under the folds of the Stars and Stripes, the flag that during a lonely and isolated life had come to be for me the symbol of home and everything I loved— and might never see again.

The thirty hours at the Pole, what with my marchings and counter-marchings, together with the observations and records, were pretty well crowded. I found time, however, to write to Mrs. Peary on a United States postal card which I had found on the ship during the winter. It had been my custom at various important stages of the journey northward to write such a note in order that, if anything serious happened to me, these brief communications might ultimately reach her at the hands of survivors. This was the card, which later reached Mrs. Peary at Sydney:—

90 North
April 7th

My dear Jo,

I have won out at last. Have been here a day. I start for home and you in an hour. Love to the "kidsies."

Bert

In the afternoon of the 7th, after flying our flags and taking our photographs, we went into our igloos and tried to sleep a little, before starting south again.

CHAPTER SIX

My Attainment of the Pole, 1907–1909

Frederick A. Cook

I Was First

My claim of being first to reach the North Pole will rest upon the data I have presented.

My last word to all—to friends and enemies—is, if you must pass judgment, study the problem carefully. You are as capable of forming a correct judgment as the self-appointed experts. One of Peary's captains has said "that he knew, but never would admit, that Peary did not reach the Pole." Rear Admiral Chester has said the same about me, but he "admits" it in big, flaming type. With due respect to these men, in justice to the cause, I am bound to say that these, and others of their kind, who necessarily have a blinding bias, are not better able to judge than the average American citizen.

Since my account was written and printed first, the striking analogy apparent in the Peary pages either proves my position at the Pole or it convicts Peary of using my data to fill out and impart verisimilitude to his own story of a second victory.

Much against my will I find myself compelled to uncover the dark pages of the selfish unfairness of rival interests. In doing so my aim is not to throw doubt and distrust on Mr. Peary's success, but to show his incentive and his methods in attempting to leave the sting of discredit upon me. I would prefer to close my eye to a long series of wrong-doings as I have done in the passing years, but the Polar controversy cannot be understood unless we get the perspective of the man who has forced it.

Heretofore I have allowed others to expend their argumentative ammunition. The questions which I have raised are minor points. On the main question of Polar attainment there is not now room for doubt. The Pole has been honestly reached—the American Eagle has spread its wings of glory over the world's top. Whether there is room for one or two or more under those wings, I am content to let the future decide.

Frederick A. Cook
The Waldorf-Astoria
New York, June 15, 1911

Dr. Cook Is Vindicated. His Discovery of the North Pole Is Endorsed by the Explorers of All the World

In placing Dr. Cook on the Chautauqua platform as a lecturer, we have been compelled to study the statements issued for and against the rival polar claims with special reference to the facts bearing upon the present status of the Polar Controversy.

Though the question has been argued during four years, we find that it is almost the unanimous opinion of arctic explorers today, that Dr. Cook reached the North Pole on April 21, 1909.

With officer Peary's first announcement he chose to force a press campaign to deny Dr. Cook's success and to proclaim himself as the sole Polar Victor. Peary aimed to be retired as a Rear-Admiral on a pension of $6,000 per year. This ambition was granted; but the American Congress rejected his claim for priority by eliminating from the pension bill the words "Discovery of the Pole." The European geographical societies, forced under diplomatic pressure to honor Peary, have also refused him the title of "Discoverer." By a final verdict of the American government and of the highest European authorities, Peary is therefore denied the assumption of being the discoverer of the Pole, though his claim as a re-discoverer is allowed. The evasive inscriptions on the Peary medals prove this statement.

Following the acute excitement of the first announcement, it seemed to be desirable to bring the question to a focus by submitting to some authoritative body for decision. Such an institution, however, did not exist. Previously, explorers had been rated by the slow process of historic digestion and assimilation of the facts offered, but it was thought that an academic examination would meet the demands.

Officer Peary first submitted his case to a commission appointed by the National Geographic Society of Washington, D.C. This jury promptly said that in their "opinion" Peary reached the Pole on April 6, 1909; but a year later in Congress the same men unwillingly admitted that in the Peary proofs there was no positive proof.

Dr. Cook's data was sent to a commission appointed by the University of Copenhagen. The Danes reported that the material presented was incomplete and did not constitute positive proof. This verdict, however, did not carry the interpretation that the Pole had not been reached. The Danes have never said, as they have been quoted by the press, that Dr. Cook did not reach the Pole; quite to the contrary, the University of Copenhagen conferred the degree of Ph.D. and the Royal Danish Geographical Society gave a gold medal, both in recognition of the merits of the Polar effort.

May 22, 1913
The Chautauqua Managers' Association

To the Pole—The Last Hundred Miles

I shall never forget that dismal hour. I shall never forget that desolate drab scene about us—those endless stretches of gray and dead-white ice, that drab dull sky, that thickening blackness in the west which entered into and made gray and black our souls, that ominous, eerie and dreadful wind, betokening a terrorizing Arctic storm.

I shall never forget the mournful group before me, in itself an awful picture of despair, of man's ambition failing just as victory is within his grasp. Ah-we-lah, a thin, half-starved figure in worn furs, lay over his sled, limp, dispirited, broken. In my ears I can now hear his low sobbing words, I can see the tears on his yellow fissured face. I can see E-tuk-i-shook standing gaunt and grim, and as he gazed yearningly onward to the south, sighing pitifully, shudderingly for the home, the loved one, An-na-do-a, left behind, whom, I could tell, he did not expect to see again.

It was a critical moment. Up to this time, during the second week of April, we had, by intense mental force, goaded our wearied legs onward to the limit of endurance. With a cutting wind in our faces, feeling with each step the cold more severely to the marrow of our bones, with our bodily energy and our bodily heat decreasing, we had traveled persistently, suffering intolerable pains with every breath.

Despite increasing despair, I had cheered my companions as best I could; I had impressed upon them the constant nearing of my goal. I had encouraged in them the belief of nearness of land; each day I had gone on, fearing what had now come, the utter breaking of their spirits.

"*Unne-sinikpo-ashuka.*" (Yes, it is well to die.)

"*Awonga-up-dow-epuksha!*" (Yesterday I, too, felt that way), I said to myself. The sudden extinction of consciousness, I thought, might be indeed a blessed relief. But as long as life persisted, as long as human endurance could be strained, I determined to continue. Desperate as was my condition, and suffering hellish tortures, the sight of the despair of my companions re-aroused me. Should we fail now, after our long endurance, now, when the goal was so near?

The Pole was only 100 miles beyond. The attainment seemed almost certain.

I knew my companions were brave. I was certain of their fidelity. Could their mental despair be alleviated, I felt convinced they could brace themselves for another effort. I spoke kindly to them; I told them what we had accomplished, that they were good and brave, that their parents and their sweethearts would be proud of them, and that as a matter of honor we must not now fail.

"*Tigishu-conitu,*" I said. (The Pole is near.)

Then I said, "The ice is flat, the snow is good, the sky is clear, the Great Spirit is with us, the Pole is near!"

Ah-we-lah dully nodded his head. I noticed, however, he wiped his eyes.

As I spoke my own spirits rose to the final effort, my lassitude gave way to a new enthusiasm. I felt the fire kindling for many years aglow within me. The goal was near; there remained but one step to the apex of my ambition. I spoke hurriedly. The two sat up and listened. Slowly they became inspired with my intoxication. Never did I speak so vehemently.

With snapping whip we were off for that last hundred miles.

The animals pricked their ears, re-curled their tails, and pulled at the traces. Shouting to keep up the forced enthusiasm, we bounded forward on the last lap. A sort of wild gratification filled my heart. I knew that only mental enthusiasm would now prevent the defeat which might yet come from our own bodies refusing to go farther. Brain must now drive muscle. Fortunately the sense of final victory imparted a supernormal mental stimulus.

On April 14, my observations gave latitude, 88°21"; longitude, 95°52". The wind came with a satanic cut from the west. There had been little drift. But with a feeling of chagrin I saw that the ice before us displayed signs of recent activity. It was more irregular, with open cracks here and there. These we had to avoid, but the sleds glided with less friction, and the weary dogs maintained a better speed.

With set teeth and newly sharpened resolutions, we continued mile after mile of that last one hundred. More dogs had gone into the stomachs of their hungry companions, but there still remained a sufficient pull of well-tried brute force for each sled. Although their noisy vigor had been gradually lost in the long drag, they still broke the frigid silence with an occasional outburst of howls. Any fresh enthusiasm from the drivers was quickly responded to by canine activity.

We were in good trim to cover distance economically. Our sledges were light, our bodies were thin. We had lost, since leaving winter camp, judging from appearances, from twenty-five to forty pounds each. All our muscles had shriveled. The dogs retained strength that was amazing. Stripped for the last lap, one horizon after another was lifted.

In the forced effort which followed we frequently became overheated. The temperature was steady at forty-four degrees below zero Fahrenheit. Perspiration came with ease, and with a certain amount of pleasure. Later followed a train of suffering for many days. The delight of the birdskin shirt gave place to the chill of a wet blanket. Our coats and trousers hardened to icy suits of armor. It became quite impossible to dress after a sleep without softening the stiffened furs with the heat of our bare skin. Mittens, boots and fur stockings became quite useless until dried out.

Fortunately, at this time the rays of the sun were warm enough to dry the furs in about three days, if lashed to the sunny side of a sled as we marched along, and strangely enough, the furs dried out without apparent thawing. In these last days we felt more keenly the pangs of perspiration than in all our earlier adventures. We persistently used the amber-colored goggles. They afforded protection to the eyes, but in spite of every precaution, our distorted, frozen, burned and withered faces lined a map in relief, of the hardships endured en route.

We were curious-looking savages. The perpetual glitter of the snows induced a squint of our eyes which distorted our faces in a remarkable manner. The strong light reflected from the crystal surface threw the muscles about the eyes into a state of chronic contraction. The iris was reduced to a mere pinhole.

The strong winds and drifting snows necessitated the habit of peeping out of the corners of the eyes. Nature, in attempting to keep the ball from hardening, flushed it at all times with blood. To keep the seeing windows of the mind open required a constant exertion of willpower. The effect was a set of expressions of hardship and wrinkles which might be called the boreal squint.

This boreal squint is a part of the russet-bronze physiognomy which falls to the lot of every Arctic explorer. The early winds, with a piercing temperature, start a flush of scarlet, while frequent frostbites leave figures in black. Later the burning sun browns the skin; subsequently, strong winds sap the moisture, harden the skin and leave open fissures on the face. The human face takes upon itself the texture and configuration of the desolate, wind-driven world upon which it looks.

Hard work and reduced nourishment contract the muscles, dispel the fat and leave the skin to shrivel in folds. The imprint of the goggles, the set expression of hard times, and the mental blank of the environment remove all spiritual animation. Our faces assumed the color and lines of old, withering, russet apples, and would easily pass for the mummied countenances of the prehistoric progenitors of man.

In enforced efforts to spread out our stiffened legs over the last reaches, there was left no longer sufficient energy at camping times to erect snow shelters. Our silk tent was pressed into use. Although the temperature was still very low, the congenial rays pierced the silk fabric and rested softly on our eyelids closed in heavy slumber. In strong winds it was still necessary to erect a sheltering wall, whereby to shield the tent.

As we progressed over the last one hundred mile step, my mind was divested of its lethargy. Unconsciously I braced myself. My senses became more keen. With a careful scrutiny I now observed the phenomena of the strange world into which fortune had pressed us—first of all men.

Step by step, I invaded a world untrodden and unknown. Dulled as I was by hardship, I thrilled with the sense of the explorer in new lands, with the thrill of discovery and conquest. "Then," as Keats says, "felt I like some watcher of the skies, when a new planet swims into his ken." In this land of ice I was master, I was sole invader. I strode forward with an undaunted glory in my soul.

Signs of land, which I encouraged my companions to believe were real, were still seen every day, but I knew, of course, they were deceptive. It now seemed to me that something unusual must happen, that some line must cross our horizon to mark the important area into which we were passing.

Through vapor-charged air of crystal, my eyes ran over plains moving in brilliant waves of running colors toward dancing horizons. Mirages turned things topsy-turvy. Inverted lands and queer objects ever rose and fell, shrouded in mystery. All of this was due to the atmospheric magic of the continued glory of midnight suns in throwing piercing beams of light through superimposed strata of air of varying temperature and density.

Daily, by careful measurements, I found that our night shadows shortened and became more uniform during the passing hours of the day, as the shadow dial was marked.

With a lucky series of astronomical observations our position was fixed for each stage of progress.

Nearing the Pole, my imagination quickened. A restless, almost hysterical excitement came over all of us. My boys fancied they saw bears and seals. I had new lands under observation frequently, but with a change in the direction of light the horizon cleared. We became more and more eager to push further into the mystery. Climbing the long ladder of latitudes, there was always the feeling that each hour's work was bringing us nearer the Pole—the Pole which men had sought for three centuries, and which, fortune favoring, should be mine!

From the 88th to the 89th parallel the ice lay in large fields, the surface was less irregular than formerly. In other respects it was about the same as below the 87th. I observed here also, an increasing extension of the range of vision. I seemed to scan longer distances, and the ice along the horizon had a less angular outline.

The color of the sky and the ice changed to deeper purple-blues. I had no way of checking these impressions by other observations; the eagerness to find something unusual may have fired my imagination, but since the earth is flattened at the Pole, perhaps a widened horizon would naturally be detected there.

At eight o'clock on the morning of April 19, we camped on a picturesque old field, with convenient hummocks, to the top of which we could easily rise for the frequent outlook which we now maintained. We pitched our tent and silenced the dogs by blocks of pemmican. New enthusiasm was aroused by a liberal pot of pea soup and a few chips of frozen meat. Then we bathed in life-giving sunbeams, screened from the piercing air by the strands of the silk-walled tent.

The day was beautiful. Had our sense of appreciation not been blunted by accumulated fatigue we should have greatly enjoyed the play of light and color in the ever-changing scene of sparkle. But in our condition it was but an inducement to keep the eyes open and to pro-long interest long enough to dispel the growing complaint of aching muscles.

Ah-we-lah and E-tuk-i-shook were soon lost in profound sleep, the only comfort in their hard lives. I remained awake, as had been my habit for many preceding days, to get nautical observations. My longitude calculations lined us at 94°3". At noon the sun's altitude was carefully set on the sextant, and the latitude, quickly reduced, gave 89°31". The drift had carried us too far east, but our advance was encouraging.

I put down the instrument, wrote the reckonings in my book. Then I gazed, with a sort of fascination, at the figures. My heart began to thump wildly. Slowly my brain whirled with exultation. I arose jubilant. We were only twenty-nine miles from the North Pole!

I tried to explain to them that the Pole is not visible to the eye, and that its position is located only by a repeated use of the various instruments. Although this was quite beyond their comprehension the explanation entirely satisfied their curiosity. They burst out in hurrahs of joy. For two hours they chanted, danced and shouted the passions of wildlife. Their joy, however, was in the thought of a speedy turning back homeward, I surmised.

With the Pole only twenty-nine miles distant, more sleep was quite impossible. We brewed an extra pot of tea, prepared a favorite broth of pemmican, dug up a surprise of fancy biscuits and filled up on good things to the limit of the allowance for our final feast days. The dogs, which had joined the chorus of gladness, were given an extra lump of pemmican. A few hours more were agreeably spent in the tent. Then we started out with new spirit for the uttermost goal of our world.

Bounding joyously forward, with a stimulated mind, I reviewed the journey. Obstacle after obstacle had been overcome. Each battle won gave a spiritual thrill, and courage to scale the next barrier. Thus had been ever, and was still, in the unequal struggles between human and inanimate nature, an incentive to go onward, ever onward, up the stepping-stones to ultimate success. And now, after a life-denying struggle in a world where every element of Nature is against the life and progress of man, triumph came with steadily measured reaches of fifteen miles a day!

We were excited to fever heat. Our feet were light on the run. Even the dogs caught the infectious enthusiasm. They rushed along at a pace which made it difficult for me to keep a sufficient advance to set a good course. The horizon was still eagerly searched for something to mark the approaching boreal center. But nothing unusual was seen. The same expanse of moving seas of ice, on which we had gazed for 500 miles, swam about us as we drove onward.

As the day advanced beyond midnight and the splendor of the summer night ran into a clearer continued day, the beams of gold on the surface snows assumed a more burning intensity. Shadows of hummocks and ice ridges became dyed with a deeper purple, and in the burning orange world loomed before us Titan shapes, regal and regally robed.

From my position, a few hundred yards ahead of the sleds, with compass and axe in hand, as usual, I could not resist the temptation to turn frequently to see the movement of the dog train with its new fire. In this backward direction the color scheme was reversed.

About the horizon the icy walls gleamed like beaten gold set with gem-spots of burning colors; the plains represented every shade of purple and blue, and over them, like vast angel wings outspread, shifted golden pinions. Through the sea of palpitating color, the dogs came, with spirited tread, noses down, tails erect and shoulders braced to the straps, like chariot horses. In the magnifying light they seemed many times their normal size. The young Eskimos, chanting songs of love, followed with easy, swinging steps. The long whip was swung with a brisk crack. Overall arose a cloud of frosted breath, which, like incense smoke, became silvered in the light, a certain signal of efficient motive power.

With our destination reachable over smooth ice, in these brighter days of easier travel our long-chilled blood was stirred to double action, our eyes opened to beauty and color, and a normal appreciation of the wonders of this new strange and wonderful world.

As we lifted the midnight's sun to the plane of the midday sun, the shifting Polar desert became floored with a sparkling sheen of millions of diamonds, through which we fought a way to ulterior and greater glory.

Our leg cramps eased and our languid feet lifted buoyantly from the steady drag as the soul arose to effervescence. Fields of rich purple, lined with running liquid gold, burning with flashes of iridescent colors, gave a sense of gladness long absent from our weary life. The ice was much better. We still forced a way over large fields, small pressure areas and narrow leads.

Camp was pitched early in the morning of April 20. The sun was northeast, the pack glowed in tones of lilac, the normal westerly air brushed our frosty faces. Our surprising burst of enthusiasm had been nursed to its limits. Under it a long march had been made over average ice, with the usual result of overpowering fatigue. Too tired and sleepy to wait for a cup of tea, we poured melted snow into our stomach and pounded the pemmican with an axe to ease the task of the jaws. Our eyes closed before the meal was finished, and the world was lost to us for eight hours. Waking, I took observations which gave latitude 89°46".

Late at night, after another long rest, we hitched the dogs and loaded the sleds. When action began, the feeling came that no time must be lost. Feverish impatience seized me.

Cracking our whips, we bounded ahead. The boys sang. The dogs howled. Midnight of April 21 had just passed.

Over the sparkling snows the post-midnight sun glowed like at noon. I seemed to be walking in some splendid golden realms of dreamland. As we bounded onward the ice swam about me in circling rivers of gold.

We all were lifted to the paradise of winners as we stepped over the snows of a destiny for which we had risked life and willingly suffered the tortures of an icy hell. The ice under us, the goal for centuries of brave, heroic men, to reach which many had suffered terribly and terribly died, seemed almost sacred.

Constantly and carefully I watched my instruments in recording this final reach. Nearer and nearer they recorded our approach. Step by step, my heart filled with a strange rapture of conquest.

At last we step over colored fields of sparkle, climbing walls of purple and gold—finally, under skies of crystal blue, with flaming clouds of glory, we touch the mark! The soul awakens to a definite triumph; there is sunrise within us, and all the world of night-darkened trouble fades. We are at the top of the world!

The flag is flung to the frigid breezes of the North Pole!

AT THE POLE

At the Pole there were sunbursts, but because of the slight change in the sun's dip to the horizon, the prevailing light was invariably in shades running to purple. At first my imagination evoked a more glowing wonder than in reality existed; as the hours wore on, and as the wants of my body asserted themselves, I began to see the vacant spaces with a disillusionizing eye.

With the use of the sextant, the artificial horizon, pocket chronometers, and the usual instruments and methods of explorers, our observations were continued and our positions were fixed with the most painstakingly careful safeguards possible against inaccuracy. The value of all such observations as proof of a Polar success, however, is open to such interpretation as the future may determine. This applies, not only to me, but to anyone who bases any claim upon them.

To me there were many seemingly insignificant facts noted in our northward progress which left the imprint of milestones. Our footprints marked a road ever onward into the unknown. Many of these almost unconscious reckonings took the form of playful impressions and were not even at the time written down.

In the first press reports of my achievement there was not space to go into minute details, nor did the presentation of the subject permit an elaboration on all the data gathered. But now, in the light of a better perspective, it seems important that every possible phase of the minutest detail be presented. For only by a careful consideration of every phase of every phenomena en route can a true verdict be obtained upon this widely discussed subject of Polar attainment.

And now, right here, I want you to consider carefully with me one thing which made me feel sure that we had reached the Pole. This is the subject of shadows—our own shadows on the snow-covered ice. A seemingly unimportant phenomenon which had often been a topic of discussion, and so commonplace that I only rarely referred to it in my notebooks, our own shadows on the snow-cushioned ice had told of northward movement, and ultimately proved to my satisfaction that the Pole had been reached.

In our northward progress—to explain my shadow observations from the beginning—for a long time after our start from Svartevoeg, our shadows did not perceptibly shorten or brighten, to my eyes. The natives, however, got from these shadows a never-ending variety of topics of conversation. They foretold storms, located game and read the story of home entanglements. Far from land, far from every sign of a cheering, solid earth, wandering with our shadows over the hopeless desolation of the moving seas of glitter.

I, too, took a keen interest in the blue blots that represented our bodies. At noon, by comparison with later hours, they were sharp, short, of a dark, restful blue. At this time a thick atmosphere of crystals rested upon the ice pack, and when the sun sank the strongest purple rays could not penetrate the frosty haze. Long before the time for sunset, even on clear days, the sun was lost in low clouds of drifting needles.

After passing the 88th parallel there was a notable change in our shadows. The night shadow lengthened; the day shadow, by comparison, shortened. The boys saw in this something which they could not understand. The positive blue grew to a permanent purple, and the sharp outlines ran to vague, indeterminate edges.

Now at the Pole there was no longer any difference in length, color or sharpness of outline between the shadow of the day or night.

"What does it all mean?" they asked. The Eskimos looked with eager eyes at me to explain, but my vocabulary was not comprehensive enough to give them a really scientific explanation, and also my brain was too weary from the muscular poison of fatigue to frame words.

The shadows of midnight and those of midday were the same. The sun made a circle about the heavens in which the eye detected no difference in its height above the ice, either night or day. Throughout the twenty-four hours there was no perceptible rise or set in the sun's seeming movement. Now, at noon, the shadow represented in its length the altitude of the sun—about twelve degrees. At six o'clock it was the same. At midnight it was the same. At six o'clock in the morning it was the same.

There was about us no land. No fixed point. Absolutely nothing upon which to rest the eye to give the sense of location or to judge distance.

Here everything moves. The sea breathes and lifts the crust of ice which the wind stirs. The pack ever drifts in response to the pull of the air and the drive of the water. Even the sun, the only fixed dot in this stirring, restless world, where all you see is, without your seeing it, moving like a ship at sea, seems to have a rapid movement in a gold-flushed circle not far above endless fields of purple crystal; but that movement is never higher, never lower—always in the same fixed path. The instruments detect a slight spiral ascent, day after day, but the eye detects no change.

Although I had measured our shadows at times on the northward march, at the Pole these shadow notations were observed with the same care as the measured altitude of the sun by the sextant. A series was made on April 22, after E-tuk-i-shook and I had left Ah-we-lah in charge of our first camp at the Pole.

We made a little circle for our feet in the snow. E-tuk-i-shook stood in the foot circle. At midnight the first line was cut in the snow to the end of his shadow, and then I struck a deep hole with the ice-axe. Every hour a similar line was drawn out from his foot. At the end of twenty-four hours, with the help of Ah-we-lah, a circle was circumscribed along the points, which marked the end of the shadow for each hour.

In the northward march we did not stay up all of bedtime to play with shadow circles. But, at this time, to E-tuk-i-shook the thing had a spiritual interest. To me it was a part of the act of proving that the Pole had been attained. For only about the Pole, I argued, could all shadows be of equal length. Because of this combination of keen interests, we managed to find an excuse, even during sleep hours, to draw a line on our shadow circle.

Here, then, I felt, was an important observation placing me with fair accuracy at the Pole, and, unlike all other observations, it was not based on the impossible dreams of absolutely accurate time or sure corrections for refraction.

At the place where E-tuk-i-shook and I camped, four miles south of where I had left Ah-we-lah with the dogs, only two big ice hummocks were in sight. There were more spaces of open water than at our first camp. After a midnight observation—of April 22—we returned to camp. When the dogs saw us approaching in the distance they rose, and a chorus of howls rang over the regions of the Pole—regions where dogs had never howled before. All the scientific work being finished, we began hastily to make final preparations for departure.

We had spent two days about the North Pole. After the first thrills of victory, the glamor wore away as we rested and worked. Although I tried to do so, I could get no sensation of novelty as we pitched our last belongings on the sleds. The intoxication of success had gone. I suppose intense emotions are invariably followed by reactions.

Hungry, mentally and physically exhausted, a sense of the utter uselessness of this thing, of the empty reward of my endurance, followed my exhilaration. I had grasped my *ignus fatuus*. It is a misfortune for any man when his *ignus fatuus* fails to elude him.

During those last hours I asked myself why this place had so aroused an enthusiasm long-lasting through self-sacrificing years; why, for so many centuries, men had sought this elusive spot? What a futile thing, I thought, to die for! How tragically useless all those heroic efforts—efforts, in themselves, a travesty, an ironic satire, on much vainglorious human aspiration and endeavor! I thought of the enthusiasm of the people who read of the spectacular efforts of men to reach this vacant silver-shining goal of death.

I thought, too, in that hour, of the many men of science who were devoting their lives to the study of germs, the making of toxins; to the saving of men from the grip of disease—men who often lost their own lives in their experiments; whose world and work existed in unpicturesque laboratories, and for whom the laudations of people never rise. It occurred to me—and I felt the bitterness of tears in my soul—that it is often the showy and futile deeds of men which men praise; and that, after all, the only work worthwhile, the only value of a human being's efforts, lie in deeds whereby humanity benefits.

Such work as noble bands of women accomplish who go into the slums of great cities, who nurse the sick, who teach the ignorant, who engage in social service humbly, patiently, unexpectant of any reward! Such work as does the scientist who studies the depredations of malignant germs, who straightens the body of the crippled child, who precipitates a toxin which cleanses the blood of a frightful and loathsome disease!

As my eye sought the silver and purple desert about me for some stable object upon which to fasten itself, I experienced an abject abandon, an intolerable loneliness. With my two companions I could not converse; in my thoughts and emotions they could not share. I was alone. I was victorious. But how desolate, how dreadful was this victory! About us was no life, no spot to relieve the monotony of frost. We were the only pulsating creatures in a dead world of ice.

Before leaving, I enclosed a note, written on the previous day, in a metallic tube. This I buried in the surface of the Polar snows. I knew, of course, that this would not remain long at the spot, as the ice was in the grip of a slow-drifting movement. I felt the possibility of this slow movement was more important than if it remained stationary; for, if ever found in the south, the destination of the tube would indicate the ice drift from the Pole. The following is an exact copy of the original note.

COPY OF NOTE IN TUBE
April 21—at the North Pole

Accompanied by the Eskimo boys Ah-we-lah and E-tuk-i-shuk I reached at noon to-day 90° N. a spot on the polar sea 520 miles north of Svartevoeg. We were 35 days en route. Hope to return to-morrow on a line slightly west of the northward track.

New land was discovered along the 102 M. between 84 and 85. The ice proved fairly good, with few open leads, hard snow and little pressure trouble. We are in good health, and have food for forty days. This, with the meat of the dogs to be sacrificed, will keep us alive for fifty or sixty days.

This note is deposited with a small American flag in a metallic tube on the drifting ice.

Its return will be appreciated, to the International Bureau of Polar Research at the Royal Observatory, Uccle, Belgium.

(Signed) FREDERICK A. COOK

PART II

THE CALL OF THE SOUTH

CHAPTER SEVEN

The Quest for the South Pole

M. B. Synge

An American had placed the Stars and Stripes on the North Pole in 1909. It was a Norwegian who succeeded in reaching the South Pole in 1911. But the spade-work which contributed so largely to the final success had been done so enthusiastically by two Englishmen that the expeditions of Scott and Shackleton must find a place.

The crossing of the Antarctic Circle by the famous *Challenger* expedition in 1874 revived interest in the far South. The practical outcome of much discussion was the design of the *Discovery*, a ship built expressly for scientific exploration, and the appointment of Captain Scott to command an Antarctic expedition.

In August 1901, Scott left the shores of England, and by way of New Zealand crossed the Antarctic Circle on 3rd January 1902. Three weeks later he reached the Great Ice Barrier which had stopped Ross in 1840. For a week Scott steamed along the Barrier. Mounts Erebus and Terror were plainly visible, and though he could nowhere discover Parry Mountains, yet he found distant land rising high above the sea, which he named King Edward VII Land.

Scott had brought with him a captive balloon in which he now rose to a height of eight hundred feet, from which he saw an unbroken glacier stream of vast extent stretching to the south. It was now time to seek for winter quarters, and Scott, returning to McMurdo Bay named by Ross, found that it was not a bay at all, but a strait leading southward.

Here they landed their stores, set up their hut, and spent the winter, till on 2nd November 1902 all was ready for a sledge-journey to the south. For fifty-nine days Scott led his little land-party of three, with four sledges and nineteen dogs, south. But the heavy snow was too much for the dogs, and one by one died, until not one was left and the men had to drag and push the sledges themselves. Failing provisions at last compelled them to stop. Great mountain summits were seen beyond the farthest point reached.

"We have decided at last we have found something which is fitting to bear the name of him whom we most delight to honour," says Scott, "and Mount Markham it shall be called in memory of the father of the expedition."

It was 30th December when a tremendous blizzard stayed their last advance. "Chill and hungry," they lay all day in their sleeping bags, miserable at the thought of turning back, too weak and ill to go on. With only provisions for a fortnight, they at last reluctantly turned home, staggering as far as their dépôt in thirteen days.

Shackleton was smitten with scurvy; he was growing worse every day, and it was a relief when on 2nd February they all reached the ship alive, "as near spent as three persons can well be." But they had done well: they had made the first long land journey ever made in the Antarctic; they had reached a point which was farthest south; they had tested new methods of travel; they had covered 960 miles in 93 days. Shackleton was now invalided home, but it was not till 1904 that the *Discovery* escaped from the frozen harbour to make her way home.

Shackleton had returned to England in 1903, but the mysterious South Pole amid its wastes of ice and snow still called him back, and in command of the *Nimrod* he started forth in August 1907 on the next British Antarctic expedition, carrying a Union Jack, presented by the Queen, to plant on the spot farthest south. He actually placed it within ninety-seven miles of the Pole itself!

With a petrol motor car on board, Eskimo dogs, and Manchurian ponies, he left New Zealand on 1st January 1908, watched and cheered by some thirty thousand of his fellow countrymen. Three weeks later they were in sight of the Great Ice Barrier, and a few days later the huge mountains of Erebus and Terror came into sight. Shackleton had hoped to reach King Edward VII Land for winter quarters, but a formidable ice-pack prevented this, and they selected a place some twenty miles north of the *Discovery's* old winter quarters.

Getting the wild little Manchurian ponies ashore was no light job; the poor little creatures were stiff after a month's constant buffeting, for the *Nimrod's* passage had been stormy. One after another they were now led out of their stalls into a horse-box and slung over the ice. Once on *terra firma* they seemed more at home, for they immediately began pawing the snow as they were wont to do in their far-away Manchurian home.

The spacious hut, brought out by Shackleton, was soon erected. Never was such a luxurious house set up on the bleak shores of the Polar seas. There was a dark room for developing, acetylene gas for lighting, a good stove for warming, and comfortable cubicles decorated with pictures. The dark room was excellent, and never was a book of travels more beautifully illustrated than Shackleton's *Heart of the Antarctic*.

True, during some of the winter storms and blizzards the hut shook and trembled so that every moment its occupants thought it would be carried bodily away, but it stood its ground all right. The long winter was spent as usual in preparing for the spring expedition to the south, but it was 29th October 1908 before the weather made it possible to make a start. The party consisted of Shackleton, Adams, Marshall, and Wild, each leading a pony which dragged a sledge with food for ninety-one days.

"A glorious day for our start," wrote Shackleton in his diary, "brilliant sunshine and a cloudless sky. As we left the hut where we had spent so many months in comfort we had a feeling of real regret that never again would we all be together there. A clasp of the hands means more than many words, and as we turned to acknowledge the men's cheer, and saw them standing on the ice by the familiar cliffs, I felt we must try to do well for the sake of everyone concerned in the expedition."

New land in the shape of ice-clad mountains greeted the explorers on 22nd November. "It is a wonderful place we are in, all new to the world," says Shackleton. "There is an impression of limitless solitude about it that makes us feel so small as we trudge along, a few dark specks on the snowy plain."

They now had to quit the Barrier in order to travel south. Fortunately they found a gap, called the Southern Gateway, which afforded a direct line to the Pole. But their ponies had suffered badly during the march; they had already been obliged to shoot three of them, and on 7th December the last pony fell down a crevasse and was killed.

They had now reached a great plateau some seven thousand feet above the sea; it rose steadily toward the south, and Christmas Day found them "lying in a little tent, isolated high on the roof of the world, far from the ways trodden by man." With forty-eight degrees of frost, drifting snow, and a biting wind, they spent the next few days hauling their sledges up a steep incline. They had now only a month's food left. Pressing on with reduced rations, in the face of freezing winds, they reached a height of 10,050 feet.

It was the 6th of January, and they were in latitude eighty-eight degrees, when a "blinding, shrieking blizzard" made all further advance impossible. For sixty hours the four hungry explorers lay in their sleeping bags, nearly perished with cold. "The most trying day we have yet spent," writes Shackleton, "our fingers and faces being continually frostbitten. Tomorrow we will rush south with the flag. It is our last outward march."

The gale breaking, they marched on till 9th January, when they stopped within ninety-seven miles of the Pole, where they hoisted the Union Jack, and took possession of the great plateau in the King's name.

"We could see nothing but the dead-white snow plain. There was no break in the plateau as it extended towards the Pole. I am confident that the Pole lies on the great plateau we have discovered miles and miles from any outstanding land."

And so the four men turned homewards. "Whatever our regret may be, we have done our best," said the leader somewhat sadly. Blinding blizzards followed them as they made their way slowly back. On 28th January they reached the Great Ice Barrier. Their food was well-nigh spent; their daily rations consisted of six biscuits and some horse meat in the shape of the Manchurian ponies they had shot and left the November before. But it disagreed with most of them, and it was four very weak and ailing men who staggered back to the *Nimrod* toward the end of February 1909.

Shackleton reached England in the autumn of 1909 to find that another Antarctic expedition was to leave our shores in the following summer under the command of Scott, in the *Terra Nova*. It was one of the best-equipped expeditions that ever started; motor-sledges had been specially constructed to go over the deep snow, which was fatal to the motor car carried by Shackleton. There were fifteen ponies and thirty dogs. Leaving England in July 1910, Scott was established in winter quarters in McMurdo Sound by 26th January 1911. It was November before he could start on the southern expedition.

We left Hut Point on the evening of 2nd November. For sixty miles we followed the track of the motors (sent on five days before). The ponies are going very steadily. We found the motor party awaiting us in latitude 80½ degrees south. The motors had proved entirely satisfactory, and the machines dragged heavy loads over the worst part of the Barrier surface, crossing several crevasses. The sole cause of abandonment was the overheating of the air-cooled engines. We are building snow cairns at intervals of four miles to guide homeward parties and leaving a week's provisions at every degree of latitude. As we proceeded the weather grew worse, and snowstorms were frequent. The sky was continually overcast, and the land was rarely visible. The ponies, however, continued to pull splendidly.

As they proceeded south they encountered terrific storms of wind and snow, out of which they had constantly to dig the ponies. Christmas passed and the New Year of 1912 dawned. On 3rd January when 150 miles from the Pole, "I am going forward," says Scott, "with a party of five men with a month's provisions, and the prospect of success seems good, provided that the weather holds and no unforeseen obstacles arise."

Scott and his companions successfully attained the object of their journey. They reached the South Pole on 17th January only to find that they had been forestalled by others! And it is remarkable to note that so correct were their observations, the two parties located the Pole within half a mile of one another.

Scott's return journey ended disastrously. Blinding blizzards prevented rapid progress; food and fuel ran short; still the weakened men struggled bravely forward till, within a few miles of a dépôt of supplies, death overtook them.

Scott's last message can never be forgotten. "I do not regret this journey which has shown that Englishmen can endure hardship, help one another, and meet death with as great fortitude as ever in the past. . . . Had we lived, I should have had a tale to tell of the hardihood, endurance, and courage of my companions which would have stirred the heart of every Englishman. These rough notes and our dead bodies must tell the tale; but surely, surely, a great, rich country like ours will see that those who are dependent upon us are properly provided for."

It was on 14th December 1911 that Captain Amundsen had reached the Pole. A Norwegian, fired by the example of his fellow countryman, Nansen, Amundsen had long been interested in both Arctic and Antarctic exploration. In a ship of only forty-eight tons, he had, with six others, made a survey of the North Magnetic Pole, sailed through the Behring Strait, and accomplished the Northwest Passage, for which he was awarded the Royal Medal of the Royal Geographical Society. On his return he planned an expedition to the North Pole. He had made known his scheme, and, duly equipped for North Polar expedition in Nansen's little *Fram*, Amundsen started. Suddenly the world rang with the news that Peary had discovered the North Pole, and that Amundsen had turned his prow southwards and was determined to make a dash for the South Pole. Landing in Whales Bay some 400 miles to the east of Scott's winter quarters, his first visitors were the Englishmen on board the *Terra Nova*, who were taking their ship to New Zealand for the winter.

Making a hut on the shore, Amundsen had actually started on his journey to the Pole before Scott heard of his arrival.

"I am fully alive to the complication in the situation arising out of Amundsen's presence in the Antarctic," wrote the English explorer, "but as any attempt at a race might have been fatal to our chance of getting to the Pole at all, I decided to do exactly as I should have done had not Amundsen been here. If he gets to the Pole he will be bound to do it rapidly with dogs, and one foresees that success will justify him."

Although the Norwegian explorer left his winter quarters on 8th September for his dash to the Pole, he started too early; three of his party had their feet frostbitten, and the dogs suffered severely, so he turned back, and it was not till 20th October, just a week before Scott's start, that he began in real earnest his historic journey. He was well off for food, for whales were plentiful on the shores of the Bay, and seals, penguins, and gulls abounded. The expedition was well equipped, with eight explorers, four sledges, and thirteen dogs attached to each.

"Amundsen is a splendid leader, supreme in organisation, and the essential in Antarctic travel is to think out the difficulties before they arise." So said those who worked with him on his most successful journey.

Through dense fog and blinding blizzards the Norwegians now made their way south, their Norwegian skis and sledges proving a substantial help. The crevasses in the ice were very bad; one dog dropped in and had to be abandoned; another day the dogs got across, but the sledge fell in, and it was necessary to climb down the crevasse, unpack the sledge, and pull up piece by piece till it was possible to raise the empty sledge. So intense was the cold that the very brandy froze in the bottle and was served out in lumps.

"It did not taste much like brandy then," said the men, "but it burnt our throats as we sucked it."

The dogs travelled well. Each man was responsible for his own team; he fed them and made them fond of him. Thus all through November the Norwegians travelled south, till they reached the vast plateau described by Shackleton. One tremendous peak, fifteen thousand feet high, they named "Frithjof Nansen."

On 14th December they reached their goal; the weather was beautiful, the ground perfect for sledging.

"At 3 p.m. we made halt," says Amundsen. "According to our reckoning, we had reached our destination. All of us gathered round the colours—a beautiful silken flag; all hands took hold of it, and, planting it on the spot, we gave the vast plateau on which the Pole is situate the name of 'The King Haakon VII.' It was a vast plain, alike in all directions, mile after mile."

Here in brilliant sunshine the little party camped, taking observations till 17th December, when, fastening to the ground a little tent with the Norwegian flag and the *Fram* pennant, they gave it the name "Polheim" and started for home.

So the North and South Poles yielded up their well-hoarded secrets after centuries of waiting, within two and a half years of one another.

They had claimed more lives than any exploration had done before—or is ever likely to do again.

And so ends the last of these great earth stories—stories which have made the world what it is today—and we may well say with one of the most successful explorers of our times, "The future may give us thrilling stories of the conquest of the air, but the spirit of man has mastered the earth."

CHAPTER EIGHT

The Worst Journey in the World

Apsley Cherry-Garrard

Note: Apsley Cherry-Garrard was one of the youngest members of Robert Falcon Scch the South Pole, the Terra Nova expedition.

THE SEARCH JOURNEY

OCTOBER 28, 1912. HUT POINT. A BEAUTIFUL DAY. WE FINISHED DIGGING out the stable for the mules this morning and brought in some blubber this afternoon. The Bluff has its cap on, but otherwise the sky is nearly clear: there is a little cumulus between White Island and the Bluff, the first I have seen this year on the Barrier. It is most noticeable how much snow has disappeared off the rocks and shingle here.

October 29. Hut Point. The mule party, under Wright, consisting of Gran, Nelson, Crean, Hooper, Williamson, Keohane, and Lashly, left Cape Evans at 10:30 and arrived here at 5 p.m. after a good march in perfect weather. They leave Debenham and Archer at the hut, and I am afraid it will be dull work for them the next three months. Archer turned out early and made some cakes which they have brought with them. They camped for lunch seven miles from Cape Evans.

This is the start of the Search Journey. Everything which forethought can do has been done, and to a point twelve miles south of Corner Camp the mules will be travelling light owing to the depots which have been laid. The barometer has been falling the last few days and is now low, while the Bluff is overcast. Yet it does not look like a blizzard to come.

Two Adélie penguins, the first, came to Cape Evans yesterday, and a skua was seen there on the 24th: so summer is really here.

October 30. Hut Point. It is now 8 p.m., and the mules are just off, looking very fit, keeping well together, and giving no trouble at the start. Their leaders turned in this afternoon, and tonight begins the new routine of night marching, just the same as last year. It did look thick on the Barrier this afternoon, and it was quite a question whether it was advisable for them to start. But it is rolling away now, being apparently only fog, which is now disappearing before some wind, or perhaps because the sun is losing its power. I think they will have a good march.

November 2, 5 a.m. Biscuit Depôt. Atkinson, Dimitri, and I, with two dog teams, left Hut Point last night at 8:30. We have had a coldish night's run, minus twenty-one degrees when we left after lunch, minus seventeen degrees now. The surface was very heavy for the dogs, there being a soft coating of snow over everything since we last came this way, due no doubt to the foggy days we have been having lately. The sledge-meter makes it nearly sixteen miles.

The mule party has two days' start on us, and their programme is to do twelve miles a day to One Ton Depôt. Their tracks are fairly clear, but there has been some drift from the east since they passed. We picked up our cairns well. We are pretty wet, having been running nearly all the way.

November 3. Early morning. 14½ miles. We are here at Corner Camp, but not without a struggle. We left the Biscuit Depôt at 6:30 p.m. yesterday, and it is now 4 a.m. The last six miles took us four hours, which is very bad going for dogs, and we have all been running most of the way. The surface was very bad, crusty and also soft: it was blowing with some low drift, and overcast and snowing. We followed the drifted-up mule tracks with difficulty and are lucky to have got so far. The temperature has been a constant zero.

There is a note here from Wright about the mules, which left here last night. They only saw two small crevasses on the way, but Khan Sahib got into the tide-crack at the edge of the Barrier, and had to be hauled out with a rope. The mules are going fast over the first part of the day, but show a tendency to stop towards the end: they keep well together except Khan Sahib, who is a slower mule than the others. It is now blowing with some drift, but nothing bad, and beyond the Bluff it seems to be clear. We are all pretty tired.

November 4. Early morning. Well! this has been a disappointing day, but we must hope that all will turn out well. We turned out at 2 a.m. yesterday and then it was clearing all around, a mild blizzard having been blowing since we camped. We started at five in some wind and low drift. It was good travelling weather, and except for the first three miles the surface has been fair to good, and the last part very good.

Yet the dogs could not manage their load, which according to programme should go up a further 150 lbs. each team here at Dimitri Depôt. One of our dogs, Kusoi, gave out, but we managed to get him along tied to the stern of the sledge, because the team behind tried to get at him and he realized he had better mend his ways. We camped for lunch when Tresor also was pretty well done.

We were then on a very good surface, but were often pushing the sledge to get it along. The mule party was gone when we started again, and probably did not see us. We came on to the depôt, but we cannot hope to get along far on bad surfaces if we cannot get along on good ones. The note left by Wright states that their sledge-meter has proved useless, and this leaves all three parties of us with only one, which is not very reliable now.

So it has been decided that the dogs must return from 80°30", or 81° at the farthest, and instead of four mules, as was intended, going on from there, five must go on instead. The dogs can therefore now leave behind much of their own weights and take on the mules' weights instead. And this is the part where the mules' weights are so heavy. Perhaps the new scheme is the best, but it puts everything on the mules from 80°30": if they will do it all is well: if they won't we have nothing to fall back on.

Midnight, November 4–5. It has been blowing and drifting all day. We turned out again at mid-day on the 4th, and re-made the depôt with what we were to leave owing to the new programme. This is all rather sad, but it can't be helped. It was then blowing a summer blizzard, and we were getting frostbitten when we started, following the mule tracks.

There were plenty of cairns for us to pick up, and with the lighter loads and a very good surface we came along much better. Lunching at eight miles we arrived just as the mule party had finished their hoosh preparatory to starting, and it has been decided that the mules are not to go on tonight, but we will all start marching together tomorrow.

The news from this party is on the whole good, not the least good being that the sledge-meter is working again, though not very reliably. They are marching well, and at a great pace, except for Khan Sahib. Gulab, however, is terribly chafed both by his collar and by his breast harness, both of which have been tried. He has a great raw place where this fits on one side, and is chafed, but not so badly, on the other side. Lal Khan is pulling well, but is eating very little. Pyaree is doing very well, but has some difficulty in lifting her leg when in soft snow. Abdullah seems to be considered the best mule at present. On the whole good hearing.

Wright's sleeping bag is bad, letting in light through cracks in a good many places. But he makes very little of it and does not seem to be cold—saying it is good ventilation. The mule cloths, which have a rough lining to their outside canvas, are collecting a lot of snow, and all the mules are matted with cakes of snow. They are terrible rope-eaters, cloth-eaters, anything to eat, though they are not hungry. And they have even learnt to pull their picketing buckles undone, and go walking about the camp. Indeed Nelson says that the only time when Khan Sahib does not cast himself adrift is when he is ready to start on the march.

November 6. Early morning. We had a really good lie-in yesterday, and after the hard slogging with the dogs during the last few days I for one was very glad of it. We came on behind, and in sight of the mules this last march, and the change in the dogs was wonderful. Where it had been a job to urge them on over quite as good a surface yesterday, today for some time we could not get off the sledge except for short runs: although we had taken 312 lbs. weight off the mules and loaded it on to the dogs.

We had a most glorious night for marching, and it is now bright sunlight, and the animals' fur is quite warm where the sun strikes it. We have just had a bit of a fight over the dog food, Vaida going for Dyk, and now the others are somewhat excited, and there are constant growlings and murmurings.

The camp makes more of a mark than last year, for the mules are dark while the ponies were white or grey, and the cloths are brown instead of light green. The consequence is that the camp shows up from a long distance off. We are building cairns at regular distances, and there should be no difficulty in keeping on the course in fair weather at any rate. Now in the land of big sastrugi: Erebus is beginning to look small, but we could see an unusually big smoke from the crater all day.

November 7. Early morning. Not an easy day. It was minus nine degrees and overcast when we turned out, and the wind was then dying down, but it had been blowing up to force 5, with surface drift during the day. We started in a bad light and the surface, which was the usual hard surface common here, with big sastrugi, was covered by a thin layer of crystals which were then falling. This naturally made it very much harder pulling: we with the dogs have been running nearly all the twelve miles, and I for one am tired. At lunch Atkinson thought he saw a tent away to our right,—the very thought of it came as a shock,—but it proved to be a false alarm. We have been keeping a sharp lookout for the gear which was left about this part by the Last Return Party, but have seen no sign of it.

It is now minus fourteen degrees, but the sun is shining brightly in a clear sky, and it feels beautifully warm. It seems a very regular thing for the sky to cloud over as the sun gets low towards nightfall—and directly the sun begins to rise again the clouds disappear in a most wonderful way.

November 8. Early morning. Last night's twelve miles was quite cold for the time of year, being minus twenty-three degrees at lunch and now minus eighteen degrees. But it is calm, with bright sun, and this temperature feels warm. However, there are some frost-bites as a result, both Nelson and Hooper having swollen faces.

The same powder and crystals have been on the surface, but we have carried the good Bluff surface so far, being now four miles beyond Bluff

Depôt. This is fortunate, and to the best of my recollection we were already getting on to a soft surface at this point last summer. If so there must have been more wind here this year than last, which, according to the winter we have had, seems probable.

We made up the Bluff Depôt after lunch, putting up a new flag and building up the cairn, leaving two cases of dog-biscuit for the returning dog-teams. It is curious that the drift to leeward of the cairn, that is N.N.E., was quite soft, the snow all round and the drifts on either side being hard—exceptionally hard in fact. Why this drift should remain soft when a drift in the same place is usually hard is difficult to explain. All is happy in the mule camp. They have given Lal a drink of water and he has started to eat, which is good news. Some of the mules seem snow-blind, and they are now all wearing their blinkers. I have just heard that Gran swung the thermometer at four this morning and found it minus twenty-nine degrees. Nelson's face is a sight—his nose a mere swollen lump, frost-bitten cheeks, and his goggles have frosted him where the rims touched his face. Poor Marie!

November 11. Early morning. One Ton Depôt. Wright got a latitude sight yesterday putting us six miles from One Ton, and our sledge-meter shows 5¾, and here we are. More frostbite this morning, and it was pretty cold starting in a fair wind and minus seven degrees temperature. We have continued this really splendid surface, and now the sastrugi are pointing a little more to the south of S.W. While there are not such big mounds, the surface does not yet show any signs of getting bad.

There were the most beautiful cloud-effects as we came along—a deep black to the west, shading into long lines of grey and lemon yellow round the sun, with a vertical shaft through them, and a bright orange horizon. Now there is a brilliant parhelion. Given sun, two days here are never alike. Whatever the monotony of the Barrier may be, there is endless variety in the sky, and I do not believe that anywhere in the world such beautiful colours are to be seen.

I had a fair panic as we came up to the depôt. I did not see that one body of the ponies had gone ahead of the others and camped, but ahead of the travelling ponies was the depôt, looking very black, and I thought that there was a tent. It would be too terrible to find that, though one knew that we had done all that we could, if we had done something different we could have saved them.

And then we find that the provisions we left here for them in the tank are soaked with paraffin. How this has happened is a mystery, but I think that the oil in the XS tin, which was very full, must have forced its way out in a sudden rise of temperature in a winter blizzard, and though the tin was not touching the tank, it has found its way in.

Altogether things seemed rather dismal, but a visit to the mules is cheering, for they seem very fit as a whole and their leaders are cheerful. There are three sacks of oats here—had we known it would have saved a lot of weight—but we didn't, and we have plenty with what we have brought, so they will be of little use to us. There is no compressed fodder, which would have been very useful, for the animals which are refusing the oats would probably eat it.

Gulab has a very bad chafe, but he is otherwise fit—and it does not seem possible in this life to kill a mule because of chafing. It is a great deal to know that he does not seem to be hurt by it, and pulls away gallantly. Crean says he had to run a mile this morning with Rani. Marie says he is inventing some new ways of walking, one step forward and one hop back, in order to keep warm when leading Khan Sahib. Up to date we cannot say that the Fates have been unkind to us.

November 12. Early morning. Lunch, 2:30 a.m. I am afraid our sledge-meters do not agree over this morning's march. The programme is to do thirteen miles a day if possible from here: that is 7½ before lunch and 5½ afterwards. We could see two cairns of last year on our right as we came along.

We have got on to a softer surface now and there is bad news of Lal Khan, and it will depend on this after-lunch march whether he must be shot this evening or not. It was intended to shoot a mule two marches from One Ton, but till just lately it had not been thought that it must be Lal Khan. He is getting very slow, and came into camp with Khan Sahib: the trouble of course is that he will not eat: he has hardly eaten, they say, a day's ration since he left Hut Point, and he can't work on nothing. It is now minus sixteen degrees, with a slight southerly wind.

Nearly mid-day. 11–12 miles south of One Ton. We have found them—to say it has been a ghastly day cannot express it—it is too bad for words. The tent was there, about half-a-mile to the west of our course, and close to a drifted-up cairn of last year. It was covered with snow and looked just like a cairn, only an extra gathering of snow showing where the ventilator was, and so we found the door.

It was drifted up some two to three feet to windward. Just by the side two pairs of ski sticks, or the topmost half of them, appeared over the snow, and a bamboo which proved to be the mast of the sledge.

Their story I am not going to try and put down. They got to this point on March 21, and on the 29th all was over.

Nor will I try and put down what there was in that tent. Scott lay in the centre, Bill on his left, with his head towards the door, and Birdie on his right, lying with his feet towards the door.

Bill especially had died very quietly with his hands folded over his chest. Birdie also quietly.

Oates' death was a very fine one. We go on tomorrow to try and find his body. He was glad that his regiment would be proud of him.

They reached the Pole a month after Amundsen.

We have everything—records, diaries, etc. They have among other things several rolls of photographs, a meteorological log kept up to March 13, and, considering all things, a great many geological specimens. *And they have stuck to everything.* It is magnificent that men in such case should go on pulling everything that they have died to gain. I think they realized their coming end a long time before. By Scott's head was tobacco: there is also a bag of tea.

Atkinson gathered everyone together and read to them the account of Oates' death given in Scott's Diary: Scott expressly states that he wished it known. His (Scott's) last words are:

"For God's sake take care of our people."

Then Atkinson read the lesson from the Burial Service from Corinthians. Perhaps it has never been read in a more magnificent cathedral and under more impressive circumstances—for it is a grave which kings must envy. Then some prayers from the Burial Service: and there with the floor-cloth under them and the tent above we buried them in their sleeping bags—and surely their work has not been in vain.

That scene can never leave my memory. We with the dogs had seen Wright turn away from the course by himself and the mule party swerve right-handed ahead of us. He had seen what he thought was a cairn, and then something looking black by its side. A vague kind of wonder gradually gave way to a real alarm. We came up to them all halted. Wright came across to us. "It is the tent." I do not know how he knew. Just a waste of snow: to our right the remains of one of last year's cairns, a mere mound: and then three feet of bamboo sticking quite alone out of the snow: and then another mound, of snow, perhaps a trifle more pointed. We walked up to it. I do not think we quite realized—not for very long—but someone reached up to a projection of snow, and brushed it away. The green flap of the ventilator of the tent appeared, and we knew that the door was below.

Two of us entered, through the funnel of the outer tent, and through the bamboos on which was stretched the lining of the inner tent. There was some snow—not much—between the two linings. But inside we could see nothing—the snow had drifted out the light. There was nothing to do but to dig the tent out. Soon we could see the outlines. There were three men here.

Bowers and Wilson were sleeping in their bags. Scott had thrown back the flaps of his bag at the end. His left hand was stretched over Wilson, his lifelong friend. Beneath the head of his bag, between the bag and the floor-cloth, was the green wallet in which he carried his diary. The brown books of diary were inside: and on the floor-cloth were some letters.

Everything was tidy. The tent had been pitched as well as ever, with the door facing down the sastrugi, the bamboos with a good spread, the tent itself taut and shipshape. There was no snow inside the inner lining. There were some loose pannikins from the cooker, the ordinary tent gear, the personal belongings, and a few more letters and records—personal and scientific.

Near Scott was a lamp formed from a tin and some lamp wick off a finnesko. It had been used to burn the little methylated spirit which remained. I think that Scott had used it to help him to write up to the end. I feel sure that he had died last—and once I had thought that he would not go so far as some of the others. We never realized how strong that man was, mentally and physically, until now.

We sorted out the gear, records, papers, diaries, spare clothing, letters, chronometers, finnesko, socks, a flag. There was even a book which I had lent Bill for the journey—and he had brought it back. Somehow we learnt that Amundsen had been to the Pole, and that they too had been to the Pole, and both items of news seemed to be of no importance whatever. There was a letter there from Amundsen to King Haakon. There were the personal chatty little notes we had left for them on the Beardmore—how much more important to us than all the royal letters in the world.

We dug down the bamboo which had brought us to this place. It led to the sledge, many feet down, and had been rigged there as a mast. And on the sledge were some more odds and ends—a piece of paper from the biscuit box; Bowers' meteorological log; and the geological specimens, thirty pounds of them, all of the first importance. Drifted over also were the harnesses, ski, and ski-sticks.

Hour after hour, so it seemed to me, Atkinson sat in our tent and read. The finder was to read the diary and then it was to be brought home—these were Scott's instructions written on the cover. But Atkinson said he was only going to read sufficient to know what had happened—and after that they were brought home unopened and unread. When he had the outline we all gathered together and he read to us the Message to the Public, and the account of Oates' death, which Scott had expressly wished to be known.

We never moved them. We took the bamboos of the tent away, and the tent itself covered them. And over them we built the cairn.

I do not know how long we were there, but when all was finished, and the chapter of Corinthians had been read, it was midnight of some day. The sun was dipping low above the Pole, the Barrier was almost in shadow. And the sky was blazing—sheets and sheets of iridescent clouds. The cairn and cross stood dark against a glory of burnished gold.

COPY OF NOTE LEFT AT THE CAIRN, OVER THE BODIES
November 12th, 1912
Lat. 79'50" S

This Cross and Cairn are erected over the bodies of Capt. Scott, C.V.O., R.N.; Dr. E. A. Wilson, M.B., B.A. Cantab.; Lt. H. R. Bowers, Royal Indian Marines. A slight token to perpetuate their gallant and successful attempt to reach the Pole. This they did on the 17th January 1912 after the Norwegian expedition had already done so. Inclement weather and lack of fuel was the cause of their death.

Also to commemorate their two gallant comrades, Capt. L. E. G. Oates of the Inniskilling Dragoons, who walked to his death in a blizzard to save his comrades, about eighteen miles south of this position; also of Seaman Edgar Evans, who died at the foot of the Beardmore Glacier.

The Lord gave and the Lord taketh away. Blessed be the name of the Lord.

Relief Expedition
(Signed by all members of the party.)

Midnight, November 12–13. I cannot think that anything which could be done to give these three great men—for great they were—a fitting grave has been left undone.

A great cairn has been built over them, a mark which must last for many years. That we can make anything that will be permanent on this Barrier is impossible, but as far as a lasting mark can be made it has been done. On this a cross has been fixed, made out of ski. On either side are the two sledges, fixed upright and dug in.

The whole is very simple and most impressive.

On a bamboo standing by itself is left the record which I have copied into this book, and which has been signed by us all.

We shall leave some provisions here, and go on lightly laden to see if we can find Titus Oates' body: and so give it what burial we can.

We start in about an hour, and I for one shall be glad to leave this place.

I am very very sorry that this question of the shortage of oil has arisen. We in the First Return Party were most careful with our measurement—having a ruler of Wright's and a piece of bamboo with which we did it, measuring the total height of oil in each case, and then dividing up the stick accordingly with the ruler, and we were *always* careful to take *a little less than we were entitled to*, which was stated to me, and stated by Birdie in his depôt notes, to be one-third of everything in the depôt.

How the shortage arose is a mystery. And they eleven miles from One Ton and plenty!

Titus did not show his foot till about three days before he died. The foot was then a great size, and almost every night it would be frost-bitten again. Then the last day at lunch he said he could go on no more—but they said he must: he wanted them to leave him behind in his bag. That night he turned in, hoping never to wake, but he woke, and then he asked their advice, they said they must all go on together. A thick blizzard was blowing, and he said, after a bit, "Well, I am just going outside, and I may be some time."

They searched for him but could not find him.

They had a terrible time from 80°30" on to their last camp. There Bill was very bad, and Birdie and the Owner had to do the camping.

And then, eleven miles from plenty, they had *nine days of blizzard, and that was the end.*

They had a good spread on their tent, and their ski-sticks were standing, but their skis were drifted up on the ground.

The tent was in excellent condition—only down some of the poles there were some chafes.

They had been trying a spirit lamp when all the oil was gone.

At 88° or so they were getting temperatures from minus twenty to minus thirty degrees. At eight-two degrees, 10,000 feet lower, it was regularly down to minus forty-seven degrees in the nighttime, and minus thirty degrees during the day, for no explainable reason.

Bill's and Birdie's feet got bad—the Owner's feet got bad last.

It is all too horrible—I am almost afraid to go to sleep now.

November 14. Early morning. It has been a miserable march. We had to wait some time after hoosh to let the mules get ahead. Then we went on in a cold raw fog and some headwind, with constant frost-bites. The surface has been very bad all day for the thirteen miles: if we had been walking in arrowroot it would have been much like this was. At lunch the temperature was minus 14.7 degrees.

Then on when it was drifting with the wind in our faces and in a bad light. What we took to be the mule party ahead proved to be the old pony walls twenty-six miles from One Ton. There was here a bit of sacking on the cairn, and Oates' bag. Inside the bag was the theodolite, and his finnesko and socks. One of the finnesko was slit down the front as far as the leather beckets, evidently to get his bad foot into it.

This was fifteen miles from the last camp, and I suppose they had brought on his bag for three or four miles in case they might find him still alive. Half a mile from our last camp there was a very large and quite unmistakable undulation, one-quarter to one-third of a mile from crest to crest: the pony walls behind us disappeared almost as soon as we started to go down, and reappeared again on the other side. There were, I feel sure, other rolls, but this was the largest. We have seen no sign of Oates' body.

About half an hour ago it started to blow a blizzard, and it is now thick, but the wind is not strong. The mules, which came along well considering the surface, are off their feed, and this may be the reason.

Dimitri saw the Cairn with the Cross more than eight miles away this morning, and in a good light it would be seen from much farther off.

November 15. Early morning. We built a cairn to mark the spot near which Oates walked out to his death, and we placed a cross on it. Lashed to the cross is a record, as follows:

Hereabouts died a very gallant gentleman, Captain L. E. G. Oates of the Inniskilling Dragoons. In March 1912, returning from the Pole, he walked willingly to his death in a blizzard to try and save his comrades, beset by hardship. This note is left by the Relief Expedition. 1912.

This was signed by Atkinson and myself.

We saw the cairn for a long way in a bad light as we came back today.

The original plan with which we started from Cape Evans was, if the party was found where we could still bear out sufficiently to the eastward to have a good chance of missing the pressure caused by the Beardmore, to go on and do what we could to survey the land south of the Beardmore: for this was the original plan of Captain Scott for this year's sledging. But as things are I do not think there can be much doubt that we are doing right in losing no time in going over to the west of McMurdo Sound to see whether we can go up to Evans Coves, and help Campbell and his party.

We brought on Oates' bag. The theodolite was inside.

A thickish blizzard blew all day yesterday, but it was clear and there was only surface drift when we turned out for the night march. Then again as we came along, the sky became overcast—all except over the land, which remains clear these nights when everything else is obscured. We noticed the same thing last year. Now the wind, which had largely dropped, has started again and it is drifting. We have had wind and drift on four out of the last five days.

November 17. Early morning. I think we are all going crazy together—at any rate things are pretty difficult. The latest scheme is to try and find a way over the plateau to Evans Coves, trying to strike the top of a glacier and go down it. There can be no good in it: if ever men did it, they would arrive about the time the ship arrived there too, and their labour would be in vain. If they got there and the ship did not arrive, there is another party stranded. They would have to wait till February 15 or 20 to see if the ship was coming, and then there would be no travelling back over the plateau, even if we could do it those men there could not.

It was almost oppressively hot yesterday—but I'll never grumble about heat again. It has now cleared a lot and we came along on the cairns easily—but on a very soft downy surface, and the travelling has not been fast. We bring with us the Southern Party's gear. The sledge, which was the ten-foot which they brought on from the bottom of the glacier, has been left.

November 18. Early morning. I am thankful to say that the plateau journey idea has been given up.

Once more we have come along in thick, snowy weather. If we had not men on ski to steer we could never keep much of a course, but Wright is steering us very straight, keeping a check on the course by watching the man behind, and so far we have been picking up all the cairns. This morning we passed the pony walls made on November 10. And yet they were nearly level with the ground; so they are not much of a mark. Yank has just had a disagreement with Kusoi—for Kusoi objected to his trying to get at the meat on the sledge. The mules have been sinking in a long way, and are marching very slowly. Pyaree eats the tea-leaves after meals: Rani and Abdullah divide a rope between them at the halts; and they have eaten the best part of a trace since our last camp. These animals eat anything but their proper food, and this some of them will hardly touch.

It cleared a bit for our second march, and we have done our thirteen miles, but it was very slow travelling. Now it is drifting as much as ever. Yank, that redoubtable puller, has just eaten himself loose for the third time since hoosh. This time I had to go down to the pony walls to get him.

We have had onions for the first time tonight in our hoosh—they are most excellent. Also we have been having some Nestlé's condensed milk from One Ton Depôt—which I do not want to see again, the depôt I mean. Peary must know what he is about, taking milk as a ration: the sweetness is a great thing, but it would be heavy: we have been having it with temperature down to minus fourteen degrees, when it was quite manageable, but I don't know what it would be like in colder temperatures.

November 19. Early morning. We have done our thirteen miles today and have got on to a much better surface. By what we and others have seen before, it seems that last winter must have generally been an exceptional one. There have been many parties out here: we have never before seen this wind-swept surface, on which it is often too slippery to walk comfortably. I do not know what temperatures the Discovery had in April, but it was much colder last April than it was the year before. And then nothing had been experienced down here to compare with the winds last winter.

There was a high wind and a lot of drift yesterday during the day, and now it is blowing and drifting as usual. During the last nine days there has only been one, the day we found the tent, when it has not been drifting during all or part of the day. It is all right for travelling north, but we should be having very uncomfortable marches if we were marching the other way.

November 20. Early morning. Today we have seemed to be walking in circles through space. Wright, by dint of having a man behind to give him a fixed point to steer upon, has steered us quite straight, and we have picked up every cairn. The pony party camped for lunch by two cairns, but they never knew the two cairns were there until a piece of paper blew away and had to be fetched; and it was caught against one of the cairns.

They left a flag there to guide us, and though we saw and brought along the flag, we never saw the cairns. The temperature is minus 22.5 degrees, and it is now blowing a full blizzard. All this snow has hitherto been lying on the ground and making a very soft surface, for though the wind has always been blowing it has never been very strong. This snow and wind, which have now persisted for nine out of the last ten days, make most dispiriting marches; for there is nothing to see, and finding tracks or steering is a constant strain. We are certainly lucky to have been able to march as we have.

Note on Mules.—The most ardent admirer of mules could not say that they were a success. The question is whether they might be made so. There was really only one thing against them but that is a very important one—they would not eat on the Barrier. From the time they went away to the day they returned (those that did return, poor things) they starved themselves, and yet they pulled biggish loads for thirty days.

If they would have eaten they would have been a huge success. They travelled faster than the ponies and, with one exception, kept together better than the ponies. If both were eating their ration it is questionable whether a good mule or a good pony is to be preferred. Our mules were of the best, and they were beautifully trained and equipped by the Indian Government: yet on November 13, a fortnight from the start, Wright records, "mules are a poor substitute for ponies. Not many will see Hut Point again, I think. Doubt if any would have got much farther than this if surfaces had been as bad this year as last."

Though they would not eat oats, compressed fodder, and oil-cake, they were quite willing to eat all kinds of other things. If we could have arrived at the mule equivalent to a vegetarian diet they might have pulled to the Beardmore without stopping. The nearest to this diet at which we could arrive was saennegrass, tea-leaves, tobacco ash, and rope— all of which were eaten with gusto.

But supplies were very limited. They ate dog-biscuit as long as they thought we were not looking—but as soon as they realized they were meant to eat it they went on a hunger-strike again. But during halts at cairns Rani and Pyaree would stand solemnly chewing the same piece of rope from different ends. Abdullah always led the line, and followed Wright's ski tracks faithfully, so that if another man was ahead and Wright turned aside Abdullah always turned too. It was quite a manœuvre for Wright to read the sledge-meter at the back of the sledge. As for Begum: "Got Begum out of a soft patch by rolling her over."

On the whole the mules failed to adapt themselves to this life, and as such must at present be considered to be a failure for Antarctic work. Certainly those of our ponies which had the best chance to adapt themselves went farthest, such as Nobby and Jimmy Pigg, both of whom had experience of Barrier sledging before they started on the Polar Journey.

November 22. Early morning. We could not have had a more perfect night to march. Yesterday at 4 p.m., holding the thermometer in the sun, the spirit rose to thirty degrees: it was almost too warm in the tent. The cairns show very plainly—in such weather navigation of this kind would be dead easy. But they are already being eaten away and toppling. The pony walls are drifted level—huge drifts, quite hard, running up to windward and down to lee.

The dogs are getting more hungry, and want to get at the mules, which makes them go better. They went very well today, but too fast once, for we had a general mix-up: Bieliglass under the sledge and the rest all tangled up and ready for a fight at the first chance. How one of the front pair of dogs got under the sledge is a mystery.

Among the Polar Party's gear is a letter to the King of Norway. It was left by the Norwegians for Scott to take back. It is wrapped in a piece of thin windcloth with one dark check line in it. Coarser and rougher and, I should say, heavier than our Mandelbergs.

November 24. Early morning. A glut of foot-walloping in soft snow and breaking crusts. We have done between seventeen and eighteen miles today. We saw no crevasses, and have marked the course well, building up the cairns and leaving two flags—so the mule party should be all right. The dogs were going well behind the ponies, but directly we went ahead they seemed to lose heart. I think they are tired of the Barrier: a cairn now awakens little interest: they know it is only a mark and it does not mean a camp: they are all well fed, and fairly fat and in good condition. With a large number of dogs I suppose one team can go ahead when it is going well—changing places with another—each keeping the others going. But I do not think that these dogs now will do much more; but they have already done as much as any dogs of which we have any record.

The land is clearing gradually. I have never seen such contrasts of black rock and white snow, and White Island was capped with great ranges of black cumulus, over which rose the pure white peaks of the Royal Society Range in a blue sky. The Barrier itself was quite a deep grey, making a beautiful picture. And now Observation Hill and Castle Rock are in front. I don't suppose I shall ever see this view again: but it is associated with many memories of returning to home and plenty after some long and hard journeys: in some ways I feel sorry— but I have seen it often enough.

November 25. Early morning. We came in twenty-four miles with our loads, to find the best possible news—Campbell's Party, all well, are at Cape Evans. They arrived here on November 6, starting from Evans Coves on September 30. What a relief it is, and how different things seem now! It is the first real bit of good news since February last—it seems an age. We mean to get over the sea-ice, if possible, as soon as we can, and then we shall hear their story.

November 26. Early morning. Starting from Hut Point about 6:45 p.m. last evening, we came through by about 9 p.m., and sat up talking and hearing all the splendid news till past 2 a.m. this morning.

All the Northern Party look very fat and fit, and they are most cheerful about the time they have had, and make light of all the anxious days they must have spent and their hard times.

I cannot write all their story. When the ship was battling with the pack to try and get in to them they had open water in Terra Nova Bay to the horizon, as seen from two hundred feet high. They prepared for the winter, digging their hut into a big snowdrift a mile from where they were landed. They thought that the ship had been wrecked—or that everyone had been taken off from here, and that then the ship had been blown north by a succession of furious gales which they had and could not get back. They never considered seriously the possibility of sledging down the coast before the winter. They got settled in and were very warm—so warm that in August they did away with one door, of which they had three, of biscuit boxes and sacking.

Their stove was the bottom of an oil tin, and they cooked by dripping blubber on to seal bones, which became soaked with the blubber, and Campbell tells me they cooked almost as quickly as a primus. Of course they were filthy. Their main difficulty was dysentery and ptomaine poisoning.

Their stories of the winter are most amusing—of "Placing the Plug, or Sports in the Antarctic"; of lectures; of how dirty they were; of their books, of which they had four, including David Copperfield. They had a spare tent, which was lucky, for the bamboos of one of theirs were blown in during a big wind, and the men inside it crept along the piedmont on hands and knees to the igloo and slept two in a bag.

How the seal seemed as if they would give out, and they were on half rations and very hungry: and they were thinking they would have to come down in the winter, when they got two seals: of the fish they got from the stomach of a seal—"the best feed they had"—the blubber they have eaten.

But they were buried deep in the snow and quite warm. Big winds all the time from the W.S.W., cold winds off the plateau—in the igloo they could hear almost nothing outside—how they just had a biscuit a day at times, sugar on Sundays, etc.

And so all is well in this direction, and we have done right in going south, and we have at least succeeded in getting all records. I suppose any news is better than no news.

Evening. The Pole Party photos of themselves at the Pole and at the Norwegian cairn (a Norwegian tent, post and two flags) are very good indeed—one film is unused, one used on these two subjects: taken with Birdie's camera. All the party look fit and well, and their clothes are not iced up. It was calm at the time: the surface looks rather soft.

Atkinson and Campbell have gone to Hut Point with one dog team, and we are all to forgather here. The ice still seems good from here to Hut Point: all else open water as far as can be seen.

A steady southerly wind has been blowing here for three days now. The mules should get into Hut Point today.

It is the happiest day for nearly a year—almost the only happy one.

CHAPTER NINE

We Succeed

Roald Amundsen

AT LAST WE GOT AWAY, ON OCTOBER 19, 1911. THE WEATHER FOR THE past few days had not been altogether reliable; now windy, now calm—now snowing, now clear: regular spring weather, in other words. That day it continued unsettled; it was misty and thick in the morning, and did not promise well for the day, but by 9:30 there was a light breeze from the east, and at the same time it cleared.

There was no need for a prolonged inquiry into the sentiments of the party.—What do you think? Shall we start?—"Yes, of course. Let's be jogging on." There was only one opinion about it. Our coursers were harnessed in a jiffy, and with a little nod—as much as to say, "See you tomorrow"—we were off. I don't believe Lindström even came out of doors to see us start. "Such an everyday affair: what's the use of making a fuss about it?"

There were five of us—Hanssen, Wisting, Hassel, Bjaaland, and myself. We had four sledges, with thirteen dogs to each. At the start our sledges were very light, as we were only taking supplies for the trip to S 80°, where all our cases were waiting for us; we could therefore sit on the sledges and flourish our whips with a jaunty air. I sat astride on Wisting's sledge, and anyone who had seen us would no doubt have thought a polar journey looked very inviting.

The going was excellent, but the atmosphere became thicker as we went inland. For the first twelve miles from the edge of the Barrier I had been sitting with Hassel, but, seeing that Wisting's dogs could manage two on the sledge better than the others, I moved. Hanssen drove first; he had to steer by compass alone, as the weather had got thicker. After him came Bjaaland, then Hassel, and, finally, Wisting and me. We had just gone up a little slope, when we saw that it dropped rather steeply on the other side; the descent could not be more than twenty yards long. I sat with my back to the dogs, looking aft, and was enjoying the brisk drive. Then suddenly the surface by the side of the sledge dropped perpendicularly, and showed a yawning black abyss, large enough to have swallowed us all, and a little more. A few inches more to one side, and we should have taken no part in the polar journey.

We had then covered seventeen miles, and we camped, well pleased with the first day of our long journey. My belief that, with all in one tent, we should manage our camping and preparations much better than before was fully justified. The tent went up as though it arose out of the ground, and everything was done as though we had had long practice. We found we had ample room in the tent, and our arrangements worked splendidly the whole time.

The bindings were taken off all our ski, and either stowed with other loose articles in a provision-case, or hung up together with the harness on the top of the ski, which were lashed upright to the front of the sledge. The tent proved excellent in every way; the dark colour subdued the light, and made it agreeable.

Neptune, a fine dog, was let loose when we had come six miles over the plain; he was so fat that he could not keep up. We felt certain that he would follow us, but he did not appear. We then supposed that he had turned back and made for the flesh-pots, but, strangely enough, he did not do that either. He never arrived at the station; it is quite a mystery what became of him.

During the night it blew a gale from the east, but it moderated in the morning, so that we got away at 10 a.m. The weather did not hold for long; the wind came again with renewed force from the same quarter, with thick driving snow. However, we went along well, and passed flag after flag. After going nineteen and a quarter miles, we came to a snow beacon that had been erected at the beginning of April, and had stood for seven months; it was still quite good and solid. This gave us a good deal to think about: so we could depend upon these beacons; they would not fall down. From the experience thus gained, we afterwards erected the whole of our extensive system of beacons on the way south.

The next day, the 21st, brought very thick weather: a strong breeze from the southeast, with thick driving snow. It would not have been a day for crossing the trap if we had not found our old tracks. It was true that we could not see them far, but we could still see the direction they took. So as to be quite safe, I now set our course northeast by east—two points east was the original course. And compared with our old tracks, this looked right, as the new course was considerably more easterly than the direction of the tracks. One last glance over the camping-ground to see whether anything was forgotten, and then into the blizzard. It was really vile weather, snowing from above and drifting from below, so that one was quite blinded. We could not see far; very often we on the last sledge had difficulty in seeing the first. Bjaaland was next in front of us. For a long time we had been going markedly downhill, and this was not in accordance with our reckoning; but in that weather one could not make much of a reckoning. We had several times passed over crevasses, but none of any size. Suddenly we saw Bjaaland's sledge sink over. He jumped off and seized the trace. The sledge lay on its side for a few seconds, then began to sink more and more, and finally disappeared altogether. Bjaaland had got a good purchase in the snow, and the dogs lay down and dug their claws in. The sledge sank more and more—all this happened in a few moments.

"Now I can't hold it any longer." We—Wisting and I—had just come up. He was holding on convulsively, and resisting with all his force, but it was no use—inch by inch the sledge sank deeper. The dogs, too, seemed to understand the gravity of the situation; stretched out in the snow, they dug their claws in, and resisted with all their strength. But still, inch by inch, slowly and surely, it went down into the abyss. Bjaaland was right enough when he said he couldn't hold on any longer. A few seconds more, and his sledge and thirteen dogs would never have seen the light of day again. Help came at the last moment. Hanssen and Hassel, who were a little in advance when it happened, had snatched an Alpine rope from a sledge and came to his assistance. They made the rope fast to the trace, and two of us—Bjaaland and I—were now able, by getting a good purchase, to hold the sledge suspended. First the dogs were taken out; then Hassel's sledge was drawn back and placed across the narrowest part of the crevasse, where we could see that the edges were solid. Then by our combined efforts the sledge, which was dangling far below, was hoisted up as far as we could get it, and made fast to Hassel's sledge by the dogs' traces. Now we could slack off and let go: one sledge hung securely enough by the other. We could breathe a little more freely.

The next thing to be done was to get the sledge right, up, and before we could manage that it had to be unloaded. A man would have to go down on the rope, cast off the lashings of the cases, and attach them again for drawing up.

"We've been lucky," said Wisting; "this is the only place where the crevasse is narrow enough to put a sledge across. If we had gone a little more to the left"—Hanssen looked eagerly in that direction—"none of us would have escaped. There is no surface there; only a crust as thin as paper. It doesn't look very inviting down below, either; immense spikes of ice sticking up everywhere, which would split you before you got very far down."

There could be no question of going farther into the trap, for we had long ago come to the conclusion that, in spite of our precautions, we had arrived at this ugly place. We should have to look about for a place for the tent, but that was easier said than done. There was no possibility of finding a place large enough for both the tent and the guy-ropes; the tent was set up on a small, apparently solid spot, and the guys stretched across crevasses in all directions. We were beginning to be quite familiar with the place. That crevasse ran there and there, and it had a side-fissure that went so and so—just like schoolboys learning a lesson.

By 4 p.m. it cleared, and a small reconnoitring party, composed of three, started to find a way out of this. I was one of the three, so we had a long Alpine rope between us; I don't like tumbling in, if I can avoid it by such simple means. We set out to the east—the direction that had brought us out of the same broken ground before—and we had not gone more than a few paces when we were quite out of it. It was now clear enough to look about us. Our tent stood at the northeastern corner of a tract that was full of hummocks; we could decide beyond a doubt that this was the dreaded trap. We continued a little way to the east until we saw our course clearly, and then returned to camp. We did not waste much time in getting things ready and leaving the place. It was a genuine relief to find ourselves once more on good ground, and we resumed our journey southward at a brisk pace.

That we were not quite out of the dangerous zone was shown by a number of small hummocks to the south of us. They extended across our course at right angles. We could also see from some long but narrow crevasses we crossed that we must keep a good lookout. When we came into the vicinity of the line of hummocks that lay in our course, we stopped and discussed our prospects. Then suddenly Hanssen's three leading dogs disappeared, and the others stopped abruptly. He got them hauled up without much trouble and came over. We others, who were following, crossed without accident, but our further progress seemed doubtful, for after a few more paces the same three dogs fell in again. We were now in exactly the same kind of place as before; crevasses ran in every direction, like a broken pane of glass.

I had had enough, and would take no more part in this death-ride. I announced decisively that we must turn back, follow our tracks, and go round it all.

We could now see all our surroundings clearly. This place lay, as we had remarked before, in a hollow; we followed it round, and came up the rise on the south without accident. Here we caught sight of one of our flags; it stood to the east of us, and thus confirmed our suspicion that we had been going too far to the west. We had one more contact with the broken ground, having to cross some crevasses and pass a big hole; but then it was done, and we could once more rejoice in having solid ice beneath us. Hanssen, however, was not satisfied till he had been to look into the hole. In the evening we reached the two snow-huts we had built on the last trip, and we camped there, twenty-six miles from the depot. The huts were drifted up with snow, so we left them in peace, and as the weather was now so mild and fine, we preferred the tent.

It was a treat to get into the tent; the day had been a bitter one. During the night the wind went round to the north, and all the snow that had been blown northward by the wind of the previous day had nothing to do but to come back again; the road was free. And it made the utmost use of its opportunity; nothing could be seen for driving snow when we turned out next morning.

We had decided to cover the distance between 80° and 82° S in daily marches of seventeen miles. We could easily have done twice this, but as it was more important to arrive than to show great speed, we limited the distance; besides which, here between the depots we had sufficient food to allow us to take our time. We were interested in seeing how the dogs would manage the loaded sledges. We expected them to do well, but not as well as they did.

On October 25 we left 80° S with a light northwesterly breeze, clear and mild.

On the following day we were already in sight of the large pressure-ridges on the east, which we had seen for the first time on the second depot journey between 81° and 82° S, and this showed that the atmosphere must be very clear. We could not see any greater number than the first time, however. From our experience of beacons built of snow, we could see that if we built such beacons now, on our way south, they would be splendid marks for our return journey; we therefore decided to adopt this system of landmarks to the greatest possible extent. We built in all 150 beacons, six feet high, and used in their construction nine thousand blocks, cut out of the snow with specially large snow-knives. In each of them was deposited a paper, giving the number and position of the beacon, and indicating the distance and the direction to be taken to reach the next beacon to the north.

The next day was brilliant—calm and clear. The sun really baked the skin of one's face. We put all our skin clothing out to dry; a little rime will always form at the bottom of a sleeping-bag. We also availed ourselves of this good opportunity to determine our position and check our compasses; they proved to be correct. We replaced the provisions we had consumed on the way, and resumed our journey on October 31.

There was a thick fog next morning, and very disagreeable weather; perhaps we felt it more after the previous fine day.

From 81° S we began to erect beacons at every nine kilometres. The next day we observed the lowest temperature of the whole of this journey: minus 30.1 degrees Fahrenheit. The wind was south-southeast, but not very strong. It did not feel like summer, all the same. We now adopted the habit which we kept up all the way to the south—of taking our lunch while building the beacon that lay halfway in our day's march. It was nothing very luxurious—three or four dry oatmeal biscuits, that was all. If one wanted a drink, one could mix snow with the biscuit—"bread and water." It is a diet that is not much sought after in our native latitudes, but latitude makes a very great difference in this world. If anybody had offered us more "bread and water," we should gladly have accepted it.

That day we crossed the last crevasse for a long time to come, and it was only a few inches wide. The surface looked grand ahead of us; it went in very long, almost imperceptible undulations. We could only notice them by the way in which the beacons we put up often disappeared rather rapidly.

On November 2 we had a gale from the south, with heavy snow. The going was very stiff, but the dogs got the sledges along better than we expected. The temperature rose, as usual, with a wind from this quarter: plus 14° F. It was a pleasure to be out in such a temperature, although it did blow a little. The day after we had a light breeze from the north. The heavy going of the day before had completely disappeared; instead of it we had the best surface one could desire, and it made our dogs break into a brisk gallop. That was the day we were to reach the depot in 82° S, but as it was extremely thick, our chances of doing so were small.

At four o'clock next morning the sun broke through. We let it get warm and disperse the fog, and then went out. What a morning it was—radiantly clear and mild. So still, so still lay the mighty desert before us, level and white on every side. But, no; there in the distance the level was broken: there was a touch of colour on the white. The third important point was reached, the extreme outpost of civilization. Our last depot lay before us; that was an unspeakable relief. The victory now seemed half won.

In the fog we had come about three and a half miles too far to the west; but we now saw that if we had continued our march the day before, we should have come right into our line of flags. There they stood, flag after flag, and the little strip of black cloth seemed to wave quite proudly, as though it claimed credit for the way in which it had discharged its duty. Here, as at the depot in 81° S, there was hardly a sign of snowfall. The drift round the depot had reached the same height as there—one and half feet. Clearly the same conditions of weather had prevailed all over this region. The depot stood as we had made it, and the sledge as we had left it. Falling snow and drift had not been sufficient to cover even this. The little drift that there was offered an excellent place for the tent, being hard and firm.

Next day we stayed here to give the dogs a thorough rest for the last time. We took advantage of the fine weather to dry our outfit and check our instruments. When evening came we were all ready, and now we could look back with satisfaction to the good work of the autumn; we had fully accomplished what we aimed at—namely, transferring our base from 78°38" to 82° S.

On November 6, at 8 a.m., we left 82° S. Now the unknown lay before us; now our work began in earnest. The appearance of the Barrier was the same everywhere—flat, with a splendid surface. At the first beacon we put up we had to shoot Lucy. We were sorry to put an end to this beautiful creature, but there was nothing else to be done. Her friends—Karenius, Sauen, and Schwartz—scowled up at the beacon where she lay as they passed, but duty called, and the whip sang dangerously near them, though they did not seem to hear it. We had now extended our daily march to twenty-three miles; in this way we should do a degree in three days.

On the 7th we decided to stop for a day's rest. The dogs had been picking up wonderfully every day, and were now at the top of their condition, as far as health and training went. With the greatest ease they covered the day's march at a pace of seven and a half kilometres (four miles and two-thirds) an hour. As for ourselves, we never had to move a foot; all we had to do was to let ourselves be towed.

On the 12th we reached 84° S. On that day we made the interesting discovery of a chain of mountains running to the east; this, as it appeared from the spot where we were, formed a semicircle, where it joined the mountains of South Victoria Land. This semicircle lay true south, and our course was directed straight towards it.

In the depot in 84° S we left, besides the usual quantity of provisions for five men and twelve dogs for four days, a can of paraffin, holding seventeen litres (about thirty-four gallons). We had an abundance of matches, and could therefore distribute them over all the depots. The Barrier continued as flat as before, and the going was as good as it could possibly be. We had thought that a day's rest would be needed by the dogs for every degree of latitude, but this proved superfluous; it looked as if they could no longer be tired. Without any longer stay, then, we left 84° S the next day, and steered for the bay ahead.

That day we went twenty-three miles in thick fog, and saw nothing of the land.

On November 15 we reached 85° S, and camped at the top of one of these swelling waves. The valley we were to cross next day was fairly broad, and rose considerably on the other side. On the west, in the direction of the nearest land, the undulation rose to such a height that it concealed a great part of the land from us. During the afternoon we built the usual depot, and continued our journey on the following day. As we had seen from our camping-ground, it was an immense undulation that we had to traverse; the ascent on the other side felt uncomfortably warm in the powerful sun, but it was no higher than three hundred feet by the aneroid. From the top of this wave the Barrier stretched away before us, flat at first, but we could see disturbances of the surface in the distance. Now we are going to have some fun in getting to land, I thought, for it seemed very natural that the Barrier, hemmed in as it was here, would be much broken up. The disturbances we had seen consisted of some big, old crevasses, which were partly filled up; we avoided them easily. Now there was another deep depression before us; with a correspondingly high rise on the other side. We went over it capitally; the surface was absolutely smooth, without a sign of fissure or hole anywhere. Then we shall get them when we are on the top, I thought. It was rather stiff work uphill, unaccustomed as we were to slopes. I stretched my neck more and more to get a view. At last we were up; and what a sight it was that met us! Not an irregularity, not a sign of disturbance; quietly and evenly the ascent continued. I believe that we were then already above land; the large crevasses that we had avoided down below probably formed the boundary.

We were now immediately below the ascent, and made the final decision of trying it here. This being settled, we pitched our camp. It was still early in the day, but we had a great deal to arrange before the morrow. Here we should have to overhaul our whole supply of provisions, take with us what was absolutely necessary for the remainder of the trip, and leave the rest behind in depot. First, then, we camped, worked out our position, fed the dogs and let them loose again, and then went into our tent to have something to eat and go through the provision books.

We had now reached one of the most critical points of our journey. Our plan had now to be laid so that we might not only make the ascent as easily as possible, but also get through to the end. Our calculations had to be made carefully, and every possibility taken into account. As with every decision of importance, we discussed the matter jointly. The distance we had before us, from this spot to the Pole and back, was 683 miles. Reckoning with the ascent that we saw before us, with other unforeseen obstructions, and finally with the certain factor that the strength of our dogs would be gradually reduced to a fraction of what it now was, we decided to take provisions and equipment for sixty days on the sledges, and to leave the remaining supplies—enough for thirty days—and outfit in depot. We calculated, from the experience we had had, that we ought to be able to reach this point again with twelve dogs left. We now had forty-two dogs. Our plan was to take all the forty-two up to the plateau; there twenty-four of them were to be slaughtered, and the journey continued with three sledges and eighteen dogs. Of these last eighteen, it would be necessary, in our opinion, to slaughter six in order to bring the other twelve back to this point.

When all this was finished, three of us put on our ski and made for the nearest visible land. This was a little peak, a mile and three-quarters away—Mount Betty. Running on ski felt quite strange, although I had now covered 385 miles on them; but we had driven the whole way, and were somewhat out of training. We could feel this, too, as we went up the slope that afternoon. After Mount Betty the ascent became rather steep, but the surface was even, and the going splendid, so we got on fast.

First we came up a smooth mountain-side, about 1,200 feet above the sea, then over a little plateau; after that another smooth slope like the first, and then down a rather long, flat stretch, which after a time began to rise very gradually, until it finally passed into small glacier formations. Our reconnaissance extended to these small glaciers. We had ascertained that the way was practicable, as far as we were able to see; we had gone about five and a half miles from the tent, and ascended two thousand feet. On the way back we went gloriously; the last two slopes down to the Barrier gave us all the speed we wanted. Bjaaland and I had decided to take a turn round by Mount Betty for the sake of having real bare ground under our feet; we had not felt it since Madeira in September 1910, and now we were in November 1911.

Mount Betty offered no perpendicular crags or deep precipices to stimulate our desire for climbing; we only had to take off our ski, and then we arrived at the top. It consisted of loose screes, and was not an ideal promenade for people who had to be careful of their boots. It was a pleasure to set one's foot on bare ground again, and we sat down on the rocks to enjoy the scene. The rocks very soon made themselves felt, however, and brought us to our feet again. We photographed each other in "picturesque attitudes," took a few stones for those who had not yet set foot on bare earth, and strapped on our ski.

The dogs, after having been so eager to make for bare land when they first saw it, were now not the least interested in it; they lay on the snow, and did not go near the top. Between the bare ground and the snow surface there was bright, blue-green ice, showing that at times there was running water here.

By this time the dogs had already begun to be very voracious. Everything that came in their way disappeared; whips, ski-bindings, lashings, etc., were regarded as delicacies. If one put down anything for a moment, it vanished. With some of them this voracity went so far that we had to chain them.

On November 17 we began the ascent. To provide for any contingency, I left in the depot a paper with information of the way we intended to take through the mountains, together with our plan for the future, our outfit, provisions, etc. The weather was fine, as usual, and the going good. Our distance this first day was eleven and a half miles, with a rise of two thousand feet. Our camp that evening lay on a little glacier among huge crevasses; on three sides of us were towering summits.

On November 20, we were up and away at the usual time, about 8 a.m. The weather was splendid, calm and clear. Getting up over the saddle was a rough beginning of the day for our dogs, and they gave a good account of themselves, pulling the sledges up with single teams this time. The going was heavy, as on the preceding day, and our advance through the loose snow was not rapid. We did not follow our tracks of the day before, but laid our course directly for the place where we had decided to attempt the ascent. As we approached Mount Ole Engelstad, under which we had to pass in order to come into the arm of the glacier between it and Mount Nansen, our excitement began to rise. What does the end look like? Does the glacier go smoothly on into the plateau, or is it broken up and impassable? We rounded Mount Engelstad more and more; wider and wider grew the opening. The surface looked extremely good as it gradually came into view, and it did not seem as though our assumption of the previous day would be put to shame. At last the whole landscape opened out, and without obstruction of any kind whatever the last part of the ascent lay before us. It was both long and steep from the look of it, and we agreed to take a little rest before beginning the final attack.

We stopped right under Mount Engelstad in a warm and sunny place, and allowed ourselves on this occasion a little lunch, an indulgence that had not hitherto been permitted. The cooking-case was taken out, and soon the Primus was humming in a way that told us it would not be long before the chocolate was ready. It was a heavenly treat, that drink. We had all walked ourselves warm, and our throats were as dry as tinder. The contents of the pot were served round by the cook—Hanssen. It was no use asking him to share alike; he could not be persuaded to take more than half of what was due to him—the rest he had to divide among his comrades. The drink he had prepared this time was what he called chocolate, but I had some difficulty in believing him. He was economical, was Hanssen, and permitted no extravagance; that could be seen very well by his chocolate. Well, after all, to people who were accustomed to regard "bread and water" as a luxury, it tasted, as I have said, heavenly. It was the liquid part of the lunch that was served extra; if anyone wanted something to eat, he had to provide it himself—nothing was offered him. Happy was he who had saved some biscuits from his breakfast! Our halt was not a very long one. It is a queer thing that, when one only has on light underclothing and windproof overalls, one cannot stand still for long without feeling cold. Although the temperature was no lower than minus 4° F, we were glad to be on the move again.

Saturday, November 25, was a grand day in many respects. I had already seen proofs on several occasions of the kind of men my comrades were, but their conduct that day was such that I shall never forget it, to whatever age I may live. In the course of the night the wind had gone back to the north, and increased to a gale. It was blowing and snowing so that when we came out in the morning we could not see the sledges; they were half snowed under. The dogs had all crept together, and protected themselves as well as they could against the blizzard. The temperature was not so very low (minus 16.6° F), but low enough to be disagreeably felt in a storm. We had all taken a turn outside to look at the weather, and were sitting on our sleeping bags discussing the poor prospect.

No sooner was the proposal submitted than it was accepted unanimously and with acclamation. When I think of my four friends of the southern journey, it is the memory of that morning that comes first to my mind. All the qualities that I most admire in a man were clearly shown at that juncture: courage and dauntlessness, without boasting or big words. Amid joking and chaff, everything was packed, and then— out into the blizzard.

It was practically impossible to keep one's eyes open; the fine drift snow penetrated everywhere, and at times one had a feeling of being blind. The tent was not only drifted up, but covered with ice, and in taking it down we had to handle it with care so as not to break it in pieces. The dogs were not much inclined to start, and it took time to get them into their harness, but at last we were ready. One more glance over the camping-ground to see that nothing we ought to have with us had been forgotten. The fourteen dogs' carcasses that were left were piled up in a heap, and Hassel's sledge was set up against it as a mark. The spare sets of dog-harness, some Alpine ropes, and all our crampons for ice-work, which we now thought would not be required, were left behind. The last thing to be done was planting a broken ski upright by the side of the depot. It was Wisting who did this, thinking, presumably, that an extra mark would do no harm. That it was a happy thought the future will show.

And then we were off: It was a hard pull to begin with, both for men and beasts, as the high sastrugi continued towards the south, and made it extremely difficult to advance. Those who had sledges to drive had to be very attentive, and support them so that they did not capsize on the big waves, and we who had no sledges found great difficulty in keeping our feet, as we had nothing to lean against. We went on like this, slowly enough, but the main thing was that we made progress. The ground at first gave one the impression of rising, though not much. The going was extremely heavy; it was like dragging oneself through sand.

At three in the morning the sun cut through the clouds and we through the tent door. To take in the situation was more than the work of a moment. The sun showed as yet like a pat of butter, and had not succeeded in dispersing the thick mists; the wind had dropped somewhat, but was still fairly strong. This is, after all, the worst part of one's job—turning out of one's good, warm sleeping bag, and standing outside for some time in thin clothes, watching the weather. We knew by experience that a gleam like this, a clearing in the weather, might come suddenly, and then one had to be on the spot. The gleam came; it did not last long, but long enough. We lay on the side of a ridge that fell away pretty steeply. The descent on the south was too abrupt, but on the southeast it was better and more gradual, and ended in a wide, level tract. We could see no crevasses or unpleasantness of any kind. It was not very far that we could see, though; only our nearest surroundings.

The weather, which had somewhat improved during the night, had now broken loose again, and the northeaster was doing all it could. However, it would take more than storm and snow to stop us now, since we had discovered the nature of our immediate surroundings; if we once got down to the plain, we knew that we could always feel our way on.

After putting ample brakes on the sledge-runners, we started off downhill in a southeasterly direction. The slight idea of the position that we had been able to get in the morning proved correct. The descent was easy and smooth, and we reached the plain without any adventure. We could now once more set our faces to the south, and in thick driving snow we continued our way into the unknown, with good assistance from the howling northeasterly gale. We now recommenced the erection of beacons, which had not been necessary during the ascent. In the course of the forenoon we again passed over a little ridge, the last of them that we encountered. The surface was now fine enough, smooth as a floor and without a sign of sastrugi. If our progress was nevertheless slow and difficult, this was due to the wretched going, which was real torture to all of us. A sledge journey through the Sahara could not have offered a worse surface to move over. Now the forerunners came into their own, and from here to the Pole Hassel, and I took it in turns to occupy the position.

The weather improved in the course of the day, and when we camped in the afternoon it looked quite smiling. The sun came through and gave a delightful warmth after the last few bitter days. It was not yet clear, so that we could see nothing of our surroundings. The distance according to our three sledge-meters was eighteen and a half miles; taking the bad going into consideration, we had reason to be well satisfied with it. Our altitude came out at 9,475 feet above the sea, or a drop of 825 feet in the course of the day. This surprised me greatly. What did it mean? Instead of rising gradually, we were going slowly down. Something extraordinary must await us farther on, but, what? According to dead reckoning our latitude that evening was 86° S.

November 27 did not bring us the desired weather; the night was filled with sharp gusts from the north; the morning came with a slack wind, but accompanied by mist and snowfall. This was abominable; here we were, advancing over absolutely virgin ground, and able to see nothing. The surface remained about the same—possibly rather more undulating. That it had been blowing here at some time, and violently too, was shown by the under-surface, which was composed of sastrugi as hard as iron. Luckily for us, the snowfall of the last few days had filled these up, so as to present a level surface. It was heavy going, though better than on the previous day.

As we were advancing, still blindly, and fretting at the persistently thick weather, one of us suddenly called out: "Hullo, look there!" A wild, dark summit rose high out of the mass of fog to the east-southeast. It was not far away—on the contrary, it seemed threateningly near and right over us. We stopped and looked at the imposing sight, but Nature did not expose her objects of interest for long. The fog rolled over again, thick, heavy and dark, and blotted out the view. We knew now that we had to be prepared for surprises. After we had gone about ten miles the fog again lifted for a moment, and we saw quite near—a mile or so away—two long, narrow mountain ridges to the west of us, running north and south, and completely covered with snow. These—Helland Hansen's Mountains—were the only ones we saw on our right hand during the march on the plateau; they were between nine thousand and ten thousand feet high, and would probably serve as excellent landmarks on the return journey.

We set to work at once to build the depot; the snow here was excellent for this purpose—as hard as glass. In a short time an immense erection of adamantine blocks of snow rose into the air, containing provisions for five men for six days and for eighteen dogs for five days. A number of small articles were also left behind.

While we were thus occupied, the fog had been coming and going; some of the intervals had been quite clear, and had given me a good view of the nearest part of the range. It appeared to be quite isolated, and to consist of four mountains; one of these—Mount Helmer Hanssen—lay separated from the rest. The other three—Mounts Oscar Wisting, Sverre Hassel, and Olav Bjaaland—lay closer together.

Behind this group the air had been heavy and black the whole time, showing that more land must be concealed there. Suddenly, in one of the brightest intervals, there came a rift in this curtain, and the summits of a colossal mountain mass appeared. Our first impression was that this mountain—Mount Thorvald Nilsen—must be something over twenty thousand feet high; it positively took our breath away, so formidable did it appear. But it was only a glimpse that we had, and then the fog enclosed it once more. We had succeeded in taking a few meagre bearings of the different summits of the nearest group; they were not very grand, but better ones were not to be obtained. For that matter, the site of the depot was so well marked by its position under the foot of the glacier that we agreed it would be impossible to miss it.

Having finished the edifice, which rose at least 6 feet into the air, we put one of our black provision cases on the top of it, so as to be able to see it still more easily on the way back. An observation we had contrived to take while the work was in progress gave us our latitude as 86°21" S. This did not agree very well with the latitude of our dead reckoning—86°23" S. Meanwhile the fog had again enveloped everything, and a fine, light snow was falling. We had taken a bearing of the line of glacier that was most free of crevasses, and so we moved on again. It was some time before we felt our way up to the glacier. The crevasses at its foot were not large, but we had no sooner entered upon the ascent than the fun began. There was something uncanny about this perfectly blind advance among crevasses and chasms on all sides. We examined the compass from time to time, and went forward cautiously.

Hassel and I went in front on a rope; but that, after all, was not much of a help to our drivers. We naturally glided lightly on our ski over places where the dogs would easily fall through. This lowest part of the glacier was not entirely free from danger, as the crevasses were often rendered quite invisible by a thin overlying layer of snow. In clear weather it is not so bad to have to cross such a surface, as the effect of light and shade is usually to show up the edges of these insidious pitfalls, but on a day like this, when everything looked alike, one's advance is doubtful. We kept it going, however, by using the utmost caution. Wisting came near to sounding the depth of one of these dangerous crevasses with sledge, dogs and all, as the bridge he was about to cross gave way. Thanks to his presence of mind and a lightning-like movement—some would call it luck—he managed to save himself. In this way we worked up about two hundred feet, but then we came upon such a labyrinth of yawning chasms and open abysses that we could not move. There was nothing to be done but to find the least disturbed spot, and set the tent there.

As soon as this was done Hanssen and I set out to explore. We were roped, and therefore safe enough. It required some study to find a way out of the trap we had run ourselves into. Towards the group of mountains last described—which now lay to the east of us—it had cleared suffi- ciently to give us a fairly good view of the appearance of the glacier in that direction. What we had before seen at a distance was now confirmed. The part extending to the mountains was so ground up and broken that there was positively not a spot where one could set one's foot. It looked as if a battle had been fought here, and the ammunition had been great blocks of ice. They lay pell-mell, one on the top of another, in all directions, and evoked a picture of violent confusion. Thank God we were not here while this was going on, I thought to myself, as I stood looking out over this battlefield; it must have been a spectacle like doomsday, and not on a small scale either. To advance in that direction, then, was hopeless, but that was no great matter, since our way was to the south. On the south we could see nothing; the fog lay thick and heavy there. All we could do was to try to make our way on, and we therefore crept southward.

On leaving our tent we had first to cross a comparatively narrow snow-bridge, and then go along a ridge or saddle, raised by pressure, with wide open crevasses on both sides. This ridge led us on to an icewave about twenty-five feet high—a formation which was due to the pressure having ceased before the wave had been forced to break and form hummocks. We saw well enough that this would be a difficult place to pass with sledges and dogs, but in default of anything better it would have to be done. From the top of this wave formation we could see down on the other side, which had hitherto been hidden from us. The fog prevented our seeing far, but the immediate surroundings were enough to convince us that with caution we could beat up farther. From the height on which we stood, every precaution would be required to avoid going down on the other side; for there the wave ended in an open crevasse, specially adapted to receive any drivers, sledges or dogs that might make a slip.

November 29 brought considerably clearer weather, and allowed us a very good survey of our position. We could now see that the two mountain ranges uniting in 86° S were continued in a mighty chain running to the southeast, with summits from 10,000 to 15,000 feet. Mount Thorvald Nilsen was the most southerly we could see from this point. Mounts Hanssen, Wisting, Bjaaland, and Hassel formed, as we had thought the day before, a group by themselves, and lay separated from the main range.

The drivers had a warm morning's work. They had to drive with great circumspection and patience to grapple with the kind of ground we had before us; a slight mistake might be enough to send both sledge and dogs with lightning rapidity into the next world. It took, nevertheless, a remarkably short time to cover the distance we had explored on the previous evening; before we knew it, we were at Hell's Gate.

It was no very great distance that we put behind us that day—nine and a quarter miles in a straight line. But, taking into account all the turns and circuits we had been compelled to make, it was not so short after all. We set our tent on a good, solid foundation, and were well pleased with the day's work. The altitude was 8,960 feet above the sea. The sun was now in the west, and shining directly upon the huge mountain masses. It was a fairy landscape in blue and white, red and black, a play of colours that defies description. Clear as it now appeared to be, one could understand that the weather was not all that could be wished, for the southeastern end of Mount Thorvald Nilsen lost itself in a dark, impenetrable cloud, which led one to suspect a continuation in that direction, though one could not be certain.

Mount Nilsen—ah! anything more beautiful, taking it altogether, I have never seen. Peaks of the most varied forms rose high into the air, partly covered with driving clouds.

Our prospects of advancing were certainly not bright; as far as we could see in the line of our route one immense ridge towered above another, concealing on their farther sides huge, wide chasms, which all had to be avoided. We went forward—steadily forward—though the way round was both long and troublesome. We had no rope on this time, as the irregularities were so plain that it would have been difficult to go into them. It turned out, however, at several points, that the rope would not have been out of place. We were just going to cross over one of the numerous ridges—the surface here looked perfectly whole—when a great piece broke right under the back half of Hanssen's ski. We could not deny ourselves the pleasure of glancing down into the hole. The sight was not an inviting one, and we agreed to avoid this place when we came on with our dogs and sledges. Every day we had occasion to bless our ski. We often used to ask each other where we should now have been without these excellent appliances. The usual answer was: Most probably at the bottom of some crevasse. When we first read the different accounts of the aspect and nature of the Barrier, it was clear to all of us, who were born and bred with ski on our feet, that these must be regarded as indispensable. This view was confirmed and strengthened every day, and I am not giving too much credit to our excellent ski when I say that they not only played a very important part, but possibly the most important of all, on our journey to the South Pole. Many a time we traversed stretches of surface so cleft and disturbed that it would have been an impossibility to get over them on foot. I need scarcely insist on the advantages of ski in deep, loose snow.

After advancing for two hours, we decided to return. From the raised ridge on which we were then standing, the surface ahead of us looked more promising than ever; but we had so often been deceived on the glacier that we had now become definitely sceptical. How often, for instance, had we thought that beyond this or that undulation our trials would be at an end, and that the way to the south would lie open and free; only to reach the place and find that the ground behind the ridge was, if possible, worse than what we had already been struggling with. But this time we seemed somehow to feel victory in the air. The formations appeared to promise it, and yet—had we been so often deceived by these formations that we now refused to offer them a thought? Was it possibly instinct that told us this? I do not know, but certain it is that Hanssen and I agreed, as we stood there discussing our prospects, that behind the farthest ridge we saw, we should conquer the glacier. We had a feverish desire to go and have a look at it; but the way round the many crevasses was long, and—I may as well admit it—we were beginning to get tired. The return, downhill as it was, did not take long, and soon we were able to tell our comrades that the prospects for the morrow were very promising.

During the night a gale sprang up from the southeast, and blew so that it howled in the guy-ropes of the tent; it was well that the tent pegs had a good hold. In the morning, while we were at breakfast, it was still blowing, and we had some thoughts of waiting for a time; but suddenly, without warning, the wind dropped to such an extent that all our hesitation vanished. What a change the southeast wind had produced! The splendid covering of snow that the day before had made ski-running a pleasure, was now swept away over great stretches of surface, exposing the hard substratum. Our thoughts flew back; the crampons we had left behind seemed to dance before my eyes, backwards and forwards, grinning and pointing fingers at me.

Meanwhile, we packed and made everything ready. The tracks of the day before were not easy to follow; but if we lost them now and again on the smooth ice surface, we picked them up later on a snow wave that had resisted the attack of the wind. It was hard and strenuous work for the drivers. The sledges were difficult to manage over the smooth, sloping ice; sometimes they went straight, but just as often cross-wise, requiring sharp attention to keep them from capsizing.

The glacier that day presented the worst confusion we had yet had to deal with. Hassel and I went in front, as usual, with the rope on. Up to the spot Hanssen and I had reached the evening before our progress was comparatively easy; one gets on so much quicker when one knows that the way is practicable. After this point it became worse; indeed, it was often so bad that we had to stop for a long time and try in various directions, before finding a way. More than once the axe had to be used to hack away obstructions. At one time things looked really serious; chasm after chasm, hummock after hummock, so high and steep that they were like mountains. Here we went out and explored in every direction to find a passage; at last we found one, if, indeed, it deserved the name of a passage. It was a bridge so narrow that it scarcely allowed room for the width of the sledge; a fearful abyss on each side. The crossing of this place reminded me of the tight-rope walker going over Niagara. It was a good thing none of us was subject to giddiness, and that the dogs did not know exactly what the result of a false step would be.

On the other side of this bridge we began to go downhill, and our course now lay in a long valley between lofty undulations on each side. It tried our patience severely to advance here, as the line of the hollow was fairly long and ran due west. We tried several times to lay our course towards the south and clamber up the side of the undulation, but these efforts did not pay us. We could always get up on to the ridge, but we could not come down again on the other side; there was nothing to be done but to follow the natural course of the valley until it took us into the tract lying to the south. It was especially the drivers whose patience was sorely tried, and I could see them now and then take a turn up to the top of the ridge, not satisfied with the exploration Hassel and I had made. But the result was always the same; they had to submit to Nature's caprices and follow in our tracks.

As we progressed, it could be seen that we had really come upon another kind of ground; for once we had not been made fools of. Not that we had an unbroken, level surface to go upon—it would be a long time before we came to that—but we were able to keep our course for long stretches at a time. The huge crevasses became rarer, and so filled up at both ends that we were able to cross them without going a long way round. There was new life in all of us, both dogs and men, and we went rapidly southward. As we advanced, the conditions improved more and more. We could see in the distance some huge dome-shaped formations, that seemed to tower high into the air: these turned out to be the southernmost limit of the big crevasses and to form the transition to the third phase of the glacier.

It was a stiff climb to get up these domes, which were fairly high and swept smooth by the wind. They lay straight in our course, and from their tops we had a good view. The surface we were entering upon was quite different from that on the northern side of the domes. Here the big crevasses were entirely filled with snow and might be crossed anywhere. What specially attracted one's attention here was an immense number of small formations in the shape of haycocks. Great stretches of the surface were swept bare, exposing the smooth ice.

December 1, was a very fatiguing one for us all. From early morning a blinding blizzard raged from the southeast, with a heavy fall of snow. The going was of the very worst kind—polished ice. I stumbled forward on ski, and had comparatively easy work. The drivers had been obliged to take off their ski and put them on the loads, so as to walk by the side, support the sledges, and give the dogs help when they came to a difficult place; and that was pretty often, for on this smooth ice surface there were a number of small scattered sastrugi, and these consisted of a kind of snow that reminded one more of fish-glue than of anything else when the sledges came in contact with it. The dogs could get no hold with their claws on the smooth ice, and when the sledge came on to one of these tough little waves, they could not manage to haul it over, try as they might. The driver then had to put all his strength into it to prevent the sledge stopping. Thus in most cases the combined efforts of men and dogs carried the sledge on.

In the course of the afternoon the surface again began to be more disturbed, and great crevasses crossed our path time after time. These crevasses were really rather dangerous; they looked very innocent, as they were quite filled up with snow, but on a nearer acquaintance with them we came to understand that they were far more hazardous than we dreamed of at first. It turned out that between the loose snow-filling and the firm ice edges there was a fairly broad, open space, leading straight down into the depths. The layer of snow which covered it over was in most cases quite thin. In driving out into one of these snow-filled crevasses nothing happened as a rule; but it was in getting off on the other side that the critical moment arrived. For here the dogs came up on to the smooth ice surface, and could get no hold for their claws, with the result that it was left entirely to the driver to haul the the sledge up. The strong pull he then had to give sent him through the thin layer of snow. Under these circumstances he took a good, firm hold of the sledge-lashing, or of a special strap that had been made with a view to these accidents. But familiarity breeds contempt, even with the most cautious, and some of the drivers were often within an ace of going down into "the cellar."

If this part of the journey was trying for the dogs, it was certainly no less so for the men. If the weather had even been fine, so that we could have looked about us, we should not have minded it so much, but in this vile weather it was, indeed, no pleasure.

At this camp we left behind all our delightful reindeer-skin clothing, as we could see that we should have no use for it, the temperature being far too high. We kept the hoods of our reindeer coats, however; we might be glad of them in going against the wind. Our day's march was not to be a long one; the little slackening of the wind about midday was only a joke. It soon came on again in earnest, with a sweeping blizzard from the same quarter—the southeast. If we had known the ground, we should possibly have gone on; but in this storm and driving snow, which prevented our keeping our eyes open, it was no use. A serious accident might happen and ruin all. Two and half miles was therefore our whole distance. The temperature when we camped was minus 5.8°F. Height above the sea, 9,780 feet.

In the course of the night the wind veered from southeast to north, falling light, and the weather cleared. This was a good chance for us, and we were not slow to avail ourselves of it. A gradually rising ice surface lay before us, bright as a mirror. As on the preceding days, I stumbled along in front on ski, while the others, without their ski, had to follow and support the sledges. The surface still offered filled crevasses, though perhaps less frequently than before. Meanwhile small patches of snow began to show themselves on the polished surface, and soon increased in number and size, until before very long they united and covered the unpleasant ice with a good and even layer of snow. Then ski were put on again, and we continued our way to the south with satisfaction.

We were all rejoicing that we had now conquered this treacherous glacier, and congratulating ourselves on having at last arrived on the actual plateau. As we were going along, feeling pleased about this, a ridge suddenly appeared right ahead, telling us plainly that perhaps all our sorrows were not yet ended. The ground had begun to sink a little, and as we came nearer we could see that we had to cross a rather wide, but not deep, valley before we arrived under the ridge. Great lines of hummocks and haycock-shaped pieces of ice came in view on every side; we could see that we should have to keep our eyes open.

And now we came to the formation in the glacier that we called the Devil's Ballroom. Little by little the covering of snow that we had praised in such high terms disappeared, and before us lay this wide valley, bare and gleaming. At first it went well enough; as it was downhill, we were going at a good pace on the smooth ice. Suddenly Wisting's sledge cut into the surface, and turned over on its side. We all knew what had happened—one of the runners was in a crevasse.

On December 4, at 87° S—according to dead reckoning—we saw the last of the land to the northeast. The atmosphere was then apparently as clear as could be, and we felt certain that our view covered all the land there was to be seen from that spot. We were deceived again on this occasion, as will be seen later. Our distance that day (December 4) was close upon twenty-five miles; height above the sea, 10,100 feet.

On December 5 there was a gale from the north, and once more the whole plain was a mass of drifting snow. In addition to this there was thick falling snow, which blinded us and made things worse, but a feeling of security had come over us and helped us to advance rapidly and without hesitation, although we could see nothing. That day we encountered new surface conditions—big, hard snow-waves (sastrugi). These were anything but pleasant to work among, especially when one could not see them. It was of no use for us "forerunners" to think of going in advance under these circumstances, as it was impossible to keep on one's feet. Three or four paces was often the most we managed to do before falling down. The sastrugi were very high, and often abrupt; if one came on them unexpectedly, one required to be more than an acrobat to keep on one's feet. The plan we found to work best in these conditions was to let Hanssen's dogs go first; this was an unpleasant job for Hanssen, and for his dogs too, but it succeeded, and succeeded well. An upset here and there was, of course, unavoidable, but with a little patience the sledge was always righted again. The drivers had as much as they could do to support their sledges among these sastrugi, but while supporting the sledges, they had at the same time a support for themselves. It was worse for us who had no sledges, but by keeping in the wake of them we could see where the irregularities lay, and thus get over them.

December 6 brought the same weather: thick snow, sky and plain all one, nothing to be seen. Nevertheless we made splendid progress. The sastrugi gradually became levelled out, until the surface was perfectly smooth; it was a relief to have even ground to go upon once more. These irregularities that one was constantly falling over were a nuisance; if we had met with them in our usual surroundings it would not have mattered so much; but up here on the high ground, where we had to stand and gasp for breath every time we rolled over, it was certainly not pleasant.

That day we passed 88° S, and camped in 88°9" S. A great surprise awaited us in the tent that evening. I expected to find, as on the previous evening, that the boiling-point had fallen somewhat; in other words, that it would show a continued rise of the ground, but to our astonishment this was not so. The water boiled at exactly the same temperature as on the preceding day. I tried it several times, to convince myself that there was nothing wrong, each time with the same result. There was great rejoicing among us all when I was able to announce that we had arrived on the top of the plateau.

December 7 began like the 6th, with absolutely thick weather, but, as they say, you never know what the day is like before sunset. Possibly I might have chosen a better expression than this last—one more in agreement with the natural conditions—but I will let it stand. Though for several weeks now the sun had not set, my readers will not be so critical as to reproach me with inaccuracy. With a light wind from the northeast, we now went southward at a good speed over the perfectly level plain, with excellent going. The uphill work had taken it out of our dogs, though not to any serious extent. They had turned greedy—there is no denying that—and the half kilo of pemmican they got each day was not enough to fill their stomachs. Early and late they were looking for something—no matter what—to devour. To begin with they contented themselves with such loose objects as ski-bindings, whips, boots, and the like; but as we came to know their proclivities, we took such care of everything that they found no extra meals lying about. But that was not the end of the matter. They then went for the fixed lashings of the sledges, and—if we had allowed it—would very quickly have resolved the various sledges into their component parts. But we found a way of stopping that: every evening, on halting, the sledges were buried in the snow, so as to hide all the lashings. That was successful; curiously enough, they never tried to force the "snow rampart." I may mention as a curious thing that these ravenous animals, that devoured everything they came across, even to the ebonite points of our ski-sticks, never made any attempt to break into the provision cases. They lay there and went about among the sledges with their noses just on a level with the split cases, seeing and scenting the pemmican, without once making a sign of taking any. But if one raised a lid, they were not long in showing themselves. Then they all came in a great hurry and flocked about the sledges in the hope of getting a little extra bit. I am at loss to explain this behaviour; that bashfulness was not at the root of it, I am tolerably certain.

During the forenoon the thick, grey curtain of cloud began to grow thinner on the horizon, and for the first time for three days we could see a few miles about us. The feeling was something like that one has on waking from a good nap, rubbing one's eyes and looking around. We had become so accustomed to the grey twilight that this positively dazzled us. Meanwhile, the upper layer of air seemed obstinately to remain the same and to be doing its best to prevent the sun from showing itself. We badly wanted to get a meridian altitude, so that we could determine our latitude. Since 86°47" S we had had no observation, and it was not easy to say when we should get one. Hitherto, the weather conditions on the high ground had not been particularly favourable. Although the prospects were not very promising, we halted at 11 a.m. and made ready to catch the sun if it should be kind enough to look out. Hassel and Wisting used one sextant and artificial horizon, Hanssen and I the other set.

I don't know that I have ever stood and absolutely pulled at the sun to get it out as I did that time. If we got an observation here which agreed with our reckoning, then it would be possible, if the worst came to the worst, to go to the Pole on dead reckoning; but if we got none now, it was a question whether our claim to the Pole would be admitted on the dead reckoning we should be able to produce. Whether my pulling helped or not, it is certain that the sun appeared. It was not very brilliant to begin with, but, practised as we now were in availing ourselves of even the poorest chances, it was good enough. Down it came, was checked by all, and the altitude written down. The curtain of cloud was rent more and more, and before we had finished our work—that is to say, caught the sun at its highest, and convinced ourselves that it was descending again—it was shining in all its glory. We had put away our instruments and were sitting on the sledges, engaged in the calculations. I can safely say that we were excited. What would the result be, after marching blindly for so long and over such impossible ground, as we had been doing? We added and subtracted, and at last there was the result. We looked at each other in sheer incredulity: the result was as astonishing as the most consummate conjuring trick—88°16" S, precisely to a minute the same as our reckoning, 88°16" S. If we were forced to go to the Pole on dead reckoning, then surely the most exacting would admit our right to do so. We put away our observation books, ate one or two biscuits, and went at it again.

We had a great piece of work before us that day nothing less than carrying our flag farther south than the foot of man had trod. We had our silk flag ready; it was made fast to two ski-sticks and laid on

Hanssen's sledge. I had given him orders that as soon as we had covered the distance to 88° S, which was Shackleton's farthest south, the flag was to be hoisted on his sledge. It was my turn as forerunner, and I pushed on. There was no longer any difficulty in holding one's course; I had the grandest cloud-formations to steer by, and everything now went like a machine. First came the forerunner for the time being, then Hanssen, then Wisting, and finally Bjaaland. The forerunner who was not on duty went where he liked; as a rule he accompanied one or other of the sledges. I had long ago fallen into a reverie—far removed from the scene in which I was moving; what I thought about I do not remember now, but I was so preoccupied that I had entirely forgotten my surroundings. Then suddenly I was roused from my dreaming by a jubilant shout, followed by ringing cheers. I turned round quickly to discover the reason of this unwonted occurrence, and stood speechless and overcome.

I find it impossible to express the feelings that possessed me at this moment. All the sledges had stopped, and from the foremost of them the Norwegian flag was flying. It shook itself out, waved and flapped so that the silk rustled; it looked wonderfully well in the pure, clear air and the shining white surroundings. 88°23" was past; we were farther south than any human being had been. No other moment of the whole trip affected me like this. The tears forced their way to my eyes; by no effort of will could I keep them back. It was the flag yonder that conquered me and my will. Luckily I was some way in advance of the others, so that I had time to pull myself together and master my feelings before reaching my comrades. We all shook hands, with mutual congratulations; we had won our way far by holding together, and we would go farther yet—to the end.

We did not pass that spot without according our highest tribute of admiration to the man, who—together with his gallant companions—had planted his country's flag so infinitely nearer to the goal than any of his precursors. Sir Ernest Shackleton's name will always be written in the annals of Antarctic exploration in letters of fire. Pluck and grit can work wonders, and I know of no better example of this than what that man has accomplished.

December 9 arrived with the same fine weather and sunshine. True, we felt our frost-sores rather sharply that day, with minus 18.4°F and a little breeze dead against us, but that could not be helped. We at once began to put up beacons—a work which was continued with great regularity right up to the Pole. These beacons were not so big as those we had built down on the Barrier; we could see that they would be quite large enough with a height of about three feet, as it was, very easy to see the slightest irregularity on this perfectly flat surface. While thus engaged we had an opportunity of becoming thoroughly acquainted with the nature of the snow. Often—very often indeed—on this part of the plateau, to the south of 88°25", we had difficulty in getting snow good enough—that is, solid enough for cutting blocks. The snow up here seemed to have fallen very quietly, in light breezes or calms. We could thrust the tent pole, which was six feet long, right down without meeting resistance, which showed that there was no hard layer of snow. The surface was also perfectly level; there was not a sign of sastrugi in any direction.

Every step we now took in advance brought us rapidly nearer the goal; we could feel fairly certain of reaching it on the afternoon of the 14th. It was very natural that our conversation should be chiefly concerned with the time of arrival. None of us would admit that he was nervous, but I am inclined to think that we all had a little touch of that malady. What should we see when we got there? A vast, endless plain, that no eye had yet seen and no foot yet trodden; or—No, it was an impossibility; with the speed at which we had travelled, we must reach the goal first, there could be no doubt about that. And yet—and yet—Wherever there is the smallest loophole, doubt creeps in and gnaws and gnaws and never leaves a poor wretch in peace. "What on earth is Uroa scenting?" It was Bjaaland who made this remark, on one of these last days, when I was going by the side of his sledge and talking to him. "And the strange thing is that he's scenting to the south. It can never be—" Mylius, Ring, and Suggen, showed the same interest in the southerly direction; it was quite extraordinary to see how they raised their heads, with every sign of curiosity, put their noses in the air, and sniffed due south. One would really have thought there was something remarkable to be found there.

From 88°25" S the barometer and hypsometer indicated slowly but surely that the plateau was beginning to descend towards the other side. This was a pleasant surprise to us; we had thus not only found the very summit of the plateau, but also the slope down on the far side. This would have a very important bearing for obtaining an idea of the construction of the whole plateau. On December 9 observations and dead reckoning agreed within a mile. The same result again on the 10th: observation two kilometres behind reckoning. The weather and going remained about the same as on the preceding days: light southeasterly breeze, temperature minus 18.4°F. The snow surface was loose, but ski and sledges glided over it well. On the 11th, the same weather conditions. Temperature minus 13°F. Observation and reckoning again agreed exactly. Our latitude was 89°15" S. On the 12th we reached 89°30", reckoning one kilometre behind observation. Going and surface as good as ever. Weather splendid—calm with sunshine. The noon observation on the 13th gave 89°37" S. Reckoning 89°38.5" S. We halted in the afternoon, after going eight geographical miles, and camped in 89°45", according to reckoning.

The weather during the forenoon had been just as fine as before; in the afternoon we had some snow-showers from the southeast. It was like the eve of some great festival that night in the tent. One could feel that a great event was at hand. Our flag was taken out again and lashed to the same two ski-sticks as before. Then it was rolled up and laid aside, to be ready when the time came. I was awake several times during the night, and had the same feeling that I can remember as a little boy on the night before Christmas Eve—an intense expectation of what was going to happen. Otherwise I think we slept just as well that night as any other.

On the morning of December 14 the weather was of the finest, just as if it had been made for arriving at the Pole. I am not quite sure, but I believe we despatched our breakfast rather more quickly than usual and were out of the tent sooner, though I must admit that we always accomplished this with all reasonable haste.

The going on that day was rather different from what it had been; sometimes the ski went over it well, but at others it was pretty bad. We advanced that day in the same mechanical way as before; not much was said, but eyes were used all the more. Hanssen's neck grew twice as long as before in his endeavour to see a few inches farther. I had asked him before we started to spy out ahead for all he was worth, and he did so with a vengeance. But, however keenly he stared, he could not descry anything but the endless flat plain ahead of us. The dogs had dropped their scenting, and appeared to have lost their interest in the regions about the earth's axis.

At three in the afternoon a simultaneous "Halt!" rang out from the drivers. They had carefully examined their sledge-meters, and they all showed the full distance—our Pole by reckoning. The goal was reached, the journey ended. I cannot say—though I know it would sound much more effective—that the object of my life was attained. That would be romancing rather too bare-facedly. I had better be honest and admit straight out that I have never known any man to be placed in such a diametrically opposite position to the goal of his desires as I was at that moment. The regions around the North Pole—well, yes, the North Pole itself—had attracted me from childhood, and here I was at the South Pole. Can anything more topsy-turvy be imagined?

We reckoned now that we were at the Pole. Of course, every one of us knew that we were not standing on the absolute spot; it would be an impossibility with the time and the instruments at our disposal to ascertain that exact spot. But we were so near it that the few miles which possibly separated us from it could not be of the slightest importance. It was our intention to make a circle round this camp, with a radius of twelve and a half miles (twenty kilometres), and to be satisfied with that. After we had halted we collected and congratulated each other. We had good grounds for mutual respect in what had been achieved, and I think that was just the feeling that was expressed in the firm and powerful grasps of the fists that were exchanged. After this we proceeded to the greatest and most solemn act of the whole journey—the planting of our flag. Pride and affection shone in the five pairs of eyes that gazed upon the flag, as it unfurled itself with a sharp crack, and waved over the Pole. I had determined that the act of planting it—the historic event—should be equally divided among us all. It was not for one man to do this; it was for all who had staked their lives in the struggle, and held together through thick and thin. This was the only way in which I could show my gratitude to my comrades in this desolate spot. I could see that they understood and accepted it in the spirit in which it was offered. Five weather-beaten, frost-bitten fists they were that grasped the pole, raised the waving flag in the air, and planted it as the first at the geographical South Pole. "Thus we plant thee, beloved flag, at the South Pole, and give to the plain on which it lies the name of King

Haakon VII's Plateau." That moment will certainly be remembered by all of us who stood there.

One gets out of the way of protracted ceremonies in those regions—the shorter they are the better.

Of course, there was a festivity in the tent that evening—not that champagne corks were popping and wine flowing—no, we contented ourselves with a little piece of seal meat each, and it tasted well and did us good. There was no other sign of festival indoors. Outside we heard the flag flapping in the breeze. Conversation was lively in the tent that evening, and we talked of many things. Perhaps, too, our thoughts sent messages home of what we had done.

Everything we had with us had now to be marked with the words "South Pole" and the date, to serve afterwards as souvenirs. Wisting proved to be a first-class engraver, and many were the articles he had to mark. Tobacco—in the form of smoke—had hitherto never made its appearance in the tent. From time to time I had seen one or two of the others take a quid, but now these things were to be altered. I had brought with me an old briar pipe, which bore inscriptions from many places in the Arctic regions, and now I wanted it marked "South Pole." When I produced my pipe and was about to mark it, I received an unexpected gift Wisting offered me tobacco for the rest of the journey. He had some cakes of plug in his kit-bag, which he would prefer to see me smoke. Can anyone grasp what such an offer meant at such a spot, made to a man who, to tell the truth, is very fond of a smoke after meals? There are not many who can understand it fully. I accepted the offer, jumping with joy, and on the way home I had a pipe of fresh, fine-cut plug every evening. Ah! That Wisting, he spoiled me entirely. Not only did he give me tobacco, but every evening—and I must confess I yielded to the temptation after a while, and had a morning smoke as well—he undertook the disagreeable work of cutting the plug and filling my pipe in all kinds of weather.

But we did not let our talk make us forget other things. As we had got no noon altitude, we should have to try and take one at midnight. The weather had brightened again, and it looked as if midnight would be a good time for the observation. We therefore crept into our bags to get a little nap in the intervening hours. In good time—soon after 11 p.m.—we were out again, and ready to catch the sun; the weather was of the best, and the opportunity excellent. We four navigators all had a share in it, as usual, and stood watching the course of the sun. This was a labour of patience, as the difference of altitude was now very slight. The result at which we finally arrived was of great interest, as it clearly shows how unreliable and valueless a single observation like this is in these regions. At 12:30 a.m. we put our instruments away, well satisfied with our work, and quite convinced that it was the midnight altitude that we had observed. The calculations which were carried out immediately afterwards gave us S 89°56". We were all well pleased with this result.

Early next morning, December 16, we were on our feet again. Bjaaland, who had now left the company of the drivers and been received with jubilation into that of the forerunners, was immediately entrusted with the honourable task of leading the expedition forward to the Pole itself. I assigned this duty, which we all regarded as a distinction, to him as a mark of gratitude to the gallant Telemarkers for their pre-eminent work in the advancement of ski spot. The leader that day had to keep as straight as a line, and if possible to follow the direction of our meridian. A little way after Bjaaland came Hassel, then Hanssen, then Wisting, and I followed a good way behind. I could thus check the direction of the march very accurately, and see that no great deviation was made. Bjaaland on this occasion showed himself a matchless forerunner; he went perfectly straight the whole time. Not once did he incline to one side or the other, and when we arrived at the end of the distance, we could still clearly see the sledge we had set up and take its bearing. This showed it to be absolutely in the right direction.

It was 11 a.m. when we reached our destination. While some of us were putting up the tent, others began to get everything ready for the coming observations. A solid snow pedestal was put up, on which the artificial horizon was to be placed, and a smaller one to rest the sextant on when it was not in use. At 11:30 a.m. the first observation was taken. We divided ourselves into two parties—Hanssen and I in one, Hassel and Wisting in the other. While one party slept, the other took the observations, and the watches were of six hours each. The weather was altogether grand, though the sky was not perfectly bright the whole time. A very light, fine, vaporous curtain would spread across the sky from time to time, and then quickly disappear again. This film of cloud was not thick enough to hide the sun, which we could see the whole time, but the atmosphere seemed to be disturbed. The effect of this was that the sun appeared not to change its altitude for several hours, until it suddenly made a jump.

Observations were now taken every hour through the whole twenty-four. It was very strange to turn in at 6 p.m., and then on turning out again at midnight to find the sun apparently still at the same altitude, and then once more at 6 a.m. to see it still no higher. The altitude had changed, of course, but so slightly that it was imperceptible with the naked eye. To us it appeared as though the sun made the circuit of the heavens at exactly the same altitude. The times of day that I have given here are calculated according to the meridian of Framheim; we continued to reckon our time from this. The observations soon told us that we were not on the absolute Pole, but as close to it as we could hope to get with our instruments.

On December 17 at noon we had completed our observations, and it is certain that we had done all that could be done. In order if possible to come a few inches nearer to the actual Pole, Hanssen and Bjaaland went out four geographical miles (seven kilometres) in the direction of the newly found meridian.

Bjaaland astonished me at dinner that day. Speeches had not hitherto been a feature of this journey, but now Bjaaland evidently thought the time had come, and surprised us all with a really fine oration. My amazement reached its culmination when, at the conclusion of his speech, he produced a cigar-case full of cigars and offered it round. A cigar at the Pole! What do you say to that? But it did not end there. When the cigars had gone round, there were still four left. I was quite touched when he handed the case and cigars to me with the words: "Keep this to remind you of the Pole." I have taken good care of the case, and shall preserve it as one of the many happy signs of my comrades' devotion on this journey. The cigars I shared out afterwards, on Christmas Eve, and they gave us a visible mark of that occasion.

When this festival dinner at the Pole was ended, we began our preparations for departure. First we set up the little tent we had brought with us in case we should be compelled to divide into two parties. It had been made by our able sailmaker, Rionne, and was of very thin windproof gabardine. Its drab colour made it easily visible against the white surface. Another pole was lashed to the tent-pole, making its total height about thirteen feet. On the top of this a little Norwegian flag was lashed fast, and underneath it a pennant, on which "Fram" was painted. The tent was well secured with guy-ropes on all sides. Inside the tent, in a little bag, I left a letter, addressed to H.M. the King, giving information of what we had accomplished. The way home was a long one, and so many things might happen to make it impossible for us to give an account of our expedition. Besides this letter, I wrote a short epistle to Captain Scott, who, I assumed, would be the first to find the tent. Other things we left there were a sextant with a glass horizon, a hypsometer case, three reindeer-skin foot-bags, some kamiks and mits.

When everything had been laid inside, we went into the tent, one by one, to write our names on a tablet we had fastened to the tent pole. On this occasion we received the congratulations of our companions on the successful result, for the following messages were written on a couple of strips of leather, sewed to the tent

"Good luck," and "Welcome to 90°." These good wishes, which we suddenly discovered, put us in very good spirits. They were signed by Beck and Rönne. They had good faith in us. When we had finished this we came out, and the tent-door was securely laced together, so that there was no danger of the wind getting a hold on that side.

And so goodbye to Polheim. It was a solemn moment when we bared our heads and bade farewell to our home and our flag. And then the travelling tent was taken down and the sledges packed. Now the homeward journey was to begin—homeward, step by step, mile after mile, until the whole distance was accomplished. We drove at once into our old tracks and followed them. Many were the times we turned to send a last look to Polheim. The vaporous, white air set in again, and it was not long before the last of Polheim, our little flag, disappeared from view.

CHAPTER TEN

Loss of the *Endurance*

Sir Ernest Shackleton

PREFACE

AFTER THE CONQUEST OF THE SOUTH POLE BY AMUNDSEN, WHO, BY A narrow margin of days only, was in advance of the British Expedition under Scott, there remained but one great main object of Antarctic journeyings—the crossing of the South Polar continent from sea to sea.

When I returned from the *Nimrod* Expedition on which we had to turn back from our attempt to plant the British flag on the South Pole, being beaten by stress of circumstances within ninety-seven miles of our goal, my mind turned to the crossing of the continent, for I was morally certain that either Amundsen or Scott would reach the Pole on our own route or a parallel one. After hearing of the Norwegian success I began to make preparations to start a last great journey—so that the first crossing of the last continent should be achieved by a British Expedition.

I think our story of high adventure, strenuous days, lonely nights, unique experiences, and, above all, records of unflinching determination, supreme loyalty, and generous self-sacrifice on the part of my men which, even in these days that have witnessed the sacrifices of nations and regardlessness of self on the part of individuals, still will be of interest to readers who now turn gladly from the red horror of war and the strain of the last five years to read, perhaps with more understanding minds, the tale of the White Warfare of the South.

The struggles, the disappointments, and the endurance of this small party of Britishers, hidden away for nearly two years in the fastnesses of the Polar ice, striving to carry out the ordained task and ignorant of the crises through which the world was passing, make a story which is unique in the history of Antarctic exploration.

LOCKED IN

The ice did not trouble us again seriously until the end of September, though during the whole month the floes were seldom entirely without movement. The roar of pressure would come to us across the otherwise silent ice fields, and bring with it a threat and a warning. Watching from the crow's-nest, we could see sometimes the formation of pressure ridges. The sunshine glittered on newly riven ice surfaces as the masses of shattered floe rose and fell away from the line of pressure.

The area of disturbance would advance towards us, recede, and advance again. The routine of work and play on the *Endurance* proceeded steadily. Our plans and preparations for any contingency that might arise during the approaching summer had been made, but there seemed always plenty to do in and about our prisoned ship. Runs with the dogs and vigorous games of hockey and football on the rough snow-covered floe kept all hands in good fettle. The record of one or two of these September days will indicate the nature of our life and our surroundings:

September *4.—Temperature,* −14.1° Fahr. Light easterly breeze, blue sky, and stratus clouds. During forenoon notice a distinct terra-cotta or biscuit colour in the stratus clouds to the north. This travelled from east to west and could conceivably have come from some of the Graham Land volcanoes, now about 300 miles distant to the northwest. The upper current of air probably would come from that direction. Heavy rime. Pack unbroken and unchanged as far as visible. No land for 22 miles. No animal life observed.

September *7.—Temperature,* −10.8° Fahr. Moderate easterly to southerly winds, overcast and misty, with light snow till midnight, when weather cleared. Blue sky and fine clear weather to noon. Much rime aloft. Thick fresh snow on ship and floe that glistens brilliantly in the morning sunlight. Little clouds of faint violet-coloured mist rise from the lower and brinier portions of the pack, which stretches unbroken to the horizon.

Very great refraction all round. A tabular berg about fifty feet high ten miles west is a good index of the amount of refraction. On ordinary days it shows from the masthead, clear-cut against the sky; with much refraction, the pack beyond at the back of it lifts up into view; today a broad expanse of miles of pack is seen above it. Numerous other bergs generally seen in silhouette are, at first sight, lost, but after a closer scrutiny they appear as large lumps or dark masses well below the horizon.

Refraction generally results in too big an altitude when observing the sun for position, but today, the horizon is thrown up so much that the altitude is about twelve feet too small. No land visible for twenty miles. No animal life observed. Lower Clark's tow-net with 566 fathoms of wire, and hoist it up at two and a half miles an hour by walking across the floe with the wire.

Results rather meagre—jelly-fish and some fish larvæ. Exercise dogs in sledge teams. The young dogs, under Crean's care, pull as well, though not so strongly, as the best team in the pack. Hercules for the last fortnight or more has constituted himself leader of the orchestra. Two or three times in the twenty-four hours he starts a howl—a deep, melodious howl— and in about thirty seconds he has the whole pack in full song, the great deep, booming, harmonious song of the half-wolf pack.

By the middle of September we were running short of fresh meat for the dogs. The seals and penguins seemed to have abandoned our neighbourhood altogether. Nearly five months had passed since we killed a seal, and penguins had been seen seldom. Clark, who was using his trawl as often as possible, reported that there was a marked absence of *plankton* in the sea, and we assumed that the seals and the penguins had gone in search of their accustomed food.

The men got an emperor on the 23rd. The dogs, which were having their sledging exercise, became wildly excited when the penguin, which had risen in a crack, was driven ashore, and the best efforts of the drivers failed to save it alive. On the following day Wild, Hurley, Macklin, and McIlroy took their teams to the Stained Berg, about seven miles west of the ship, and on their way back got a female crab-eater, which they killed, skinned, and left to be picked up later.

They ascended to the top of the berg, which lay in about lat. 69°30" S, long. 51° W, and from an elevation of 110 feet could see no land. Samples of the discoloured ice from the berg proved to contain dust with black gritty particles or sand grains. Another seal, a bull Weddell, was secured on the 26th. The return of seal life was opportune, since we had nearly finished the winter supply of dog-biscuit and wished to be able to feed the dogs on meat.

The seals meant a supply of blubber, moreover, to supplement our small remaining stock of coal when the time came to get up steam again. We initiated a daylight-saving system on this day by putting forward the clock one hour. "This is really pandering to the base but universal passion that men, and especially seafarers, have for getting up late, otherwise we would be honest and make our routine earlier instead of flogging the clock."

During the concluding days of September the roar of the pressure grew louder, and I could see that the area of disturbance was rapidly approaching the ship. Stupendous forces were at work and the fields of firm ice around the *Endurance* were being diminished steadily.

September 30 was a bad day. It began well, for we got two penguins and five seals during the morning. Three other seals were seen. But at 3 p.m. cracks that had opened during the night alongside the ship commenced to work in a lateral direction. The ship sustained terrific pressure on the port side forward, the heaviest shocks being under the forerigging. It was the worst squeeze we had experienced. The decks shuddered and jumped, beams arched, and stanchions buckled and shook.

I ordered all hands to stand by in readiness for whatever emergency might arise. Even the dogs seemed to feel the tense anxiety of the moment. But the ship resisted valiantly, and just when it appeared that the limit of her strength was being reached the huge floe that was pressing down upon us cracked across and so gave relief.

"The behaviour of our ship in the ice has been magnificent," wrote Worsley. "Since we have been beset her staunchness and endurance have been almost past belief again and again. She has been nipped with a million-ton pressure and risen nobly, falling clear of the water out on the ice. She has been thrown to and fro like a shuttlecock a dozen times. She has been strained, her beams arched upwards, by the fearful pressure; her very sides opened and closed again as she was actually bent and curved along her length, groaning like a living thing. It will be sad if such a brave little craft should be finally crushed in the remorseless, slowly strangling grip of the Weddell pack after ten months of the bravest and most gallant fight ever put up by a ship."

The *Endurance* deserved all that could be said in praise of her. Shipwrights had never done sounder or better work; but how long could she continue the fight under such conditions? We were drifting into the congested area of the western Weddell Sea, the worst portion of the worst sea in the world, where the pack, forced on irresistibly by wind and current, impinges on the western shore and is driven up in huge corrugated ridges and chaotic fields of pressure.

The vital question for us was whether or not the ice would open sufficiently to release us, or at least give us a chance of release, before the drift carried us into the most dangerous area. There was no answer to be got from the silent bergs and the grinding floes, and we faced the month of October with anxious hearts.

The leads in the pack appeared to have opened out a little on October 1, but not sufficiently to be workable even if we had been able to release the *Endurance* from the floe. The day was calm, cloudy and misty in the forenoon and clearer in the afternoon, when we observed well-defined parhelia. The ship was subjected to slight pressure at intervals.

Two bull crab-eaters climbed on to the floe close to the ship and were shot by Wild. They were both big animals in prime condition, and I felt that there was no more need for anxiety as to the supply of fresh meat for the dogs. Seal-liver made a welcome change in our own menu. The two bulls were marked, like many of their kind, with long parallel scars about three inches apart, evidently the work of the killers. A bull we killed on the following day had four parallel scars, sixteen inches long, on each side of its body; they were fairly deep and one flipper had been nearly torn away.

The creature must have escaped from the jaws of a killer by a very small margin. Evidently life beneath the pack is not always monotonous. We noticed that several of the bergs in the neighbourhood of the ship were changing their relative positions more than they had done for months past. The floes were moving.

THE BEGINNING OF THE END

Our position on Sunday, October 3, was lat. 69°14" S, long. 51°8" W. During the night the floe holding the ship aft cracked in several places, and this appeared to have eased the strain on the rudder. The forenoon was misty, with falls of snow, but the weather cleared later in the day and we could see that the pack was breaking. New leads had appeared, while several old leads had closed. Pressure ridges had risen along some of the cracks. The thickness of the season's ice, now about 230 days old, was four feet five inches under seven or eight inches of snow. This ice had been slightly thicker in the early part of September, and I assumed that some melting had begun below.

Clark had recorded plus temperatures at depths of 150 and 200 fathoms in the concluding days of September. The ice obviously had attained its maximum thickness by direct freezing, and the heavier older floes had been created by the consolidation of pressure-ice and the overlapping of floes under strain. The air temperatures were still low, minus 24.5°F being recorded on October 4.

The movement of the ice was increasing. Frost-smoke from opening cracks was showing in all directions during October 6. It had the appearance in one place of a great prairie fire, rising from the surface and getting higher as it drifted off before the wind in heavy, dark, rolling masses. At another point there was the appearance of a train running before the wind, the smoke rising from the locomotive straight upwards; and the smoke columns elsewhere gave the effect of warships steaming in line ahead.

During the following day the leads and cracks opened to such an extent that if the *Endurance* could have been forced forward for thirty yards we could have proceeded for two or three miles; but the effort did not promise any really useful result. The conditions did not change materially during the rest of that week. The position on Sunday, October 10, was lat. 69°21" S, long. 50°34" W. A thaw made things uncomfortable for us that day. The temperature had risen from minus 10°F to plus 29.8°F, the highest we had experienced since January, and the ship got dripping wet between decks.

The upperdeck was clear of ice and snow and the cabins became unpleasantly messy. The dogs, who hated wet, had a most unhappy air. Undoubtedly one grows to like familiar conditions. We had lived long in temperatures that would have seemed distressingly low in civilized life, and now we were made uncomfortable by a degree of warmth that would have left the unaccustomed human being still shivering. The thaw was an indication that winter was over, and we began preparations for reoccupying the cabins on the main deck.

I had the shelter-house round the stern pulled down on the 11th and made other preparations for working the ship as soon as she got clear. The carpenter had built a wheelhouse over the wheel aft as shelter in cold and heavy weather. The ice was still loosening and no land was visible for twenty miles.

The temperature remained relatively high for several days. All hands moved to their summer quarters in the upper cabins on the 12th, to the accompaniment of much noise and laughter. Spring was in the air, and if there were no green growing things to gladden our eyes, there were at least many seals, penguins, and even whales disporting themselves in the leads. The time for renewed action was coming, and though our situation was grave enough, we were facing the future hopefully. The dogs were kept in a state of uproar by the sight of so much game. They became almost frenzied when a solemn-looking emperor penguin inspected them gravely from some point of vantage on the floe and gave utterance to an apparently derisive "Knark!"

At 7 p.m. on the 13th the ship broke free of the floe on which she had rested to starboard sufficiently to come upright. The rudder freed itself, but the propeller was found to be athwartship, having been forced into that position by the floe sometime after August 1. The water was very clear and we could see the rudder, which appeared to have suffered only a slight twist to port at the waterline. It moved quite freely. The propeller, as far as we could see, was intact, but it could not be moved by the handgear, probably owing to a film of ice in the stern gland and sleeve. I did not think it advisable to attempt to deal with it at that stage. The ship had not been pumped for eight months, but there was no water and not much ice in the bilges. Meals were served again in the wardroom that day.

The southwesterly breeze freshened to a gale on the 14th, and the temperature fell from plus 31°F to minus 1°F. At midnight the ship came free from the floe and drifted rapidly astern. Her head fell off before the wind until she lay nearly at right-angles across the narrow lead. This was a dangerous position for rudder and propeller. The spanker was set, but the weight of the wind on the ship gradually forced the floes open until the *Endurance* swung right round and drove one hundred yards along the lead.

Then the ice closed and at 3 a.m. we were fast again. The wind died down during the day and the pack opened for five or six miles to the north. It was still loose on the following morning, and I had the boiler pumped up with the intention of attempting to clear the propeller; but one of the manholes developed a leak, the packing being perished by cold or loosened by contraction, and the boiler had to be emptied out again.

The pack was rather closer on Sunday the 17th. Top-sails and head-sails were set in the afternoon, and with a moderate northeasterly breeze we tried to force the ship ahead out of the lead; but she was held fast. Later that day heavy pressure developed.

The two floes between which the *Endurance* was lying began to close and the ship was subjected to a series of tremendously heavy strains. In the engineroom, the weakest point, loud groans, crashes, and hammering sounds were heard. The iron plates on the floor buckled up and overrode with loud clangs. Meanwhile the floes were grinding off each other's projecting points and throwing up pressure ridges.

The ship stood the strain well for nearly an hour and then, to my great relief, began to rise with heavy jerks and jars. She lifted ten inches forward and three feet four inches aft, at the same time heeling six degrees to port. The ice was getting below us and the immediate danger had passed. The position was lat. 69°19" S, long. 50°40" W.

The next attack of the ice came on the afternoon of October 18th. The two floes began to move laterally, exerting great pressure on the ship. Suddenly the floe on the port side cracked and huge pieces of ice shot up from under the port bilge. Within a few seconds the ship heeled over until she had a list of thirty degrees to port, being held under the starboard bilge by the opposing floe.

The lee boats were now almost resting on the floe. The midship dog-kennels broke away and crashed down on to the lee kennels, and the howls and barks of the frightened dogs assisted to create a perfect pandemonium. Everything movable on deck and below fell to the lee side, and for a few minutes it looked as if the *Endurance* would be thrown upon her beam ends.

Order was soon restored.

I had all fires put out and battens nailed on the deck to give the dogs a foothold and enable people to get about. Then the crew lashed all the movable gear. If the ship had heeled any farther it would have been necessary to release the lee boats and pull them clear, and Worsley was watching to give the alarm. Hurley meanwhile descended to the floe and took some photographs of the ship in her unusual position. Dinner in the wardroom that evening was a curious affair. Most of the diners had to sit on the deck, their feet against battens and their plates on their knees. At 8 p.m. the floes opened, and within a few minutes the *Endurance* was nearly upright again.

Orders were given for the ice to be chipped clear of the rudder. The men poled the blocks out of the way when they had been detached from the floe with the long ice-chisels, and we were able to haul the ship's stern into a clear berth. Then the boiler was pumped up. This work was completed early in the morning of October 19, and during that day the engineer lit fires and got up steam very slowly, in order to economize fuel and avoid any strain on the chilled boilers by unequal heating.

The crew cut up all loose lumber, boxes, etc., and put them in the bunkers for fuel. The day was overcast, with occasional snowfalls, the temperature plus 12°F. The ice in our neighbourhood was quiet, but in the distance pressure was at work. The wind freshened in the evening, and we ran a wire-mooring astern. The barometer at 11 p.m. stood at 28.96, the lowest since the gales of July.

An uproar among the dogs attracted attention late in the afternoon, and we found a twenty-five-foot whale cruising up and down in our pool. It pushed its head up once in characteristic killer fashion, but we judged from its small curved dorsal fin that it was a specimen of *Balænoptera acutorostrata*, not *Orca gladiator*.

A strong southwesterly wind was blowing on October 20 and the pack was working. The *Endurance* was imprisoned securely in the pool, but our chance might come at any time. Watches were set so as to be ready for working ship. Wild and Hudson, Greenstreet and Cheetham, Worsley and Crean, took the deck watches, and the Chief Engineer and Second Engineer kept watch and watch with three of the A.B.s for stokers.

The staff and the forward hands, with the exception of the cook, the carpenter and his mate, were on "watch and watch"—that is, four hours on deck and four hours below, or off duty. The carpenter was busy making a light punt, which might prove useful in the navigation of lanes and channels. At 11 a.m. we gave the engines a gentle trial turn astern.

Everything worked well after eight months of frozen inactivity, except that the bilge-pump and the discharge proved to be frozen up; they were cleared with some little difficulty. The engineer reported that to get steam he had used one ton of coal, with wood-ashes and blubber. The fires required to keep the boiler warm consumed one and a quarter to one and a half hundred-weight of coal per day. We had about fifty tons of coal remaining in the bunkers.

October 21 and 22 were days of low temperature, which caused the open leads to freeze over. The pack was working, and ever and anon the roar of pressure came to our ears. We waited for the next move of the gigantic forces arrayed against us.

The 23rd brought a strong northwesterly wind, and the movement of the floes and pressure ridges became more formidable. Then on Sunday, October 24, there came what for the *Endurance* was the beginning of the end. The position was lat. 69°11"S., long. 51°5" W. We had now twenty-two and a half hours of daylight, and throughout the day we watched the threatening advance of the floes.

At 6:45 p.m. the ship sustained heavy pressure in a dangerous position. The onslaught was all but irresistible. The *Endurance* groaned and quivered as her starboard quarter was forced against the floe, twisting the sternpost and starting the heads and ends of planking. The ice had lateral as well as forward movement, and the ship was twisted and actually bent by the stresses. She began to leak dangerously at once.

I had the pumps rigged, got up steam, and started the bilge-pumps at 8 p.m. The pressure by that time had relaxed. The ship was making water rapidly aft, and the carpenter set to work to make a coffer-dam astern of the engines. All hands worked, watch and watch, throughout the night, pumping ship and helping the carpenter.

By morning the leak was being kept in check. The carpenter and his assistants caulked the coffer-dam with strips of blankets and nailed strips over the seams wherever possible. The main or hand pump was frozen up and could not be used at once. After it had been knocked out Worsley, Greenstreet, and Hudson went down in the bunkers and cleared the ice from the bilges.

"This is not a pleasant job," wrote Worsley. "We have to dig a hole down through the coal while the beams and timbers groan and crack all around us like pistol-shots. The darkness is almost complete, and we mess about in the wet with half-frozen hands and try to keep the coal from slipping back into the bilges. The men on deck pour buckets of boiling water from the galley down the pipe as we prod and hammer from below, and at last we get the pump clear, cover up the bilges to keep the coal out, and rush on deck, very thankful to find ourselves safe again in the open air."

Monday, October 25, dawned cloudy and misty, with a minus temperature and a strong southeasterly breeze. All hands were pumping at intervals and assisting the carpenter with the coffer-dam. The leak was being kept under fairly easily, but the outlook was bad.

Heavy pressure ridges were forming in all directions, and though the immediate pressure upon the ship was not severe, I realized that the respite would not be prolonged. The pack within our range of vision was being subjected to enormous compression, such as might be caused by cyclonic winds, opposing ocean currents, or constriction in a channel of some description. The pressure ridges, massive and threatening, testified to the overwhelming nature of the forces that were at work. Huge blocks of ice, weighing many tons, were lifted into the air and tossed aside as other masses rose beneath them.

We were helpless intruders in a strange world, our lives dependent upon the play of grim elementary forces that made a mock of our puny efforts. I scarcely dared hope now that the *Endurance* would live, and throughout that anxious day I reviewed again the plans made long before for the sledging journey that we must make in the event of our having to take to the ice. We were ready, as far as forethought could make us, for every contingency. Stores, dogs, sledges, and equipment were ready to be moved from the ship at a moment's notice.

The following day brought bright clear weather, with a blue sky. The sunshine was inspiriting. The roar of pressure could be heard all around us. New ridges were rising, and I could see as the day wore on that the lines of major disturbance were drawing nearer to the ship. The *Endurance* suffered some strains at intervals.

Listening below, I could hear the creaking and groaning of her timbers, the pistol-like cracks that told of the starting of a trenail or plank, and the faint, indefinable whispers of our ship's distress. Overhead the sun shone serenely; occasional fleecy clouds drifted before the southerly breeze, and the light glinted and sparkled on the million facets of the new pressure ridges.

The day passed slowly. At 7 p.m. very heavy pressure developed, with twisting strains that racked the ship fore and aft. The butts of planking were opened four and five inches on the starboard side, and at the same time we could see from the bridge that the ship was bending like a bow under titanic pressure.

Almost like a living creature, she resisted the forces that would crush her; but it was a one-sided battle. Millions of tons of ice pressed inexorably upon the little ship that had dared the challenge of the Antarctic. The *Endurance* was now leaking badly, and at 9 p.m. I gave the order to lower boats, gear, provisions, and sledges to the floe, and move them to the flat ice a little way from the ship. The working of the ice closed the leaks slightly at midnight, but all hands were pumping all night.

A strange occurrence was the sudden appearance of eight emperor penguins from a crack one hundred yards away at the moment when the pressure upon the ship was at its climax. They walked a little way towards us, halted, and after a few ordinary calls proceeded to utter weird cries that sounded like a dirge for the ship. None of us had ever before heard the emperors utter any other than the most simple calls or cries, and the effect of this concerted effort was almost startling.

The End

Then came a fateful day—Wednesday, October 27. The position was lat. 69°5"S, long. 51°30" W. The temperature was minus 8.5 degrees Fahrenheit, a gentle southerly breeze was blowing and the sun shone in a clear sky.

> After long months of ceaseless anxiety and strain, after times when hope beat high and times when the outlook was black indeed, the end of the Endurance has come. But though we have been compelled to abandon the ship, which is crushed beyond all hope of ever being righted, we are alive and well, and we have stores and equipment for the task that lies before us. The task is to reach land with all the members of the Expedition. It is hard to write what I feel. To a sailor his ship is more than a floating home, and in the Endurance I had centred ambitions, hopes, and desires. Now, straining and groaning, her timbers cracking and her wounds gaping, she is slowly giving up her sentient life at the very outset of her career.
>
> She is crushed and abandoned after drifting more than 570 miles in a northwesterly direction during the 281 days since she became locked in the ice. The distance from the point where she became beset to the place where she now rests mortally hurt in the grip of the floes is 573 miles, but the total drift through all observed positions has been 1,186 miles, and probably we actually covered more than 1,500 miles. We are now 346 miles from Paulet Island, the nearest point where there is any possibility of finding food and shelter.
>
> A small hut built there by the Swedish expedition in 1902 is filled with stores left by the Argentine relief ship. I know all about those stores, for I purchased them in London on behalf of the Argentine Government when they asked me to equip the relief expedition.

The distance to the nearest barrier west of us is about 180 miles, but a party going there would still be about 360 miles from Paulet Island and there would be no means of sustaining life on the barrier. We could not take from here food enough for the whole journey; the weight would be too great.

This morning, our last on the ship, the weather was clear, with a gentle south-southeasterly to south-southwesterly breeze. From the crow's-nest there was no sign of land of any sort. The pressure was increasing steadily, and the passing hours brought no relief or respite for the ship. The attack of the ice reached its climax at 4 p.m. The ship was hove stern up by the pressure, and the driving floe, moving laterally across the stern, split the rudder and tore out the rudder-post and stern-post. Then, while we watched, the ice loosened and the Endurance sank a little. The decks were breaking upwards and the water was pouring in below. Again the pressure began, and at 5 p.m. I ordered all hands on to the ice. The twisting, grinding floes were working their will at last on the ship. It was a sickening sensation to feel the decks breaking up under one's feet, the great beams bending and then snapping with a noise like heavy gunfire. The water was overmastering the pumps, and to avoid an explosion when it reached the boilers I had to give orders for the fires to be drawn and the steam let down.

The plans for abandoning the ship in case of emergency had been made well in advance, and men and dogs descended to the floe and made their way to the comparative safety of an unbroken portion of the floe without a hitch. Just before leaving, I looked down the engine-room skylight as I stood on the quivering deck, and saw the engines dropping sideways as the stays and bed-plates gave way. I cannot describe the impression of relentless destruction that was forced upon me as I looked down and around. The floes, with the force of millions of tons of moving ice behind them, were simply annihilating the ship.

Essential supplies had been placed on the floe about one hundred yards from the ship, and there we set about making a camp for the night. But about 7 p.m., after the tents were up, the ice we were occupying became involved in the pressure and started to split and smash beneath our feet. I had the camp moved to a bigger floe about two hundred yards away, just beyond the bow of the ship. Boats, stores, and camp equipment had to be conveyed across a working pressure ridge. The movement of the ice was so slow that it did not interfere much with our short trek, but the weight of the ridge had caused the floes to sink on either side and there were pools of water there. A pioneer party with picks and shovels had to build a snow-causeway before we could get all our possessions across.

By 8 p.m. the camp had been pitched again. We had two pole tents and three hoop-tents. I took charge of the small pole-tent, No. 1, with Hudson, Hurley, and James as companions; Wild had the small hoop-tent, No. 2, with Wordie, McNeish, and McIlroy. These hoop-tents are very easily shifted and set up. The eight forward hands had the large hoop-tent, No. 3; Crean had charge of No. 4 hoop-tent with Hussey, Marston, and Cheetham; and Worsley had the other pole-tent, No. 5, with Greenstreet, Lees, Clark, Kerr, Rickenson, Macklin, and Blackborrow, the last named being the youngest of the forward hands.

To-night the temperature has dropped to −16° Fahr., and most of the men are cold and uncomfortable. After the tents had been pitched I mustered all hands and explained the position to them briefly and, I hope, clearly. I have told them the distance to the Barrier and the distance to Paulet Island, and have stated that I propose to try to march with equipment across the ice in the direction of Paulet Island. I thanked the men for the steadiness and good morale they have shown in these trying circumstances, and told them I had no doubt that, provided they continued to work their utmost and to trust me, we will all reach safety in the end.

Then we had supper, which the cook had prepared at the big blubber-stove, and after a watch had been set all hands except the watch turned in. For myself, I could not sleep. The destruction and abandonment of the ship was no sudden shock. The disaster had been looming ahead for many months, and I had studied my plans for all contingencies a hundred times. But the thoughts that came to me as I walked up and down in the darkness were not particularly cheerful.

The task now was to secure the safety of the party, and to that I must bend my energies and mental power and apply every bit of knowledge that experience of the Antarctic had given me. The task was likely to be long and strenuous, and an ordered mind and a clear programme were essential if we were to come through without loss of life. A man must shape himself to a new mark directly the old one goes to ground.

At midnight I was pacing the ice, listening to the grinding floe and to the groans and crashes that told of the death-agony of the *Endurance*, when I noticed suddenly a crack running across our floe right through the camp. The alarm-whistle brought all hands tumbling out, and we moved the tents and stores lying on what was now the smaller portion of the floe to the larger portion. Nothing more could be done at that moment, and the men turned in again; but there was little sleep. Each time I came to the end of my beat on the floe I could just see in the darkness the uprearing piles of pressure-ice, which toppled over and narrowed still further the little floating island we occupied. I did not notice at the time that my tent, which had been on the wrong side of the crack, had not been erected again.

Hudson and James had managed to squeeze themselves into other tents, and Hurley had wrapped himself in the canvas of No. 1 tent. I discovered this about 5 a.m. All night long the electric light gleamed from the stern of the dying *Endurance*. Hussey had left this light switched on when he took a last observation, and, like a lamp in a cottage window, it braved the night until in the early morning the *Endurance* received a particularly violent squeeze. There was a sound of rending beams and the light disappeared. The connection had been cut.

Morning came in chill and cheerless. All hands were stiff and weary after their first disturbed night on the floe. Just at daybreak I went over to the *Endurance* with Wild and Hurley, in order to retrieve some tins of petrol that could be used to boil up milk for the rest of the men. The ship presented a painful spectacle of chaos and wreck.

The jib-boom and bowsprit had snapped off during the night and now lay at right angles to the ship, with the chains, martingale, and bob-stay dragging them as the vessel quivered and moved in the grinding pack. The ice had driven over the forecastle and she was well down by the head. We secured two tins of petrol with some difficulty and postponed the further examination of the ship until after breakfast. Jumping across cracks with the tins, we soon reached camp, and built a fireplace out of the triangular water-tight tanks we had ripped from the lifeboat. This we had done in order to make more room. Then we pierced a petrol-tin in half a dozen places with an ice-axe and set fire to it.

The petrol blazed fiercely under the five-gallon drum we used as a cooker, and the hot milk was ready in quick time. Then we three ministering angels went round the tents with the life-giving drink, and were surprised and a trifle chagrined at the matter-of-fact manner in which some of the men accepted this contribution to their comfort. They did not quite understand what work we had done for them in the early dawn, and I heard Wild say, "If any of you gentlemen would like your boots cleaned just put them outside." This was his gentle way of reminding them that a little thanks will go a long way on such occasions.

The cook prepared breakfast, which consisted of biscuit and hoosh, at 8 a.m., and I then went over to the *Endurance* again and made a fuller examination of the wreck. Only six of the cabins had not been pierced by floes and blocks of ice. Every one of the starboard cabins had been crushed. The whole of the after part of the ship had been crushed concertina fashion.

The forecastle and the Ritz were submerged, and the wardroom was three-quarters full of ice. The starboard side of the wardroom had come away. The motor-engine forward had been driven through the galley. Petrol-cases that had been stacked on the fore-deck had been driven by the floe through the wall into the wardroom and had carried before them a large picture. Curiously enough, the glass of this picture had not been cracked, whereas in the immediate neighbourhood I saw heavy iron davits that had been twisted and bent like the ironwork of a wrecked train. The ship was being crushed remorselessly.

Under a dull, overcast sky I returned to camp and examined our situation. The floe occupied by the camp was still subject to pressure, and I thought it wise to move to a larger and apparently stronger floe about two hundred yards away, off the starboard bow of the ship. This camp was to become known as Dump Camp, owing to the amount of stuff that was thrown away there. We could not afford to carry unnecessary gear, and a drastic sorting of equipment took place.

I decided to issue a complete new set of Burberrys and underclothing to each man, and also a supply of new socks. The camp was transferred to the larger floe quickly, and I began there to direct the preparations for the long journey across the floes to Paulet Island or Snow Hill.

Hurley meanwhile had rigged his kinematograph-camera and was getting pictures of the *Endurance* in her death-throes. While he was engaged thus, the ice, driving against the standing rigging and the fore-, main-, and mizzen-masts, snapped the shrouds. The foretop and topgallant mast came down with a run and hung in wreckage on the fore-, mast-, with the fore-yard vertical. The main-mast followed immediately, snapping off about ten feet above the main deck. The crow's-nest fell within ten feet of where Hurley stood turning the handle of his camera, but he did not stop the machine, and so secured a unique, though sad, picture.

The issue of clothing was quickly accomplished. Sleeping bags were required also. We had eighteen fur bags, and it was necessary, there-fore, to issue ten of the Jaeger woollen bags in order to provide for the twenty-eight men of the party. The woollen bags were lighter and less warm than the reindeer bags, and so each man who received one of them was allowed also a reindeer-skin to lie upon. It seemed fair to distribute the fur bags by lot, but some of us older hands did not join in the lottery.

We thought we could do quite as well with the Jaegers as with the furs. With quick dispatch the clothing was apportioned, and then we turned one of the boats on its side and supported it with two broken oars to make a lee for the galley. The cook got the blubber-stove going, and a little later, when I was sitting round the corner of the stove, I heard one man say, "Cook, I like my tea strong." Another joined in, "Cook, I like mine weak."

It was pleasant to know that their minds were untroubled, but I thought the time opportune to mention that the tea would be the same for all hands and that we would be fortunate if two months later we had any tea at all. It occurred to me at the time that the incident had psychological interest. Here were men, their home crushed, the camp pitched on the unstable floes, and their chance of reaching safety apparently remote, calmly attending to the details of existence and giving their attention to such trifles as the strength of a brew of tea.

During the afternoon the work continued. Every now and then we heard a noise like heavy guns or distant thunder, caused by the floes grinding together.

The pressure caused by the congestion in this area of the pack is producing a scene of absolute chaos. The floes grind stupendously, throw up great ridges, and shatter one another mercilessly. The ridges, or hedgerows, marking the pressure-lines that border the fast-diminishing pieces of smooth floe-ice, are enormous. The ice moves majestically, irresistibly. Human effort is not futile, but man fights against the giant forces of Nature in a spirit of humility. One has a sense of dependence on the higher Power. Today two seals, a Weddell and a crabeater, came close to the camp and were shot. Four others were chased back into the water, for their presence disturbed the dog teams, and this meant floggings and trouble with the harness.

The arrangement of the tents has been completed and their internal management settled. Each tent has a mess orderly, the duty being taken in turn on an alphabetical rota. The orderly takes the hoosh-pots of his tent to the galley, gets all the hoosh he is allowed, and, after the meal, cleans the vessels with snow and stores them in sledge or boat ready for a possible move.

October 29.—We passed a quiet night, although the pressure was grinding around us. Our floe is a heavy one and it withstood the blows it received. There is a light wind from the northwest to north-north-east, and the weather is fine. We are twenty-eight men with forty-nine dogs, including Sue's and Sallie's five grown-up pups.

All hands this morning were busy preparing gear, fitting boats on sledges, and building up and strengthening the sledges to carry the boats. . . . The main motor-sledge, with a little fitting from the carpenter, carried our largest boat admirably. For the next boat four ordinary sledges were lashed together, but we were dubious as to the strength of this contrivance, and as a matter of fact it broke down quickly under strain. . . . The ship is still afloat, with the spurs of the pack driven through her and holding her up. The forecastle-head is under water, the decks are burst up by the pressure, the wreckage lies around in dismal confusion, but over all the blue ensign flies still.

This afternoon Sallie's three youngest pups, Sue's Sirius, and Mrs. Chippy, the carpenter's cat, have to be shot. We could not undertake the maintenance of weaklings under the new conditions. Macklin, Crean, and the carpenter seemed to feel the loss of their friends rather badly. We propose making a short trial journey tomorrow, starting with two of the boats and the ten sledges. The number of dog teams has been increased to seven, Greenstreet taking charge of the new additional team, consisting of Snapper and Sallie's four oldest pups. We have ten working sledges to relay with five teams. Wild's and Hurley's teams will haul the cutter with the assistance of four men. The whaler and the other boats will follow, and the men who are hauling them will be able to help with the cutter at the rough places. We cannot hope to make rapid progress, but each mile counts. Crean this afternoon has a bad attack of snow-blindness.

The weather on the morning of October 30 was overcast and misty, with occasional falls of snow. A moderate northeasterly breeze was blowing. We were still living on extra food, brought from the ship when we abandoned her, and the sledging and boating rations were intact. These rations would provide for twenty-eight men for fifty-six days on full rations, but we could count on getting enough seal and penguin meat to at least double this time. We could even, if progress proved too difficult and too injurious to the boats, which we must guard as our ultimate means of salvation, camp on the nearest heavy floe, scour the neighbouring pack for penguins and seals, and await the outward rift of the pack, to open and navigable water.

> This plan would avoid the grave dangers we are now incurring of getting entangled in impassable pressure ridges and possibly irretrievably damaging the boats, which are bound to suffer in rough ice; it would also minimize the peril of the ice splitting under us, as it did twice during the night at our first camp. Yet I feel sure that it is the right thing to attempt a march, since if we can make five or seven miles a day to the northwest our chance of reaching safety in the months to come will be increased greatly.
>
> There is a psychological aspect to the question also. It will be much better for the men in general to feel that, even though progress is slow, they are on their way to land than it will be simply to sit down and wait for the tardy northwesterly drift to take us out of this cruel waste of ice. We will make an attempt to move. The issue is beyond my power either to predict or to control.

That afternoon Wild and I went out in the mist and snow to find a road to the northeast. After many devious turnings to avoid the heavier pressure-ridges, we pioneered a way for at least a mile and a half and then returned by a rather better route to the camp. The pressure now was rapid in movement and our floe was suffering from the shakes and jerks of the ice. At 3 p.m., after lunch, we got under way, leaving Dump Camp a mass of debris.

The order was that personal gear must not exceed two pounds per man, and this meant that nothing but bare necessaries was to be taken on the march. We could not afford to cumber ourselves with unnecessary weight. Holes had been dug in the snow for the reception of private letters and little personal trifles, the Lares and Penates of the members of the Expedition, and into the privacy of these white graves were consigned much of sentimental value and not a little of intrinsic worth.

I rather grudged the two pounds allowance per man, owing to my keen anxiety to keep weights at a minimum, but some personal belongings could fairly be regarded as indispensable. The journey might be a long one, and there was a possibility of a winter in improvised quarters on an inhospitable coast at the other end.

A man under such conditions needs something to occupy his thoughts, some tangible memento of his home and people beyond the seas. So sovereigns were thrown away and photographs were kept. I tore the fly-leaf out of the Bible that Queen Alexandra had given to the ship, with her own writing in it, and also the wonderful page of Job containing the verse:

Out of whose womb came the ice?
    And the hoary frost of Heaven, who hath gendered it?
    The waters are hid as with a stone,
    And the face of the deep is frozen.
    —[Job 38:29–30]

The other Bible, which Queen Alexandra had given for the use of the shore party, was down below in the lower hold in one of the cases when the ship received her death blow. Suitcases were thrown away; these were retrieved later as material for making boots, and some of them, marked "solid leather," proved, to our disappointment, to contain a large percentage of cardboard. The manufacturer would have had difficulty in convincing us at the time that the deception was anything short of criminal.

The pioneer sledge party, consisting of Wordie, Hussey, Hudson, and myself, carrying picks and shovels, started to break a road through the pressure ridges for the sledges carrying the boats. The boats, with their gear and the sledges beneath them, weighed each more than a ton.

The cutter was smaller than the whaler, but weighed more and was a much more strongly built boat. The whaler was mounted on the sledge part of the Girling tractor forward and two sledges amidships and aft. These sledges were strengthened with cross-timbers and shortened oars fore and aft. The cutter was mounted on the aero-sledge. The sledges were the point of weakness. It appeared almost hopeless to prevent them smashing under their heavy loads when travelling over rough pressure-ice which stretched ahead of us for probably 300 miles.

After the pioneer sledge had started the seven dog teams got off. They took their sledges forward for half a mile, then went back for the other sledges. Worsley took charge of the two boats, with fifteen men hauling, and these also had to be relayed. It was heavy work for dogs and men, but there were intervals of comparative rest on the backward journey, after the first portion of the load had been taken forward.

We passed over two opening cracks, through which killers were pushing their ugly snouts, and by 5 p.m. had covered a mile in a north-northwesterly direction. The condition of the ice ahead was chaotic, for since the morning increased pressure had developed and the pack was moving and crushing in all directions.

So I gave the order to pitch camp for the night on flat ice, which, unfortunately, proved to be young and salty. The older pack was too rough and too deeply laden with snow to offer a suitable camping-ground. Although we had gained only one mile in a direct line, the necessary deviations made the distance travelled at least two miles, and the relays brought the distance marched up to six miles. Some of the dog teams had covered at least ten miles. I set the watch from 6 p.m. to 7 a.m., one hour for each man in each tent in rotation.

During the night snow fell heavily, and the floor-cloths of the tents got wet through, as the temperature had risen to plus 25°F. One of the things we hoped for in those days was a temperature in the neighbourhood of zero, for then the snow surface would be hard, we would not be troubled by damp, and our gear would not become covered in soft snow. The killers were blowing all night, and a crack appeared about twenty feet from the camp at 2 a.m.

The ice below us was quite thin enough for the killers to break through if they took a fancy to do so, but there was no other camping-ground within our reach and we had to take the risk. When morning came the snow was falling so heavily that we could not see more than a few score yards ahead, and I decided not to strike camp.

A path over the shattered floes would be hard to find, and to get the boats into a position of peril might be disastrous. Rickenson and Worsley started back for Dump Camp at 7 a.m. to get some wood and blubber for the fire, and an hour later we had hoosh, with one biscuit each.

At 10 a.m. Hurley and Hudson left for the old camp in order to bring some additional dog-pemmican, since there were no seals to be found near us. Then, as the weather cleared, Worsley and I made a prospect to the west and tried to find a practicable road.

A large floe offered a fairly good road for at least another mile to the northwest, and we went back prepared for another move. The weather cleared a little, and after lunch we struck camp. I took Rickenson, Kerr, Wordie, and Hudson as a breakdown gang to pioneer a path among the pressure ridges.

Five dog teams followed. Wild's and Hurley's teams were hitched on to the cutter and they started off in splendid style. They needed to be helped only once; indeed fourteen dogs did as well or even better than eighteen men. The ice was moving beneath and around us as we worked towards the big floe, and where this floe met the smaller ones there was a mass of pressed-up ice, still in motion, with water between the ridges. But it is wonderful what a dozen men can do with picks and shovels. We could cut a road through a pressure ridge about fourteen feet high in ten minutes and leave a smooth, or comparatively smooth, path for the sledges and teams.

Ocean Camp

In spite of the wet, deep snow and the halts occasioned by thus having to cut our road through the pressure ridges, we managed to march the best part of a mile towards our goal, though the relays and the deviations again made the actual distance travelled nearer six miles. As I could see that the men were all exhausted I gave the order to pitch the tents under the lee of the two boats, which afforded some slight protection from the wet snow now threatening to cover everything.

While so engaged one of the sailors discovered a small pool of water, caused by the snow having thawed on a sail which was lying in one of the boats. There was not much—just a sip each; but, as one man wrote in his diary, "One has seen and tasted cleaner, but seldom more opportunely found water."

Next day broke cold and still with the same wet snow, and in the clearing light I could see that with the present loose surface, and considering how little result we had to show for all our strenuous efforts of the past four days, it would be impossible to proceed for any great distance.

Taking into account also the possibility of leads opening close to us, and so of our being able to row northwest to where we might find land, I decided to find a more solid floe and there camp until conditions were more favourable for us to make a second attempt to escape from our icy prison. To this end we moved our tents and all our gear to a thick, heavy old floe about one and a half miles from the wreck and there made our camp. We called this "Ocean Camp."

It was with the utmost difficulty that we shifted our two boats. The surface was terrible—like nothing that any of us had ever seen around us before. We were sinking at times up to our hips, and everywhere the snow was two feet deep.

I decided to conserve our valuable sledging rations, which would be so necessary for the inevitable boat journey, as much as possible, and to subsist almost entirely on seals and penguins.

A party was sent back to Dump Camp, near the ship, to collect as much clothing, tobacco, etc., as they could find. The heavy snow which had fallen in the last few days, combined with the thawing and consequent sinking of the surface, resulted in the total disappearance of a good many of the things left behind at this dump. The remainder of the men made themselves as comfortable as possible under the circumstances at Ocean Camp. This floating lump of ice, about a mile square at first but later splitting into smaller and smaller fragments, was to be our home for nearly two months. During these two months we made frequent visits to the vicinity of the ship and retrieved much valuable clothing and food and a few articles of personal value which in our light-hearted optimism we had thought to leave miles behind us on our dash across the moving ice to safety.

The collection of food was now the all-important consideration. As we were to subsist almost entirely on seals and penguins, which were to provide fuel as well as food, some form of blubber stove was a necessity. This was eventually very ingeniously contrived from the ship's steel ash-shoot, as our first attempt with a large iron oil drum did not prove eminently successful. We could only cook seal or penguin hooshes or stews on this stove, and so uncertain was its action that the food was either burnt or only partially cooked; and, hungry though we were, half-raw seal meat was not very appetizing.

On one occasion a wonderful stew made from seal meat, with two or three tins of Irish stew that had been salved from the ship, fell into the fire through the bottom of the oil drum that we used as a saucepan becoming burnt out on account of the sudden intense heat of the fire below. We lunched that day on one biscuit and a quarter of a tin of bully-beef each, frozen hard.

This new stove, which was to last us during our stay at Ocean Camp, was a great success. Two large holes were punched, with much labour and few tools, opposite one another at the wider or top end of the shoot. Into one of these an oil drum was fixed, to be used as the fireplace, the other hole serving to hold our saucepan.

Alongside this another hole was punched to enable two saucepans to be boiled at a time; and farther along still a chimney made from biscuit tins completed a very efficient, if not a very elegant, stove. Later on the cook found that he could bake a sort of flat bannock or scone on this stove, but he was seriously hampered for want of yeast or baking powder.

An attempt was next made to erect some sort of a galley to protect the cook against the inclemencies of the weather. The party which I had sent back under Wild to the ship returned with, amongst other things, the wheelhouse practically complete. This, with the addition of some sails and tarpaulins stretched on spars, made a very comfortable storehouse and galley. Pieces of planking from the deck were lashed across some spars stuck upright into the snow, and this, with the ship's binnacle, formed an excellent lookout from which to look for seals and penguins. On this platform, too, a mast was erected from which flew the King's flag and the Royal Clyde Yacht Club burgee.

I made a strict inventory of all the food in our possession, weights being roughly determined with a simple balance made from a piece of wood and some string, the counterweight being a sixty-pound box of provisions.

The dog teams went off to the wreck early each morning under Wild, and the men made every effort to rescue as much as possible from the ship. This was an extremely difficult task as the whole of the deck forward was under a foot of water on the port side, and nearly three feet on the starboard side. However, they managed to collect large quantities of wood and ropes and some few cases of provisions. Although the galley was under water, Bakewell managed to secure three or four saucepans, which later proved invaluable acquisitions. Quite a number of boxes of flour, etc., had been stowed in a cabin in the hold, and these we had been unable to get out before we left the ship. Having, therefore, determined as nearly as possible that portion of the deck immediately above these cases, we proceeded to cut a hole with large ice chisels through the three-inch planking of which it was formed.

As the ship at this spot was under five feet of water and ice, it was not an easy job. However, we succeeded in making the hole sufficiently large to allow some cases to come floating up. These were greeted with great satisfaction, and later on, as we warmed to our work, other cases, whose upward progress was assisted with a boat hook, were greeted with either cheers or groans according to whether they contained farinaceous food or merely luxuries such as jellies.

For each man by now had a good idea of the calorific value and nutritive and sustaining qualities of the various foods. It had a personal interest for us all. In this way we added to our scanty stock between two and three tons of provisions, about half of which was farinaceous food, such as flour and peas, of which we were so short.

This sounds a great deal, but at one pound per day it would only last twenty-eight men for three months. Previous to this I had reduced the food allowance to nine and a half ounces per man per day. Now, however, it could be increased, and "this afternoon, for the first time for ten days, we knew what it was to be really satisfied."

I had the sledges packed in readiness with the special sledging rations in case of a sudden move, and with the other food, allowing also for prospective seals and penguins, I calculated a dietary to give the utmost possible variety and yet to use our precious stock of flour in the most economical manner. All seals and penguins that appeared anywhere within the vicinity of the camp were killed to provide food and fuel.

The dog-pemmican we also added to our own larder, feeding the dogs on the seals which we caught, after removing such portions as were necessary for our own needs. We were rather short of crockery, but small pieces of venesta-wood served admirably as plates for seal steaks; stews and liquids of all sorts were served in the aluminum sledging-mugs, of which each man had one. Later on, jelly tins and biscuit-tin lids were pressed into service.

Monotony in the meals, even considering the circumstances in which we found ourselves, was what I was striving to avoid, so our little stock of luxuries, such as fish-paste, tinned herrings, etc., was carefully husbanded and so distributed as to last as long as possible.

My efforts were not in vain, as one man states in his diary:

It must be admitted that we are feeding very well indeed, considering our position. Each meal consists of one course and a beverage. The dried vegetables, if any, all go into the same pot as the meat, and every dish is a sort of hash or stew, be it ham or seal meat or half and half. The fact that we only have two pots available places restrictions upon the number of things that can be cooked at one time, but in spite of the limitation of facilities, we always seem to manage to get just enough. The milk-powder and sugar are necessarily boiled with the tea or cocoa.

We are, of course, very short of the farinaceous element in our diet, and consequently have a mild craving for more of it. Bread is out of the question, and as we are husbanding the remaining cases of our biscuits for our prospective boat journey, we are eking out the supply of flour by making bannocks, of which we have from three to four each day. These bannocks are made from flour, fat, water, salt, and a little baking-powder, the dough being rolled out into flat rounds and baked in about ten minutes on a hot sheet of iron over the fire. Each bannock weighs about one and a half to two ounces, and we are indeed lucky to be able to produce *them*.

A few boxes of army biscuits soaked with sea-water were distributed at one meal. They were in such a state that they would not have been looked at a second time under ordinary circumstances, but to us on a floating lump of ice, over 300 miles from land, and that quite hypothetical, and with the unplumbed sea beneath us, they were luxuries indeed. Wild's tent made a pudding of theirs with some dripping.

Although keeping in mind the necessity for strict economy with our scanty store of food, I knew how important it was to keep the men cheerful, and that the depression occasioned by our surroundings and our precarious position could to some extent be alleviated by increasing the rations, at least until we were more accustomed to our new mode of life. That this was successful is shown in their diaries.

Day by day goes by much the same as one another. We work; we talk; we eat. Ah, how we eat! No longer on short rations, we are a trifle more exacting than we were when we first commenced our "simple life," but by comparison with home standards we are positive barbarians, and our gastronomic rapacity knows no bounds.

All is eaten that comes to each tent, and everything is most carefully and accurately divided into as many equal portions as there are men in the tent. One member then closes his eyes or turns his head away and calls out the names at random, as the cook for the day points to each portion, saying at the same time, "Whose?"

Partiality, however unintentional it may be, is thus entirely obviated and every one feels satisfied that all is fair, even though one may look a little enviously at the next man's helping, which differs in some especially appreciated detail from one's own. We break the Tenth Commandment energetically, but as we are all in the same boat in this respect, no one says a word. We understand each other's feelings quite sympathetically.

It is just like school-days over again, and very jolly it is too, for the time being!

Later on, as the prospect of wintering in the pack became more apparent, the rations had to be considerably reduced. By that time, however, everybody had become more accustomed to the idea and took it quite as a matter of course.

Our meals now consisted in the main of a fairly generous helping of seal or penguin, either boiled or fried. As one man wrote:

We are now having enough to eat, but not by any means too much; and everyone is always hungry enough to eat every scrap he can get. Meals are invariably taken very seriously, and little talking is done till the hoosh is finished.

Our tents made somewhat cramped quarters, especially during meal-times.

Living in a tent without any furniture requires a little getting used to. For our meals we have to sit on the floor, and it is surprising how awkward it is to eat in such a position; it is better by far to kneel and sit back on one's heels, as do the Japanese.

Each man took it in turn to be the tent "cook" for one day, and one writes:

The word "cook" is at present rather a misnomer, for whilst we have a permanent galley no cooking need be done in the tent.

Really, all that the tent cook has to do is to take his two hoosh-pots over to the galley and convey the hoosh and the beverage to the tent, clearing up after each meal and washing up the two pots and the mugs. There are no spoons, etc., to wash, for we each keep our own spoon and pocket-knife in our pockets. We just lick them as clean as possible and replace them in our pockets after each meal.

Our spoons are one of our indispensable possessions here. To lose one's spoon would be almost as serious as it is for an edentate person to lose his set of false teeth.

During all this time the supply of seals and penguins, if not inexhaustible, was always sufficient for our needs.

Seal- and penguin-hunting was our daily occupation, and parties were sent out in different directions to search among the hummocks and the pressure-ridges for them. When one was found a signal was hoisted, usually in the form of a scarf or a sock on a pole, and an answering signal was hoisted at the camp.

Then Wild went out with a dog team to shoot and bring in the game. To feed ourselves and the dogs, at least one seal a day was required. The seals were mostly crab-eaters, and emperor penguins were the general rule. On November 5, however, an adelie was caught, and this was the cause of much discussion, as the following extract shows:

> The man on watch from 3 a.m. to 4 a.m. caught an adelie penguin. This is the first of its kind that we have seen since January last, and it may mean a lot. It may signify that there is land somewhere near us, or else that great leads are opening up, but it is impossible to form more than a mere conjecture at present.

No skuas, Antarctic petrels, or sea-leopards were seen during our two months' stay at Ocean Camp.

In addition to the daily hunt for food, our time was passed in reading the few books that we had managed to save from the ship. The greatest treasure in the library was a portion of the *Encyclopædia Britannica*. This was being continually used to settle the inevitable arguments that would arise.

The sailors were discovered one day engaged in a very heated discussion on the subject of *Money and Exchange*. They finally came to the conclusion that the *Encyclopædia*, since it did not coincide with their views, must be wrong.

> For descriptions of every American town that ever has been, is, or ever will be, and for full and complete biographies of every American statesman since the time of George Washington and long before, the Encyclopædia would be hard to beat. Owing to our shortage of matches we have been driven to use it for purposes other than the purely literary ones though; and one genius having discovered that the paper, used for its pages had

been impregnated with saltpetre, we can now thoroughly rec-
ommend it as a very efficient pipe-lighter.

We also possessed a few books on Antarctic exploration, a copy
of Browning and one of *The Ancient Mariner*. On reading the latter,
we sympathized with him and wondered what he had done with the
albatross; it would have made a very welcome addition to our larder.

The two subjects of most interest to us were our rate of drift and the
weather. Worsley took observations of the sun whenever possible, and his
results showed conclusively that the drift of our floe was almost entirely
dependent upon the winds and not much affected by currents.

Our hope, of course, was to drift northwards to the edge of the pack
and then, when the ice was loose enough, to take to the boats and row to
the nearest land. We started off in fine style, drifting north about twenty
miles in two or three days in a howling southwesterly blizzard.

Gradually, however, we slowed up, as successive observations showed,
until we began to drift back to the south. An increasing northeasterly wind,
which commenced on November 7 and lasted for twelve days, damped our
spirits for a time, until we found that we had only drifted back to the south
three miles, so that we were now seventeen miles to the good. This tended
to reassure us in our theories that the ice of the Weddell Sea was drifting
round in a clockwise direction, and that if we could stay on our piece long
enough we must eventually be taken up to the north, where lay the open
sea and the path to comparative safety.

The ice was not moving fast enough to be noticeable. In fact, the only
way in which we could prove that we were moving at all was by noting the
change of relative positions of the bergs around us, and, more definitely,
by fixing our absolute latitude and longitude by observations of the sun.
Otherwise, as far as actual visible drift was concerned, we might have been
on dry land.

For the next few days we made good progress, drifting seven miles
to the north on November 24 and another seven miles in the next
forty-eight hours. We were all very pleased to know that although
the wind was mainly southwest all this time, yet we had made very
little easting. The land lay to the west, so had we drifted to the east we

should have been taken right away to the centre of the entrance to the Weddell Sea, and our chances of finally reaching land would have been considerably lessened.

Our average rate of drift was slow, and many and varied were the calculations as to when we should reach the pack-edge. On December 12, 1915, one man wrote:

> Once across the Antarctic Circle, it will seem as if we are practically halfway home again; and it is just possible that with favourable winds we may cross the circle before the New Year. A drift of only three miles a day would do it, and we have often done that and more for periods of three or four weeks.
>
> We are now only 250 miles from Paulet Island, but too much to the east of it. We are approaching the latitudes in which we were at this time last year, on our way down. The ship left South Georgia just a year and a week ago, and reached this latitude four or five miles to the eastward of our present position on January 3, 1915, crossing the circle on New Year's Eve.

Thus, after a year's incessant battle with the ice, we had returned, by many strange turns of fortune's wheel, to almost identically the same latitude that we had left with such high hopes and aspirations twelve months previously; but under what different conditions now!

Our ship crushed and lost, and we ourselves drifting on a piece of ice at the mercy of the winds. However, in spite of occasional setbacks due to unfavourable winds, our drift was in the main very satisfactory, and this went a long way towards keeping the men cheerful.

As the drift was mostly affected by the winds, the weather was closely watched by all, and Hussey, the meteorologist, was called upon to make forecasts every four hours, and sometimes more frequently than that. A meteorological screen, containing thermometers and a barograph, had been erected on a post frozen into the ice, and observations were taken every four hours. When we first left the ship the weather was cold and miserable, and altogether as unpropitious as it could possibly have been for our attempted march.

Our first few days at Ocean Camp were passed under much the same conditions. At nights the temperature dropped to zero, with blinding snow and drift. One-hour watches were instituted, all hands taking their turn, and in such weather this job was no sinecure. The watchman had to be continually on the alert for cracks in the ice, or any sudden changes in the ice conditions, and also had to keep his eye on the dogs, who often became restless, fretful, and quarrelsome in the early hours of the morning. At the end of his hour he was very glad to crawl back into the comparative warmth of his frozen sleeping bag.

On November 6 a dull, overcast day developed into a howling blizzard from the southwest, with snow and low drift. Only those who were compelled left the shelter of their tent. Deep drifts formed everywhere, burying sledges and provisions to a depth of two feet, and the snow piling up around the tents threatened to burst the thin fabric. The fine drift found its way in through the ventilator of the tent, which was accordingly plugged up with a spare sock.

This lasted for two days, when one man wrote:

The blizzard continued through the morning, but cleared towards noon, and it was a beautiful evening; but we would far rather have the screeching blizzard with its searching drift and cold damp wind, for we drifted about eleven miles to the north during the night.

For four days the fine weather continued, with gloriously warm, bright sun, but cold when standing still or in the shade. The temperature usually dropped below zero, but every opportunity was taken during these fine, sunny days to partially dry our sleeping-bags and other gear, which had become sodden through our body-heat having thawed the snow which had drifted in on to them during the blizzard. The bright sun seemed to put new heart into all.

The next day brought a northeasterly wind with the very high temperature of 27° Fahr.—only 5° below freezing. "These high temperatures do not always represent the warmth which might be assumed from the thermometrical readings. They usually bring dull, overcast skies, with a raw, muggy, moisture-laden wind. The winds from the south, though colder, are nearly always coincident with sunny days and clear blue skies.

The temperature still continued to rise, reaching 33°F on November 14. The thaw consequent upon these high temperatures was having a disastrous effect upon the surface of our camp.

The surface is awful!—not slushy, but elusive. You step out gingerly. All is well for a few paces, then your foot suddenly sinks a couple of feet until it comes to a hard layer. You wade along in this way step by step, like a mudlark at Portsmouth Hard, hoping gradually to regain the surface.

Soon you do, only to repeat the exasperating performance ad lib., to the accompaniment of all the expletives that you can bring to bear on the subject. What actually happens is that the warm air melts the surface sufficiently to cause drops of water to trickle down slightly, where, on meeting colder layers of snow, they freeze again, forming a honeycomb of icy nodules instead of the soft, powdery, granular snow that we are accustomed to.

These high temperatures persisted for some days, and when, as occasionally happened, the sky was clear and the sun was shining it was unbearably hot. Five men who were sent to fetch some gear from the vicinity of the ship with a sledge marched in nothing but trousers and singlet, and even then were very hot; in fact they were afraid of getting sunstroke, so let down flaps from their caps to cover their necks.

Their sleeves were rolled up over their elbows, and their arms were red and sunburnt in consequence. The temperature on this occasion was 26°F or 6° below freezing. For five or six days more the sun continued, and most of our clothes and sleeping bags were now comparatively dry. A wretched day with rainy sleet set in on November 21, but one could put up with this discomfort as the wind was now from the south.

The wind veered later to the west, and the sun came out at 9 p.m. For at this time, near the end of November, we had the midnight sun. "A thrice-blessed southerly wind" soon arrived to cheer us all, occasioning the following remarks in one of the diaries:

Today is the most beautiful day we have had in the Antarctic—a clear sky, a gentle, warm breeze from the south, and the most brilliant sunshine. We all took advantage of it to strike tents, clean out, and generally dry and air ground-sheets and sleeping bags.

I was up early—4 a.m.—to keep watch, and the sight was indeed magnificent. Spread out before one was an extensive panorama of ice fields, intersected here and there by small broken leads, and dotted with numerous noble bergs, partly bathed in sunshine and partly tinged with the grey shadows of an overcast sky.

As one watched one observed a distinct line of demarcation between the sunshine and the shade, and this line gradually approached nearer and nearer, lighting up the hummocky relief of the ice field bit by bit, until at last it reached us, and threw the whole camp into a blaze of glorious sunshine which lasted nearly all day.

This afternoon we were treated to one or two showers of hail-like snow. Yesterday we also had a rare form of snow, or, rather, precipitation of ice-spicules, exactly like little hairs, about a third of an inch long.

The warmth in the tents at lunchtime was so great that we had all the side flaps up for ventilation, but it is a treat to get warm occasionally, and one can put up with a little stuffy atmosphere now and again for the sake of it. The wind has gone to the best quarter this evening, the southeast, and is freshening.

On these fine, clear, sunny days wonderful mirage effects could be observed, just as occur over the desert. Huge bergs were apparently resting on nothing, with a distinct gap between their bases and the horizon; others were curiously distorted into all sorts of weird and fantastic shapes, appearing to be many times their proper height. Added to this, the pure glistening white of the snow and ice made a picture which it is impossible adequately to describe.

Later on, the freshening southwesterly wind brought mild, overcast weather, probably due to the opening up of the pack in that direction.

I had already made arrangements for a quick move in case of a sudden break-up of the ice. Emergency orders were issued; each man had his post allotted and his duty detailed; and the whole was so organized that in less than five minutes from the sounding of the alarm on my whistle, tents were struck, gear and provisions packed, and the whole party was ready to move off. I now took a final survey of the men to note their condition, both mental and physical.

For our time at Ocean Camp had not been one of unalloyed bliss. The loss of the ship meant more to us than we could ever put into words. After we had settled at Ocean Camp she still remained nipped by the ice, only her stern showing and her bows overridden and buried by the relentless pack. The tangled mass of ropes, rigging, and spars made the scene even more desolate and depressing.

It was with a feeling almost of relief that the end came.

November 21, 1915.—This evening, as we were lying in our tents we heard the Boss call out, "She's going, boys!" We were out in a second and up on the lookout station and other points of vantage, and, sure enough, there was our poor ship a mile and a half away struggling in her death-agony. She went down bows first, her stern raised in the air. She then gave one quick dive and the ice closed over her forever.

It gave one a sickening sensation to see it, for, mastless and useless as she was, she seemed to be a link with the outer world. Without her our destitution seems more emphasized, our desolation more complete. The loss of the ship sent a slight wave of depression over the camp. No one said much, but we cannot be blamed for feeling it in a sentimental way. It seemed as if the moment of severance from many cherished associations, many happy moments, even stirring incidents, had come as she silently up-ended to find a last resting place beneath the ice on which we now stand.

When one knows every little nook and corner of one's ship as we did, and has helped her time and again in the fight that she made so well, the actual parting was not without its pathos, quite apart from one's own desolation, and I doubt if there was one amongst us who did not feel some personal emotion when Sir Ernest, standing on the top of the look-out, said somewhat sadly and quietly, "She's gone, boys."

It must, however, be said that we did not give way to depression for long, for soon every one was as cheery as usual. Laughter rang out from the tents, and even the Boss had a passage-at-arms with the storekeeper over the inadequacy of the sausage ration, insisting that there should be two each "because they were such little ones," instead of the one and a half that the latter proposed.

The psychological effect of a slight increase in the rations soon neutralized any tendency to downheartedness, but with the high temperatures surface-thaw set in, and our bags and clothes were soaked and sodden. Our boots squelched as we walked, and we lived in a state of perpetual wet feet. At nights, before the temperature had fallen, clouds of steam could be seen rising from our soaking bags and boots. During the night, as it grew colder, this all condensed as rime on the inside of the tent and showered down upon us if one happened to touch the side inadvertently. One had to be careful how one walked, too, as often only a thin crust of ice and snow covered a hole in the floe, through which many an unwary member went in up to his waist. These perpetual soakings, however, seemed to have had little lasting effect, or perhaps it was not apparent owing to the excitement of the prospect of an early release.

A northwesterly wind on December 7 and 8 retarded our progress somewhat, but I had reason to believe that it would help to open the ice and form leads through which we might escape to open water.

So I ordered a practice launching of the boats and stowage of food and stores in them. This was very satisfactory. We cut a slipway from our floe into a lead which ran alongside, and the boats took the water "like a bird," as one sailor remarked. Our hopes were high in anticipation of an early release. A blizzard sprang up, increasing the next day and burying tents and packing cases in the drift. On December 12 it had moderated somewhat and veered to the southeast, and the next day the blizzard had ceased, but a good steady wind from south and southwest continued to blow us north.

December 15, 1915.—The continuance of southerly winds is exceeding our best hopes, and raising our spirits in proportion. Prospects could not be brighter than they are just now. The environs of our floe are continually changing. Some days we are almost surrounded by small open leads, preventing us from crossing over to the adjacent floes.

After two more days our fortune changed, and a strong northeasterly wind brought "a beastly cold, windy day" and drove us back three and a quarter miles. Soon, however, the wind once more veered to the south and southwest. These high temperatures, combined with the strong changeable winds that we had had of late, led me to conclude that the ice all around us was rotting and breaking up and that the moment of our deliverance from the icy maw of the Antarctic was at hand.

On December 20, after discussing the question with Wild, I informed all hands that I intended to try and make a march to the west to reduce the distance between us and Paulet Island. A buzz of pleasurable anticipation went around the camp, and everyone was anxious to get on the move. So the next day I set off with Wild, Crean, and Hurley, with dog teams, to the westward to survey the route. After travelling about seven miles we mounted a small berg, and there as far as we could see stretched a series of immense flat floes from half a mile to a mile across, separated from each other by pressure ridges which seemed easily negotiable with pick and shovel. The only place that appeared likely to be formidable was a very much cracked-up area between the old floe that we were on and the first of the series of young flat floes about half a mile away.

December 22 was therefore kept as Christmas Day, and most of our small remaining stock of luxuries was consumed at the Christmas feast. We could not carry it all with us, so for the last time for eight months we had a really good meal—as much as we could eat. Anchovies in oil, baked beans, and jugged hare made a glorious mixture such as we have not dreamed of since our school days.

Everybody was working at high pressure, packing and repacking sledges and stowing what provisions we were going to take with us in the various sacks and boxes. As I looked around at the eager faces of the men I could not but hope that this time the fates would be kinder to us than in our last attempt to march across the ice to safety.

Sources

Amundsen, Roald. "We Succeed" from *The South Pole*. London: Jay Murray, 1913.

Buchan, John. "The Quest for the North Pole" from *The Last Secrets: The Final Mysteries of Exploration*. London: Thomas Nelson and Sons, 1923.

Cherry-Garrard, Apsley. "The Worst Journey in the World" from *The Worst Journey in the World*. London: Constable and Company Limited, 1922.

Cook, Frederick A. "I Was First" from *My Attainment of the Pole*. Chicago: Polar Publishing Company, 1913.

Franklin, John. "Across Barren Grounds" from *The Journey to the Polar Sea*. London: Everyman's Library, 1821.

Kane, Elisha Kent. "In Search of John Franklin" from *Explorations in the Arctic Regions*. Edinburgh: William P. Nimmo & Co., 1879.

Mudge, Rev. Z. A. "The Last Voyage of the *Polaris*" from *North-Pole Voyages*. New York: Nelson & Phillips, 1875.

Peary, Robert E. "Reaching the Pole" from *The North Pole*. New York: Greenwood Publishers, 1910.

Shackleton, Ernest. "The Loss of the *Endurance*" from *South*. London: Century Publishing, 1919.

Synge, M. B. "The Quest for the South Pole" from *A Book of Discovery: The History of the World's Exploration*. London: T. C. & E. C. Jack Limited, 1921.